A HOUSE BY THE RIVER

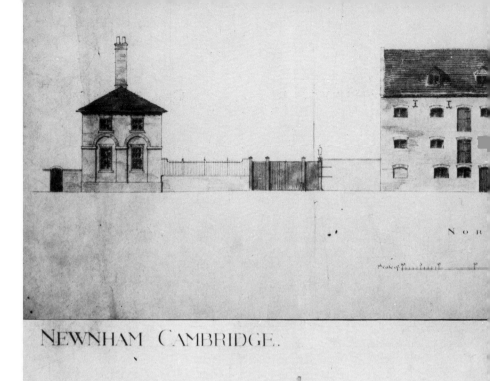

Scale of

NEWNHAM CAMBRIDGE.

.LEVATION.

Measured, January 1885.

TION.

Measured, January 1885.

A HOUSE
BY THE RIVER

*NEWNHAM GRANGE TO
DARWIN COLLEGE*

BY

MARGARET ELIZABETH
KEYNES

PRIVATELY PRINTED
CAMBRIDGE
1984

A House by the River may be obtained from
The Bursar, Darwin College, Cambridge
England CB3 9EU

Printed in England by Heffers Printers Limited Cambridge

DEDICATED

TO

THE MASTER AND FELLOWS

OF

DARWIN COLLEGE

Contents

List of Illustrations

Pen Drawings by Gwen Raverat

for her book *Period Piece*, 1952

Reproduced by kind permission of Messrs Faber & Faber

Maps

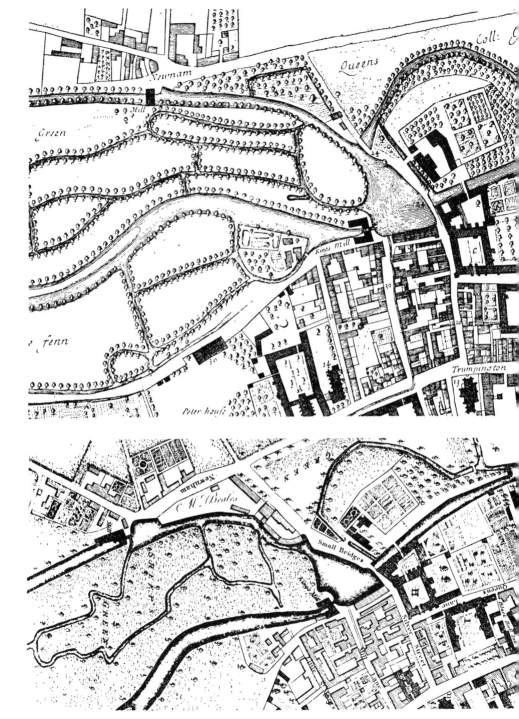

Details from the Loggan (1688) and Custance (1798) maps of Cambridge

Preface

WHEN, in 1964, Darwin College was founded at Newnham Grange by the Colleges of Caius, St John's, and Trinity, the Trustees asked me to write an account of the house and its connection with my family. I agreed, stipulating that I should include a history of the whole site and give some account of its buildings and their former inhabitants. The book therefore covers much more than the eighty years during which it belonged to my family. For the first part, my sources were limited to the histories of Cambridge, legal documents, parochial records, newspapers, etc., but as soon as I reached 1884, the year in which my father, Professor George Darwin, married and decided to buy the property, I had a wealth of information at my command. From this time until his death in 1912, my father kept his correspondence in files, so that nearly all the incoming letters about the house have been preserved. J. J. Stevenson, the architect, made some charming water-colour drawings and plans to record the buildings as they were before their alteration or demolition in 1885. Finally, my mother's letters to her home in the United States give a detailed account of how my parents bought and moved into the house, and of the first years of their life there.

Darwin College has been given its name, not only because of the association with Cambridge of Dr Erasmus Darwin and his grandson Charles Darwin, but also because Newnham Grange itself was for so long the home of Charles Darwin's son, Sir George Darwin, and his family. His widow Maud continued to live there until she died in 1947. She was succeeded by their elder son, Charles Galton Darwin, who died suddenly at the end of 1962. About a year and a half later, Darwin College was officially founded by the Nominative Trustees.

In the account I have written of my father, I give a few excerpts from letters that Charles Darwin wrote to George at Trinity, since they throw interesting light on both men and their methods of working. Charles Darwin himself, however, never set foot on the premises of Newnham Grange, as he died in 1882, three years before his son George moved into the house.

Because the Corporation used to own all the land on which Darwin College stands, my book is often as much concerned with people of the Borough as it is with members of the University. I have found names still familiar in the city constantly recurring in the annals of the past. Thus my history, though primarily a chronological record, is also a social document. I have deliberately tried to describe life in the Cambridge of former days, as what still seems to me natural and commonplace may well strike the present generation as unexpected and odd.

The practical arrangements and alterations my parents made in their property I have recorded in some detail, because my history after all chronicles the evolution of a family house to suit the needs of the inhabitants during the rapid changes brought about by the inventions of the nineteenth and twentieth centuries.

At the risk of inviting the accusation of irrelevance, I have recorded events in Cambridge, and anecdotes about some of its citizens, lest the stories should be forgotten. I also give short biographies of some of the people who played prominent roles in the history of Newnham Grange, the Old Granary and the Hermitage, buildings which with the new additions now form Darwin College.

However, Newnham Grange remains the centre of my story, with the river by which it stands playing the part of hero. My sister Gwen Raverat in her book *Period Piece* gave a vivid account of the life we led there as children; I have now tried to supply the facts about the site, the buildings, and their former occupants, bringing the history to a close at the foundation of Darwin College in 1964.

I wish to express my deep gratitude to the people who have helped me with this book. There are so many that I cannot possibly name them all.

Lammas House   *Margaret Elizabeth Keynes*
Brinkley   1974

Editor's Note

My late wife, born Margaret Elizabeth Darwin at Newnham Grange on 22 March 1890, wrote the above Preface to her book in 1974 before its completion. It had been her main interest during the last years of her life and she lived to see a draft of it finished in July 1974 before the onset of her last illness, but she was unable to give it her final revisions and polishing or to see any part of it in print. We, her family, have assumed the role of editors, though making only minor changes here and there, of which we felt that she would have approved.

She has recorded her gratitude to the many friends who assisted or advised her in the writing of her book. The editors owe a similar debt to friends who have helped in the production of this volume. Their work has been a reflection of the affection they felt for the author, and they have preferred to be nameless. We have also appreciated the care taken by the printers, and the detailed consideration which Mr Frank Collieson gave to the proofs.

Lammas House *Geoffrey Keynes*
Brinkley *July* 1976

Margaret Keynes died in December 1974 and Geoffrey in July 1982, both at Lammas House.

Newnham Grange from the front, c. 1886

CHAPTER ONE

The Site

THE site of Darwin College, owing to its position on the bank of the river and its proximity to the old Borough of Cambridge, has a remarkable history. Newnham millstream now flows down past the College to join the main river at Laundress Green near Silver Street Bridge, but in former days it diverged into another branch before reaching the Millpool. This was at a point about eighty yards to the west of the present bridge, near the east end of the Old Granary. Here, at one time, the stream crossed the line of the present road to the north-west. Nothing now remains to be seen of this ancient branch of the Cam, except the Queens' Ditch which, after making a loop westwards towards Queen's Road* (the Backs), runs north-east to rejoin the main stream of the river at the King's Bridge (as shown on map on page xiii).

Until the middle of the eighteenth century, the old branch of the river was spanned by the lesser of two Small Bridges, as they were called. The other Small Bridge was the forerunner of Silver Street Bridge. After numerous repairs, this old wooden bridge was replaced in 1841 by one of cast-iron, which served its purpose until 1959, when the present much wider stone bridge was built from a design by Sir Edwin Lutyens. Although Small Bridges Street, leading from the river to the town, had been renamed Silver Street by 1615, it was long before the bridge lost its former name and still longer before the triangular piece of land or island, along which the Causeway used to run between the two bridges, ceased to be called 'Small Bridges'.

The ancient bridges on their wooden trestles looked rather like larger many-legged versions of the willow-pattern bridge which still joins the 'Little Island' to the 'Big Island' in the garden of Darwin College. In 1475 Queens' College, in order to have room for its

* Queen's Road is written with the apostrophe *before* the s, because it was not named after the college founded by the two Queens, but to commemorate Queen Victoria's Jubilee.

I

brewhouse, stables, gardens and, later on, its grove, bought most of Small Bridges island from the Corporation, leaving the latter only a strip of land on the south between the bridges for the Causeway, which followed approximately the line of the present road. The ground was low-lying; frequent floods washed away the Causeway and destroyed the frail bridges, so that the Corporation was constantly trying to raise the height of the land. For this reason, after Queens' had bought the greater part of the island, the Corporation made the triangular piece of ground on the north of the Causeway into an official dump for the town rubbish. It must have been an unsavoury area for many years. The process of raising the level of the land to the west of Silver Street Bridge was only completed in the 1890s, when a big depression in the middle of the south part of Queens' Green was filled in to make the flat municipal meadow it now is. But in a bad flood, such as that of 1947, the road in front of the Old Granary is still covered by flood water as far as the beginning of Sidgwick Avenue.

The smaller of the two Small Bridges ceased to exist in 1756, when James Essex, the Cambridge-born architect, was building the yellow-brick Fellows' Building for Queens' at the north-east corner of Silver Street Bridge. The Corporation wished to make the second bridge unnecessary and therefore diverted the Newnham branch of the river into a tunnel to reach Queens' Green. Here the tunnel ended and the river was still further degraded by being turned into a ditch, but at least it was called the Queens' Ditch. Thus it remained unchanged until, in 1935, Queens' erected its red-brick Fisher Building nearly opposite the Old Granary, and filled in a stretch of the Ditch to form a wider frontage for its south-west corner. In 1959, while the new Silver Street Bridge was being built, some men digging a trench down the road for service pipes came across an obstruction. This proved to be the old 1756 tunnel. An eye-witness has described it as a large brick arch, but he could not see whether water was still flowing through it towards the Queens' Ditch. The men filled in the cavity with rubble and continued their pipe-laying over it. Not long after, the opening which had led the water into the tunnel from the Cam was cemented over, since it no longer served any purpose. The memory of this ancient branch of the river is preserved in the now stagnant waters of the Queens' Ditch, and it is only in the mind's eye that the second Small Bridge can still be seen, spanning the ghost of a river with its wooden struts.

Darwin College is in the parish of St Botolph's, the Church which faces the end of Silver Street. In 1922 its rector, the late A. W. Goodman, published an excellent *Little History of St Botolph's,* from which, and from Cooper's *Annals of Cambridge,* the following account of the Hermit and the Armitage (Hermitage) site is largely derived. In medieval times a Hermit looked after the Small Bridges, collected tolls for their maintenance, and sometimes even made the repairs himself. It may well be asked why hermits, so often priests, were given this mundane task. John Saltmarsh of King's has supplied the answer. In the Middle Ages a bridge was often erected as a work of piety, which a hermit might maintain. Travellers were expected to contribute to his work and to worship in his chapel.

The first mention of the Small Bridges Hermit is in the 1396 register of the Bishops of Ely, when Bishop John Fordham 'granted licence for the celebration of divine service in the Small Bridges Chapel, with an indulgence for such as should contribute to the repair of the Small Bridges'. Three years later,

the bridges and causeway between Cambridge and Barton being in very bad repair, so that casualties frequently happened to persons and carriages passing along the same, the King (Henry IV) granted to John Jaye, the hermit, for two years, certain customs on saleable articles passing along the bridges and causeway . . . to be applied to the reparation thereof.*

Another entry from Corporation Cross-book in 1428 reads:

It is ordained that all willows growing . . . on either part of the Causeway between and near the Small Bridges . . . and also in the garden and near the garden of the hermitage there . . . shall be committed to the use of the hermit there for the time being, for the reparation, amendment and sustentation of the Causeway aforesaid, his hermitage and the slippery and ruinous way near the aforesaid bridges and causeway.

* This quotation and those following all come from Cooper's *Annals.*

There are several later mentions of the hermit, but in 1549, after the Reformation, the institution came to an end. In the Corporation accounts, the receipt of £11 is noted for the sale of the Chapel, 40 shillings for a 'Sylver challys' and 20 pence for 'the Wyllowes at the Armitage'. The Chapel was presumably of stone and so was sold as valuable building material. This would account for its fetching the larger sum of £11.

Twelve years later, in 1561, the receipt of three shillings and fourpence was noted for 'the farm of a void ground' called the Armitage. This shows that no building remained. Then in 1589 the *site* of the hermitage was leased to Oliver Green.* When next the tolls at the Small Bridges are mentioned, a Corporation official collected them, and later the right to levy them was given to the highest bidder.

It is not known exactly where the Hermitage and its presumably adjoining Chapel stood. A 1494 entry in the town's accounts acknowledged the receipt of two shillings from 'Richard Dekyn, for a certain garden enclosed near the hermitage at the Small Bridges'. The proximity of the Chapel and Hermitage to the Small Bridges is constantly mentioned; the 'Armitage Site' was well defined as the narrow strip of land between the bridges, with the river on the south and the continuation of the Causeway on the north. It ended on the west side near a ditch which ran north and south to form the boundary of a grove of trees beyond, called the Holt, where the Victorian house named the Hermitage now stands. This western area was always referred to in the old documents as 'the Waste Ground' or as 'a parcel of land called the Waste Ground', but after 1851, when Newnham Terrace began to be built on it, it lost its ancient name.

The Hamond map of 1592 shows no houses west of the Small Bridges except for one building, on an island which seems to correspond to the 'Little Island' in Darwin College garden. It has sometimes been assumed that this building represents the Chapel and Hermitage. However, apart from the improbability of living on an island so difficult of access and liable to floods, the hermit would

* Dr Oliver Green of Caius also owned a meadow between Trinity Street and Sidney Street which, in the early seventeenth century, he developed as a housing estate. He built Green Street across the meadow and it still bears his name.

have been too far from his Small Bridges to intercept traffic and collect his tolls. In fact, we know that the chapel had been demolished probably in 1549, but certainly by 1561, thirty years before Hamond made his map.

We shall probably never discover the exact spot on which the Hermitage stood, but if it were not actually on the present site of the Old Granary or Newnham Grange, or between the two, it was somewhere very near them. Almost certainly it was well to the east of the modern Hermitage, for nearly the whole of that building stands outside the plot of land which has been known as the Armitage since medieval times.

Just over four hundred years ago, about five o'clock on the afternoon of Saturday 5 August 1564, anyone on the Armitage site would have witnessed the wonderful spectacle of Queen Elizabeth's entry into Cambridge. It was the beginning of her famous five-day visit to the University. Eye-witnesses have recorded it in amazing detail. She had spent the previous night in the house of one of her Gentlemen Pensioners at Haslingfield, so that her way to Cambridge next morning lay through Grantchester to Newnham, where she and her retinue were received by the Mayor and his following, and listened to the first of the innumerable orations she had to endure during her visit. Then the whole party rode on to Newnham Mill. 'And there', the account continues, 'being requested to change her horse, she alighted and went into the miller's yard and house for a short space'. (The Jolly Millers public-house, rebuilt early in the twentieth century, still stands on the site of the miller's house.) On emerging, she mounted the fresh horse, and the Mayor still 'riding with the Mace before her Majestie', rode into Cambridge followed by a great cavalcade of lords and ladies-in-waiting past the Armitage, over the Small Bridges, to turn left into Milne Street (now called Queens' Lane) at Queens' College. Here 'the trumpetters . . . by solemn blast, declared her Majestie to approach'. Thus preceded by a procession of Lords and royal officials, she rode along Milne Street between the whole university drawn up in order of seniority, the last doctor and the vice-chancellor with three 'bedells' being upon the step of the door of King's Chapel. Meanwhile, 'the bells both of the Colleges and also of the Towne were rung most part of the afternoon. . . . Order was also taken, that upon the Queen coming to the church doors, all the bells should cease, that her Majestie might heare the oration'. When, five days later, she left Cambridge, it was by the Great Bridge and Huntingdon Road, not by the Armitage and Newnham.

What a splendid sight she must have been as she rode into Cambridge! She was still a young woman, barely thirty, dressed 'in a gown of black velvet pinked: a caul upon her head, set with pearls and precious stones; a hat that was spangled with gold, and a bunch of feathers'. She had been 'attended throughout her progress from Haslingfield by a vast concourse of persons, who rent the air with acclamations of "Long Live the Queen" '.

After this stirring episode, no more events of historical interest took place near the Armitage until 1643, when the Parliamentary troops destroyed both Small Bridges. They were not restored until 1648.

The development of the Armitage site really began in 1672, with the Corporation's grant to Richard Dickinson of a twenty-one years' lease 'of the Armitage and void ground beyond the holt towards Newnham Mill'. Loggan's 1688 map shows a house standing approximately on the site of the north-eastern half of Newnham Grange. It protrudes into the road, and a line drawn across the Causeway leading to the smaller of the two Small Bridges indicates a gate. This must be the house built by Richard Dickinson when he was granted the lease of the Armitage. For obvious reasons it was called Causeway, or Causey, House.

If any further proof were needed that Newnham Grange stands on the site of Causey House it is to be found in an undated letter which Professor Kenny, Downing Professor of Laws of England, once wrote to a Cambridge paper. A newspaper cutting of this letter was found in an album at Newnham Grange.

A CAMBRIDGE STURGEON

Sir — You have given us an interesting account of the sturgeon lately taken at Hemingford Grey, and also of its predecessor captured there half a century ago. But we Cambridge folk must not forget that our own town also can boast its sturgeon.

The diary of Alderman Samuel Newton (preserved in the library of Downing College) records a capture made here in the days of Charles II. The alderman's entry is:— '1680. June 11th. At the back of Alderman Dickinson's house in Cambridge, next the causeway between Small Bridges and Newnham, there was taken by a casting-net, by Coward, a fisherman, a sturgeon of very near (if not altogether) two yards long. The waters were then pretty high about the place where the fish was taken; about four feet deep. It was thought to have been seen in Newnham Mill Pit; if so, in its return it was taken.' This entry in the diary confirms the placing of Dickinson's house in Loggan's map; the sturgeon returning downstream from Newnham Millpool was caught as it swam past the back of his house, somewhere near where the footbridge now crosses to the Little Island.

Mr Goodman in his *History of St Botolph's* records that early in the eighteenth century rates were paid on Causey House. From 1731 onwards, the house appears annually in the parochial rate-books. From 1739 to 1747 it belonged to a Mrs Lavender, a considerable property owner, since not only did she pay rates on the 'Causey' House, and her own 'Dwelling house', but she had to pay as well on four other houses. Mrs Lavender was succeeded by Mr Simeon Lord who kept a china shop in Trumpington Street near Great St. Mary's Church.* Simeon Lord, and his wife after him, remained in Causeway House for nearly thirty years.

In 1779 the house was listed in the parochial rate-books for the last time. A Mr French paid the rates on the house, which, as in Mr Lord's time, was still assessed at £5. Both their names occur again, in the *Cambridge Chronicle*, when on 17 June 1780, a Mr Patrick Beales announced that he had 'entered on Merchant's Yard at the Small Bridges lately occupied by Mr French and formerly by Mr Lord'. The Merchant's Yard was on the opposite side of the road from Causeway House, further east; later, part of it became a builder's yard. This remained in use until 1935, when it and the

* The Cambridge Folk Museum has a bill of his made out to the Duke of Bedford for a large assortment of tableware, both glass and china, purchased in 1757 for £6.6.9.

two little yellow-brick houses between it and Silver Street Bridge were swept away to make room for the red-brick Fisher Building of Queens' College. Thus, in 1780, began the association of the Beales family with the Small Bridges, and soon after with the Armitage — an association that was to last for over a hundred years.

CHAPTER TWO

The Beales Family at the Armitage: 1785–1851

In 1785 the Corporation leased the Armitage site to Patrick Beales for a term of forty years, but five years later he surrendered this lease and took two new leases, whereby in consideration of annual ground rents of 20 and 10 shillings and two 'fines' of £300 and £220, he respectively became tenant for 999 years of the 'parcel of ground called the Armitage' and 'of a certain Piece of Waste Ground at Newnham in the Parish of St Botolph, together with all the Ways Passages Waters Water Courses Easements Priviledges and appurtenances whatsoever'. Corporations were forbidden by law to sell their freehold land, so corrupt Corporations, like the one at Cambridge in those days, adopted a different method of raising money on their properties. This was to grant a lease for a portentous length of time in return for a 'fine' or lump sum and a 'peppercorn' or nominal yearly rent thereafter. In Beales's case, the rent he paid was not an actual peppercorn but a sum of twenty shillings a year.

Attached to the lease is a plan showing that the Piece of Waste Ground ended on the south at Newnham Millpool near the ford by which the cows from Newnham used to cross to their pasture on Sheep's Green.

At the northern extremity, the Beales's plot included not only the site of the little wood called the Holt, which is shown in Loggan's 1688 map, but a ditch which ran on or near its eastern boundary. In the plan attached to the Waste Ground Indenture, the Ditch, as it is carefully labelled, is shown as outside the Armitage. This ditch had disappeared by 1798, probably filled in by the Bealeses when they kept most of the north-west corner of the Waste Land down to the river to make a large garden for their house (later to be called Newnham Grange). Perhaps it was then that they planted the two large pear trees, one of which still remains in the garden of Darwin College.

By the purchase of these two leases, Patrick Beales made himself the master of a very valuable property, since he now owned the

9

entire left bank of the Cam from Newnham Millpool to the first of the two Small Bridges and still rented the Merchant's Yard on the north side of the Small Bridges.

For centuries, barges had been bringing corn and coal from King's Lynn up the rivers to Cambridge, where many of them ended their journeys and deposited their cargoes at the King's Mill, or at the quays along the east side of the Silver Street Millpool. Here, a large warehouse (now occupied mainly by the Centre of South Asian Studies and the Land Economy library) is still to be seen next to Scudamore's boathouse.

Later, the barges began coming still further upstream, as far as the Newnham Millpool, and more wharves and warehouses were needed. No buildings on the river, or the towpath, are shown on the 1790 plan of the Waste Ground, but in Custance's plan of 1798 the riverside granaries by Newnham Grange appear, though no towpath; and a long narrow building is shown close to the river in what later became the garden of the Hermitage. The development of the mercantile property was therefore probably due to the Bealeses.

The towpath may have been made for the barges, or for access to the river. In the 1851 plan of the estate, it is shown as continuing the whole way to the Newnham Millpool, and runs through the present garden along the river bank from the landing-stage to the copper-beech.

Mr Goodman tells of listening in 1921 to the reminiscences of an old inhabitant of Newnham, who recalled the days when the river from Queens' to Newnham Mill was full of barges loading and unloading at the various wharves of Patrick Beales and Co., coal and corn merchants, and he added: 'all the wharves were theirs, except Mr Brown's at the Small Bridges'. Mr Brown's wharf was on the river-bank of the present kitchen-garden on the east side of the Old Granary.

Patrick Beales did not live to see the fruition of his plans, for he died at forty-two, on 20 October 1792, only two years after buying the property. It was his younger brother, Samuel Pickering Beales, who developed the business so successfully and carried it on for the next thirty or forty years.

It is odd how difficult it is to discover the exact date of the building of an old house. Cooper, once Town-clerk of Cambridge, says in his

Memorials of Cambridge that the site of the Hermitage 'was in 1790 leased for a long term to Patrick Beales, from whom it came to his brother, S. P. Beales, Esq. who erected thereon a substantial mansion and mercantile premises now occupied by his son, Patrick Beales, alderman, who purchased the reversion from the corporation in 1839'. But Cooper gives no indication of the date for the building of the 'substantial mansion' – the future Newnham Grange – except that it must have been after 1792, when Patrick Beales died, and before the death of S. P. Beales in 1836.

The Royal Commission on Historical Monuments in its *Survey and Inventory of the City of Cambridge* states that 'the house was built early in the nineteenth century, before 1830, for the Beale[s] family, coal and corn merchants' and, after describing the exterior in detail, repeats: 'Newnham Grange is an early nineteenth-century house of gracious aspect containing fittings of the period'. But, as the existing house is clearly outlined in Custance's map of 1798, except for a slight difference in the road-frontage of the east wing, owing to its having been rebuilt in 1885, it is evident that the house must have been built in the eighteenth century.

By searching the parochial rate-books of St Botolph's, it has been possible to establish that the date of the building was 1793. S. P. Beales had been assessed at £8 for a house in St Botolph's parish in which he apparently lived from 1790 to 1793; but in the ratepayers' list of 1794 this property is marked 'Now A. Watford'. In the June quarter of 1793, Beales paid rates for the first time on an assessment of £40 and this certainly included Newnham Grange, for Beales and his sons after him continued to pay rates at the same figure of £40 for their 'house and premises' until 1838, when the assessment was suddenly increased to £350. Possibly this was a result of the Municipal Reform Act of 1835, because other large assessments in the parish also show a proportionate increase. It seems clear that Newnham Grange had been completed and occupied by the June quarter of 1793, and that by 1794 S. P. Beales had disposed of his former house to A. Watford.

The Causeway House had been assessed at £5 for many years, but the last time it was separately mentioned in the ratepayers' list is 1779. In 1780 Patrick Beales 'entered on Merchant's Yard' and from this year he was assessed at £12. Perhaps this assessment

included both the Merchant's Yard and Causeway House; but there
is no record that Patrick was in possession of the latter until 1785, so
this point remains doubtful. On his death, his brother Samuel took
his place in the list as liable for the £12 assessment. From June 1793,
however, when the new assessment at £40 first appeared in the list,
the old assessment of £12 was omitted. Did S. P. Beales then give up
renting Merchant's Yard? It is not mentioned under his name any
longer; probably he had no further use for it now that he had so much
room in which to expand his business.

It may be that the little old house was almost derelict by 1785,
when Patrick Beales first leased the Armitage. Consequently, when
in 1790 he took on the new lease for 999 years, he may have decided
to pull it down and build a 'substantial mansion' in its place.
Perhaps the plans were ready, and even the building begun, before
he was prematurely cut off at the age of forty-two. Such a large and
important house must have taken some time to build, especially as it
had to be constructed on piles, on account of the low-lying marshy site.
The Causeway House was on ground level but the main part of the
new house was built a good two feet above the ground, which
allowed headroom for the splendid range of cellars which still lie
under the main entrance floor of Newnham Grange. This was
possibly as much to raise the house above flood-level as to provide
space for extensive wine-cellars. Nothing is now recognizable of
Causeway House, unless the Beales's three-storeyed kitchen-wing
with its hipped roof and dormer windows, on the east side of the new
house, incorporated some small part of the old building. The present
big sash windows on the south and east sides would have been put
in to match with those of the new mansion. But if no use was made of
the earlier house, the Bealeses did apparently have their kitchens
built on the same site; they did not, however, keep the old name of
the house. Nor did they give it a new one, for it was only called 'Mr
Beales's house at Newnham' until it was named Newnham Grange
by Professor Darwin in 1885.

The first event to occur at the Beales's new house was chronicled
by Henry Gunning in his *Reminiscences* (1854), where at the beginning
of the second volume he writes:

A flood higher by a foot than that of October 10th, 1762, took place in February of this year (1795). . . . There was a ball given by the Freemasons on that evening, and a carriage was waiting to take Mrs Beales and her party to it. The coachman (in order to save his own life and that of his horses) was obliged to drive away, leaving the company behind. Monsieur Corneille, a celebrated hairdresser, whose presence was anxiously awaited by several parties in the town, could not leave Mr Beales's house, but was obliged to take up his residence there for the night. A member of Queens' College who left the ball about four o'clock in the morning utterly unconscious of what had taken place, sprang from the top of the steps on the left of the cloisters, and was surprised to find himself up to his waist in water. Subsequently to the setting in of the frost, there had been a heavy fall of snow and the frost broke up with a heavy rain. The bridge near Magdalene College, then called the Great Bridge, consisted of three small arches which effectually prevent the efflux of the water. The present bridge is so constructed that the flood, however large, passes under it without difficulty. Mr Beales lost many chauldrons of coals, which were carried by the flood nearly a mile from his premises, and were stopt by the shallows at Midsummer Common, where for a long time a great number of boys supported themselves by dredging for them.

Though the coal business they founded in the eighteenth century survived until 1965 under the name of Austin Beales and Company, the family of Patrick Beales apparently died out in Cambridge some forty years ago. It is strange that so little is remembered about a family once very prominent in the commercial and public life of the town; none of their personal papers or letters have turned up to help with this narrative. The one characteristic which appears to have distinguished them from other worthy citizens was their strong vein of liberalism; indeed one of them achieved some fame as a radical. This was Edmond, the third son of Samuel Pickering Beales. He was born in 1803 at Newnham—that is, in the house later called Newnham Grange. Educated at Eton and a scholar of Trinity, after leaving Cambridge he became a barrister. He is mentioned by Sir

George Otto Trevelyan in his life of Lord Macaulay, as a contemporary of Macaulay's at Trinity: 'Mr Edmond Beales, so well known to
our generation as an ardent politician'. He was 'one of the leading
members of the cleverest set of boys who ever were together at a
public school'. Foreign politics were his passion. He championed
among other causes that of the Polish refugees, and he organized
Garibaldi's visit to England. He agitated for manhood suffrage; sometimes at great public meetings he was in conflict with the police. In
spite of this he ended his career as a County Court judge in Cambridgeshire and Huntingdon. He died in 1881 in London. His father too
had fought injustice in his day. He has been called 'a merchant who
acquired local celebrity as a political reformer', though Arthur Gray
in his book on *The Town of Cambridge* says, perhaps rather unkindly,
that 'he was scarcely a disinterested Hampden'. This is on account
of the part he played in the famous Toll Cause.

By 1743, the Corporation had begun to lease to the highest bidder
the right to collect tolls at fairs and markets. Then, after some years,
the lessees, with the connivance of the Corporation, hit upon the
profitable plan of levying a toll of twopence on all carts laden with
merchandise when entering or leaving the town. The annual payment of the lessees to the Corporation rose from an average of £240
at the end of the eighteenth century to £750 by 1822. The tax caused
bitter resentment and many others besides the Bealeses refused to pay
it. The Beales's waggons went out to deliver coal and corn in all
parts of the county, and thus had frequent occasion to cross Silver
Street Bridge, where the collector was stationed. After the money had
been paid, the cart would be marked with chalk, rather as luggage
nowadays is marked when it has passed through the Customs.
The tax fell particularly heavily on the Bealeses as merchants, and on
their customers, the farmers; so eventually they determined to resist
the imposition.

In 1824 a public fund was raised to defray the costs of legal
proceedings. It is said that some of the colleges subscribed to this
fund – among them, St John's and Trinity. They were anxious to be
relieved of dealing themselves with the coal dumped on their small
college wharves, or hithes as they were called, and they had asked
S. P. Beales to handle their coal supplies for them from his own
premises.

The Bealeses had originally been corn rather than coal merchants, but like most corn merchants, in order to retain the custom of the farmers who sold them their corn, they had been obliged to supply the farmers with their coal, much of their trade being done on a barter or debit-credit system. The merchants sold coal and seed-corn to the farmer and later on took the farmer's corn in payment, which they would then sell to the millers or maltsters.

At first the Bealeses had refused the colleges' request, pleading the expense of the tolls, but when the colleges assured them of their support, should legal action about the tolls be taken, the Bealeses gave way. This is a matter of hearsay, but some substance is given to it by a recent search at Trinity, for it transpired that in December 1824 the bursar was asked to enquire after an employee of Mr Beales, Thomas Bitten, who was in hospital with injuries received in helping to fight a fire in New Court on 10 December. This indicates that, by the year in which the public fund was raised, the Bealeses were already supplying members of Trinity with coal, and ever since that time both Trinity and St John's have bought coal from the (Austin) Beales firm. After 1867 the Bealeses were no longer called corn merchants in the town directories but were described solely as coal merchants, with the occasional addition of brewers or maltsters after their name.

It was not until 1826 that the Corporation, through their lessee, Joseph Brett, brought matters to a head in an action against S. P. Beales and his son 'to recover tolls alledged to be due for loaded carts and waggons coming into or going out of the town at the rate of two-pence each cart and waggon'. The Bealeses won the case. But the next year when Brett sued another firm of merchants, he and the Corporation won. So the action against the Bealeses was brought up again; and once more the Bealeses triumphed. After this, the Corporation had to undertake to bring no further actions and to levy no such toll again. The cost of the three trials to both parties was estimated to have amounted to £8,000. The result to the Corporation was calamitous, for not only did they have to pay over £4,000 in legal dues, but they also lost their income from the lessees.

The law suit aroused great public interest, especially among legal historians, for it raised the issue: who had the right to exact tolls? Much ancient history was cited, and the fifteenth-century hermits were quoted as having been given the right to collect tolls by royal grant, and *not* by the Corporation. Thus, by an ironical twist of fate, it was the old toll-collecting hermits at the Small Bridges who helped the Bealeses to win their case.

In 1824, S. P. Beales mortgaged the Armitage and the Waste Ground to raise £7,000, either because he anticipated a legal battle, or because his business was no longer prospering. As the lawsuits are said to have cost the victorious defendants £4,000, the drain on their capital may have crippled the Bealeses for many years to come.

S. P. Beales died in 1836, aged seventy-one, and was buried in St Botolph's Church under the same tombstone as his brother Patrick. He seems to have played an active part in the parish as church-warden, and also in borough affairs. (Cooper refers to him several times in his *Annals*.) During the threat of Napoleonic invasion in 1801 he became Quartermaster in the Cambridgeshire Yeomanry Cavalry. But this patriotic venture had rather a flat ending, for, as Cooper tells, 'on finding upon a muster that their numbers were reduced from 64 to 22', he and the other three officers 'suspended any further muster till their number was sufficiently increased to render them of some utility' — and apparently they never met again. He left all his property at Newnham to his elder sons, Charles and Patrick, as tenants in common. Three years later, on payment of a 'Consideration of £80', the Corporation converted the 999 years' lease into a freehold. In 1842, the brothers dissolved their partnership. Patrick made Charles an annuity of £200 in return for which Charles granted him, among other assets, his undivided half-share in the Capital Mansion which he (Patrick) occupied. Both of them had been sent to school at Charterhouse, and Charles had a university education as a member of Peterhouse.

Judging from the numerous legal documents in the keeping of E. F. Turner and Sons, the business continued to decline, though, probably in a vain attempt to bolster it up, Patrick had added the trade of a 'Common Brewer' to his other business. But the coming of the railway to Cambridge in 1845 seems to have been a disaster to many of the inhabitants. Before that time, Cambridge had had 'the bustling activities of a busy seaport town. The business activities . . .

were mainly those incident to an emporium depending upon its water-way traffic.'* But now, 'all this was dislocated and diverted by the new intercommunications opened up by the railways. The record that over a thousand houses were empty during the years 1851–1854 furnishes evidence of the serious stress that was soon felt in the town.' Few merchants can have suffered more than Patrick Beales, who depended for his livelihood on his waterborne coal traffic and, on 2 March 1850, we find him mortgaging the Armitage and Waste Land to 'Swann Hurrell of Cambridge, Iron monger', to raise £1,000. From this point, Swann Hurrell plays a principal role in the story of the Bealeses.

* Arthur B. Gray, 'The Cambridge Business Man', *Cambridge Chamber of Commerce Journal*, 1918.

CHAPTER THREE

Swann Hurrell and the Hermitage

SWANN HURRELL was Patrick Beales's brother-in-law, his sister Katherine Frances having married Patrick in the 1830s. Born in 1816, he belonged on his mother's side to a well-known and prosperous Cambridge family, the Finches, who as early as 1688 had established themselves as ironmongers in the town. After five generations of Finches had followed each other in the business, in 1847 Swann Hurrell succeeded his uncle, Charles Finch, the last of the line. Shortly before his death in 1866, it was this Charles Finch who sold his house in Sidney Street, opposite Jesus Lane, to Dr Whewell, the Master of Trinity, for the site of Whewell's Court.

Perhaps ever since its beginning, but certainly for a very long time, the Finches' foundry had been established on what was to become the site of St John's College Chapel and the Master's Lodge. But as the Chapel was being built by 1863, the foundry must have been moved before then to its new home in Thompson's Lane, a short way downstream from the Great Bridge. It was doubtless Swann Hurrell's connection with an iron foundry rather than his likeness to the Duke of Wellington that caused him to be nicknamed the Iron Duke, though his distinguished appearance and his courteous manners probably helped to earn him this title. His photograph and that of his brother-in-law, Patrick Beales, are preserved in the Reference Library at the Guildhall. Both were Mayors of Cambridge for more than one term of office.

Patrick appears in his photograph sombre and unsmiling, with a wide, set mouth like that of the Duchess in *Alice in Wonderland,* a most formidable figure, standing very square and upright in his frockcoat, every inch a Mayor and a Victorian paterfamilias — as indeed he was, for he had not less than eleven children.

Swann Hurrell bears no kind of resemblance to his brother-in-law. Very tall and thin, he is photographed seated, with his legs crossed. His extraordinarily pale eyes gaze out of the photograph dreamily, and he has a gentle expression on his face. In spite of his vestigial white whiskers, his button boots, his furled umbrella, and the very tall top-hat on the table by his side, he does not look at all like the efficient Mayor and the good man of business he must also have been — for he it was who came to the rescue in 1850 when Patrick Beales was on the verge of bankruptcy.

By mortgaging his property to Swann Hurrell, Patrick Beales was able to pay off a thousand pounds on his father's 1824 mortgage, but far more drastic steps had to be taken to satisfy the mortgagees when they proceeded to reclaim the rest of the £7,000. Other creditors in this time of depression in Cambridge were evidently clamouring for repayment, and it was no doubt to save himself from impending bankruptcy that on 1 November 1850, he entered into articles of agreement with Swann Hurrell, John Hazard of Brentford, brewer, and Edmond Beales (his younger brother, the radical), barrister-at-law, to sell his property under their supervision for the benefit of his creditors.

It is probable that Swann Hurrell was the instigator of this move as the best way to help his brother-in-law out of his difficulties; for it was Swann Hurrell who bought Lot 1, the house and garden, at the auction, though it was specified in the advertisement that Beales should be left in occupation. The advertisement of the sale gives a marvellously detailed account of the property as it was in 1851.

One step towards freeing Beales from his debts appears to have been taken before the auction. The counting-house, yard, and business premises had been sold to Martha Edelston for £2,000. The advertisement of the auction states that

> the Purchaser of that part is bound to build a 9-inch Brick Wall, not less than 8 feet high, to divide such portion so purchased from Lot 1; such Wall commencing at the West Gable-end of the First Range of Granaries already sold, to be carried in a line across the Yard down to the River; and the purchaser of Lot 1 is to brick up and make good any of the ends of the Buildings to be separated.

St John's College possesses a copy of the advertisement of the sale and the accompanying plan for the suggested development of the Waste Ground as a building site. The auction by Wentworth and

Son took place at the Bull Hotel on Wednesday 26 March 1851, at seven o'clock in the evening.

Lot 1 Comprises a most excellent Brick-built FAMILY RESI-DENCE, opposite Queens' Green, now in the occupation of PATRICK BEALES, Esq., allowed to be one of the best built Houses in the Town, comprising on the basement, noble Entrance Hall, capital Dining Room, Two Drawing Rooms, and Breakfast Room. On the First Floor are Four Principal Bed Rooms, with the Dressing Rooms attached, and Three other Bed Rooms, and numerous Servants Rooms over. The Domestic Offices, comprise two Kitchens, Larder, Scullery, and extensive Cellarage. Together with a Range of Stables and Granaries on the left-hand side of the house, Yard behind, and an opening leading to the River. Also the Mill house (as shewn on Plan). Green-House, Shrub-beries, Lawn, and Ornamental Garden, extending to the beautiful meandering Stream forming a branch of the River Cam, across which are Two Islands, presenting altogether a most delightful Residence, suitable for a Genteel Family. The extreme Frontage of this Lot is nearly 200 Feet.

The whole of the above is Freehold except the Two Islands, which are leasehold from the Corporation of Cambridge for 40 years, from Michaelmas 1839, at a Ground Rent of Five Guineas.

The remaining fourteen lots are described at length. Lots 2, 3, and 4 are described as 'THREE VALUABLE BUILDING SITES'. One of them (lot 4) at the corner of Newnham Road possessed 'a Double Frontage opposite the contemplated picturesque Villa Residence, about to be built by Mr Edlin, Architect'. (Alas for Mr Edlin, Springfield, the house at the corner of Sidgwick Avenue and the Backs, later the home of the Jebbs, is no longer admired for its picturesque qualities.) These three small lots were to become the site of the present Hermitage. Lots 5 and 6 faced on to Newnham Road, but as Patrick Beales's garden extended right round the bend of the river, their gardens would have been short. The remaining eight lots on the other hand had long narrow gardens reaching to the river. They included the towpath, which was evidently of no further use, but was still marked on the plan. The last lot, number 15,

faced Newnham Millpool. It became the site of the Granta Brewery
and of the Granta Hotel in the 1880s.

It is not known who, if anyone, bought lots 7 to 15 at the auction.
Newnham Terrace is not mentioned in the directories until 1866,
when six houses in it, numbered 3 to 8, are listed, as well as the
Granta Brewery at the end of the row. The numbers in Newnham
Terrace have always been peculiar: even now they jump inexplic-
ably from 5 to 9—6, 7, and 8 being non-existent. But Darwin
College is not further concerned with the history of Newnham
Terrace, except in so far as lots 2 to 6 never did become part of
the terrace. Lots 2, 3, and 4 were bought by David King, solicitor
to the auctioneers. Speculative builders may well have hesitated to
buy land for development at this time of depression in Cambridge,
knowing that hundreds of houses were standing empty in the town.
Not long after the auction, David King completed his purchase of
the five lots by buying numbers 5 and 9 privately from Patrick
Beales.

In coming to the rescue of Patrick Beales, Swann Hurrell had
put the house up to auction to determine what the fair price for
it should be, and it had fallen to him for £2,310. But this is not
the end of the story. Soon afterwards he must have decided to build
himself a house next door to his brother-in-law. He was greatly
attached to his sister and to the whole Beales family. In the un-
published diary of Josiah Chater, a Cambridge accountant whose
sons founded the present firm of Chater and Myhill, Miss Enid
Porter of the Folk Museum discovered the following entry under
28 January 1847: 'Mr Swann Hurrell was married to Miss Foster
of Trumpington, at Trumpington this morning and all his men had
a supper at the Red Lion.' His wife predeceased him, probably by
many years, and they had no children. This accounts for the hold
his Beales nephews and nieces had on his interest and affection.
The second son Edward he seems to have adopted as his own, for
as soon as he was old enough, Edward was placed in his uncle's
ironmongery business and in 1870 succeeded to the Hurrell foundry,
which eventually took the name of E. Beales & Co.

In order to have a large enough site for his house, Hurrell set about buying back Lots 2 to 6 from their purchaser, David King. The negotiations about the resale of the five lots are as complicated as all the other transactions to do with the Armitage and the Waste Ground. The numerous legal papers show that by November 1852 Swann Hurrell was in possession of all five lots, for which he had paid a total of £1,010. It is not known when the present garden of the Hermitage was formed by cutting off the south-west corner of the Beales's garden, but in an 1871 plan a wall separating the two is clearly marked. The wall was removed in 1968, so that the Hermitage garden has become part of the grounds of Newnham Grange again. This compensates slightly for the loss of the lawn on which the new Rayne Building has been erected between the Hermitage and Newnham Grange.

According to the evidence in the parochial rate-books and the directories, Swann Hurrell must have built and occupied his house by 1853. Even in 1852 he had already begun to pay rates for a house and garden next door to Patrick Beales. It is impossible to decide how much of the present Hermitage forms part of the original house — it has been so much altered, added-to, and sub-divided. There had been 'substantial brick-built Stables, loose Boxes, Coach-House and Groom's Room over' on the corner three lots when David King bought them at the auction, and in 1852 it was he who had paid the rates for them. Later on, the stabling was pulled down and the three-storeyed west end of the house was built in its place, probably by Dr Parkinson. He may also have made the existing yard with perhaps a little coach house and stables on its south side. What certainly does remain of Swann Hurrell's house is the drawing-room with the bedroom over it in the big round bay facing the garden and, in all likelihood, also the long narrow verandah, supported by elegantly ornamented iron pillars, on to which the drawing-room used to open until, in 1937, it was divided into two rooms by Miss Cragoe. In some other parts of the house, a delicacy of detail and a sense of proportion are to be found that seem to indicate the same date of building. Most of the cellars must also belong to the 1853 house; they are extensive though not so lofty and fine as those built by S. P. Beales next door.

Swann Hurrell remained in his new house for about eight years, until in 1861 he moved to 30 Thompson's Lane, where his back door opened on to his foundry yard. The fine old town house still exists, but the beautiful small garden on the opposite side of the lane has long since been built over.

On leaving Newnham in 1861, Hurrell let his house to a Mrs Sarah Miller. She apparently died in 1870, for a Richard Miller, probably her son, living in Newnham Terrace, is described early in 1871 as being 'now or lately in occupation of the freehold messuage'.

Then Hurrell sold his house to Stephen Parkinson, D.D., F.R.S. He had been Senior Wrangler in 1845 and became a celebrated teacher of mathematics at St John's. As the *D.N.B.* puts it: 'In the eighteen years of his tutorship nearly a thousand pupils passed under his care, and Parkinson's Side was an important factor in the prosperity of the college. . . . He took a leading part in university affairs, and was one of the most vigorous and powerful opponents of reform and innovation.' Dr Parkinson bought the house on his marriage to Miss Elizabeth Lucy Whateley, but it was evidently not big and grand enough to suit them as it was. Miss Whateley had money, and the house was greatly enlarged and 'improved' to provide for a numerous staff. The main staircase was built in a Gothic manner; the initials SP carved on the newel of the wooden balustrade show that he was proud of his work. And the house at last received a name. Dr Parkinson must have known about the Hermitage, for that was what the house was called, though the old hermitage, as has already been stated, was almost certainly further to the east, and the Bealeses might have claimed the name for their house with greater justice. In Spalding's *Directory* of 1874, the Rev. Stephen Parkinson is listed as living in the Hermitage and so it has been called ever since. He died in 1889. An old friend and mathematical colleague of his, Dr Morgan (1830–1912), Master of Jesus College, used to tell how, after the funeral, he decided to pay a visit of condolence on the poor widow of 'Little Parkie', as Dr Parkinson was affectionately called on account of his tiny stature. Walking down the Backs, the Master of Jesus busied himself composing sympathetic remarks to make on arriving at the Hermitage. However, they were not needed, for Mrs Parkinson met him at the door, exclaiming: 'Oh, Master, wasn't it a very little coffin?'

She continued living at the Hermitage and six years later remarried, this time a Fellow of Trinity, Gerard Francis Cobb

Mrs Cobb coming out of the Hermitage

(1838–1904), a classic and moral scientist—though music was his real *forte*. He was a prolific composer of songs and set most, if not all, of Kipling's *Barrack Room Ballads* to music. Mr Cobb died in 1904 and Mrs Cobb lived on at the Hermitage in stately grandeur until her death in 1913. She left the house to the Master, Fellows, and Scholars of St John's College, and that is why it has become part of Darwin College.

On her death, St John's let the house for four years to the Rev. J. Plowden Wardlaw, Chaplain of St Edward's. Then for two years the War Office used it as a Rest Home for officers. It is said that one of them used to ride his horse through the front door along the hall and out of the garden door opposite, to graze on the lawn. In September 1919, it became a university lodging-house in the yearly tenancy of Mr H. C. H. Coppins. He had to provide not less than ten sets of rooms, the first offer to be made to St John's. In 1931, it passed from him to St Catharine's for a similar purpose and, six years later, Miss Lucy Cragoe took it over to run as a guest-house. Many distinguished people have made their homes there for a time—Dr Ramsey, lately Archbishop of Canterbury, and Dr Frisch, Nobel Prize winner, among them. Celebrated actors and actresses, such as Sir Lewis Casson and Dame Sybil Thorndike, have also been her guests. Then, in 1954, St John's allowed Miss Cragoe to assign her lease to the Association for Promoting a Third Foundation for Women in the University. Thus, the Hermitage became the birth-place of New Hall. In October 1958, Miss Cragoe's lease having terminated, St John's let the house direct to New Hall, until such time as their new buildings were ready for them.

By an odd coincidence, New Hall is also connected with the Darwins, for it was George Darwin's youngest brother Horace who, in 1882, had bought land on the Huntingdon Road for the erection of his house, the Orchard, and, some seventy years later, it was Horace and Ida Darwin's daughters, Ruth (Mrs Rees-Thomas) and Nora (Lady Barlow), who gave the house and garden for the site of the third women's college in Cambridge. New Hall has thus been established in the place where another family of Darwins once lived, for many years, whilst the Hermitage was left to become part of Darwin College.

CHAPTER FOUR

The Beales Family Again: 1851–84

Patrick Beales, like his father before him, had always played
an active part as churchwarden at St Botolph's; his name occurs
frequently in the records of parish business. He continued to occupy
the house in which he had been born and had lived for most of
his life. The directories went on describing him as a Coal and Corn
Merchant at Newnham; thus he must still have remained responsible
for the management of the coal firm. The motives of the widow,
Martha Edelston, in buying the business premises remain obscure.
To augment his income Beales had a brewery in Malting Lane and
an office in Bene't Street at which he combined the coal trade with
that of a 'Distributor of Stamps' (for legal documents). It is to
be hoped that by these means he earned enough to bring up his
large family in comfort. His wife died in 1857 when only the eldest
son, Pat, was earning his living; Mary Ellen was twenty, Edward
nineteen, and the rest were children, some of them still in the
nursery.

By the sale of his Newnham property, Patrick had realized over
£6,000, but most of this must have gone in paying off the remainder
of the 1824 mortgage. However, his financial stringency cannot
have affected his standing in the borough, for in 1856 he was elected
mayor—a position he was to fill a second time ten years later. He
continued to work for the Liberal Party and in recognition of this
was presented, in 1869, with a silver salver by a group of 'fellow
Townsmen and Friends as a mark of personal regard in acknow-
ledgment of services to the Liberal Cause', according to the inscrip-
tion engraved on the salver.

In 1874, a certain Arthur Neve (1859–1942) began work as
a junior clerk in the Beales counting house at Newnham, when he
was only fifteen. His daughters, the Misses Elsie and Winifred Neve,
who inherited the salver from their father, have kindly presented
it to the Master and Fellows of Darwin College, so that it should
return to its former home. Arthur Neve used to tell his children

26

about the fun he had there as a boy, exploring the granaries and playing on the islands. The Misses Neve knew some of Patrick Beales's daughters. The eldest, Miss M. E. Beales (1837–1918), had probably borne too much responsibility as a girl in the bringing up of the younger children after their mother's death. This may have made her the formidable lady, 'so conscious of her position', whom the Misses Neve remember with terror. She was also an exceedingly active director of the firm—so active indeed that at one time she used to have the cash book brought round to her house in Park Terrace for weekly inspection. In the late eighties she sacked the manager on the spot for drinking and forthwith appointed young Arthur Neve as his successor. He soon proved his worth and remained with the company, first as manager, and then as secretary, until he retired in 1927 at the age of sixty-eight.

The coal trade must have improved by 1864, for in that year Hurrell bought the premises back from the mysterious widow Martha Edelston, presumably in order to make his nephew Edward a partner in his father's business, for the 1866 directory described the firm as Beales, Patrick and Son. Three years later the family met with a terrible disgrace. On 21 June 1869, Josiah Chater entered in his diary: 'Heard that Pat Beales had absconded having overdrawn his account £6 or £7,000 at the bankers, he being Borough Treasurer.' He was referring to Patrick, the eldest son, who had been made Borough Treasurer in 1857 when his father was acting Deputy Mayor, during the Mayoralty of his uncle Swann Hurrell. There had been seven candidates for the post, Pat's only serious rival being a member of the well-known Cambridge family of Eaden. It was not till the fourth ballot had been taken that Pat was finally elected by the necessary majority. Perhaps his father and uncle cannot be blamed for voting for him, but later on they must have bitterly regretted having proposed their boy for the post.

The *Cambridge Chronicle* gave a long account of the meeting of the Corporation Finance Committee, at which the Town Clerk spoke of the serious duty he had to perform in reporting that Mr Patrick Beales, the Borough Treasurer, had deposited at Mortlock's Bank a bond for £7,000 bearing the Corporation Seal, which seal he,

Beales, had obtained illicitly. The Town Clerk reported that Beales had been relieved of his duties and the meeting then discussed the appointment of a successor; but it was not until November that the new treasurer did in fact take up his office, perhaps to give time for an attempt to clear up the irregularities in the accounts.

The accounts kept by Beales during his twelve years in office are in such confusion that it is impossible to know how much was due to incompetence and how much to deliberate falsification. He had opened an account at Mortlock's Bank under the name of 'Patrick Beales, Junior, Borough Treasurer', and the actual wording of this bank account led him, or permitted him, to mingle Corporation money inextricably with his own. By June 1869 the overdraft on this account had risen to over £7,000. Something desperate had to be done to deal with this situation. He therefore drew up a Corporation bond for £7,000 *plus* interest, made an impression of the Corporation Seal and deposited the bond at the bank as security. Suspicions, however, were aroused when Mortlock's noticed that, though sealed, the bond had not been properly attested with the customary signatures. Beales, realizing that awkward enquiries were being made, thereupon absconded, though not with £7,000 in his pocket as Josiah Chater implies. It appears that no attempt was made to bring him to justice. Nothing more is known about the wretched young man except that, in the next directory, his name no longer appears as the occupant of 3 Newnham Terrace, and that in 1870 his father states rather cryptically in his will that provision had been made for his son Patrick.

The bank's solicitors later on sought Counsel's opinion as to whether they had a case for suing the Corporation for the overdraft of £7,300, but owing to the ambiguity in the title of Patrick's account at the bank, Counsel considered their case was not strong enough. Eventually the Corporation agreed that a proportion of the amount owing to the bank was their liability. This amounted only to £1,000 *plus* interest. The Corporation in their turn recovered an amount almost equivalent to this sum from poor old Patrick Beales, Senior, who in 1857 had guaranteed his son on his appointment as treasurer. It is pitiful to think of the unhappiness Pat's defalcation must have caused his father and family, hitherto so justly proud of the position they held among the leading citizens of Cambridge.

After 1870, the Beales's fortunes took a turn for the better. Not only did Edward succeed to his uncle's ironmongery business, but in the following year his uncle made it possible for him to buy back the whole of the Armitage—that is, his family home, as well as the business premises.

In 1861 Hurrell had raised £2,000 by a mortgage on his Newnham property. In 1871, he redeemed this mortgage, and conveyed the freehold of 'the Hermitage'—as it would soon be called—to Dr Parkinson. He also conveyed the Beales house and garden *plus* the business premises (which he had bought back in 1864 from Mrs Edelston) to Edward for £3,750. On the following day Edward repaid his uncle this sum by means of a mortgage on his new property.

There is no knowing if his father took any part in these transactions, but he must have been glad to see the property, which he had alienated twenty years before, again in the possession of the Bealeses. He was seventy-four and had only two more years to live. By his will he left all his personal and real estate to his sons Edward and Frederick with permission to sell his estate when the trustees of his will should think it advantageous. The sons might buy in the premises at public auction if they so liked. Nothing further is known about Frederick. Edward had probably married before his father's death in 1873, for the 1874 directory shows him established at 29 Thompson's Lane in a smaller version of his uncle's fine house which it adjoined.

After their father's death, his daughters stayed on in the house for a few years. Three of them married clergymen; the others remained single. The Misses Neve remembered Emily, the youngest of the three unmarried daughters, as a friendly and rather attractive woman. She eventually left Cambridge to keep house for her uncle Swann Hurrell. He had been mayor for the third and last time in 1865, and continued living at 30 Thompson's Lane until he moved to St Leonard's in 1891.* Mr W. A. Young, who had worked in the foundry after it had been taken over by Alexander Macintosh, describes how Mr Hurrell 'was wont to look in at the foundry at times and each spring would ask whether the swallows had returned'. Young was once feeling very sore over the failure of an experiment

* *The Ironmonger*, 15 September 1934.

he had been making at the foundry. 'Mr Macintosh', he relates, 'must have mentioned the incident to Mr Hurrell because a few days later I turned into Thompson's Lane just as he was getting out of his brougham. He waited on the steps of his house and as I was passing put his hand on my shoulder and said: "Remember, Young, no man succeeds always." ' Swann Hurrell died at St Leonard's in 1897 aged eighty-one. Emily remained for the rest of her long life at St Leonard's in a house she named 'Hurrell' after him.

A distant relative of his, the late Miss Kathleen Hurrell of Newton, Cambridgeshire, told me the following anecdote about her cousin Emily. Happening to be at St Leonard's in the 1930s, by chance she passed Miss Emily's house, and was so surprised at seeing her own surname on the gate that she stopped to make enquiries from the owner as to the origin of the name. Miss Emily was delighted to receive her and soon established their relationship. The house was full of Hurrell relics — among them she remembered being shown a wooden shield with the family coat of arms of three cross-bows painted on it, 'some original pages' of Domesday Book and, even more remarkable, a silver spoon engraved with the date 1060! Miss Hurrell did not know what became of Miss Emily's treasures except that she did not bequeath any of them to the Hurrells. Doubtless they all went to the Bealeses.

By 1878, Miss Emily's sisters had moved out of their old home into 12 Newnham Terrace, where they remained for some years. The big house was let, first to a surgeon called Dr Bumpsted, and then to Mr Arthur Gray, Fellow and, many years later, Master, of Jesus College. (He was an ardent antiquary and wrote an excellent book on *The Town of Cambridge* which contains the chapter on the Tolls Cause from which I have already quoted.) During these years the Counting House, later to be incorporated in the north end of the Old Granary, remained in use as the coal office,* but coal was no longer handled on the premises, and as for the great granaries,

---

* An advertisement of the Beales business, dated June 1871, reads: 'P. Beales, COAL MERCHANT, Offices: NEWNHAM, 27 St Andrew's Street and HILLS ROAD YARD. Cash Prices: Best Duck 19s 2d (a ton) Delivery 1/- per ton.' There follows a list of the different kinds of much cheaper coal that could be supplied. It ends with Coke, costing only twopence less than the best Duck coal, which was so called because it was brought up the river by water.

they must have stood empty and deserted for years, ever since the Bealeses ceased to be corn merchants.

Edward proved in the end even less successful than his father in the management of the coal business. Matters evidently went from bad to worse until, in 1884, he was unable to meet his debts. It must have been a bitter blow for his uncle who had done so much for him ever since he was a boy. The climax was reached on 30 September when Edward entered into a Deed of Assignment for the benefit of his creditors, who, by agreeing to such a course, saved him from the stigma of formal bankruptcy. By this Deed, he handed over all his real and personal estate except the family wearing apparel and bedding, and in exchange his creditors released him from his debts. His nice little house in Thompson's Lane was sold with all its contents. Alexander Macintosh, whose family had been established as braziers and tinplaters in a shop in Market Street since 1816, bought the entire ironmongery business. The foundry was renamed the Cam Foundry and the shop and offices at 14 Market Hill became the well-known premises of Alexander Macintosh and Sons. It was not until 1962, seventy-eight years later, that this firm came to an end, much to the dismay of the older inhabitants of Cambridge. Now the familiar eighteenth-century building with its fine old red-brick façade has been demolished to make room for new shops and offices with flats over them.

Edward's coal business, however, was allowed to continue under its old name of P. Beales and Co., though he himself left Cambridge after the crash. Nothing more is known about him but his son, 'young Mr Edward', was later taken into the business. When they were children in the nineties, the Misses Neve remember seeing him sometimes in the Market Hill office, but he was young and 'larky' and they think his heart was probably not in his work, though he stuck to it for some ten years or more until his health broke down. He then retired to live in the south of England and, it is said, married his nurse. He was the last of the male Bealeses to work in the firm.

It was probably after the bankruptcy that the formidable Miss M. E. Beales stepped into the breach as managing director. Soon the business began to thrive again and it continued to flourish until by 1909 it was firmly on its feet, and became a Limited Company. Since then it has developed greatly, amalgamating with Austin & Co. and then with Coote and Warren's Cambridge Branch, 'thus effectively marrying three old-established and historical Cambridge businesses', as Mr P. G. Bailey, the present Managing Director of the firm, puts it. It is now a member of the well known Charrington group.

The family house at Newnham still belonged nominally to Edward Beales, though it was really in the hands of his Trustees. Mr Arthur Gray's lease was coming to an end in March 1885, and he did not wish to renew it. Professor George Darwin must have known this for, on 27 September 1884, he wrote to Edward Beales to ask if he might rent the house when Gray had gone. Beales referred the letter for an answer to his solicitor, John Eaden. The reply was favourable and negotiations started. Thus a new chapter opened in the history of the old house.

CHAPTER FIVE

George Howard Darwin: 1845–84

GEORGE HOWARD DARWIN, or G. H. D. as he generally signed himself, was the second son and fifth child of Charles and Emma Darwin. Both his parents were grandchildren of Josiah Wedgwood, the potter, and therefore first cousins. He was born on 9 July 1845, at his home Down House in Kent. The village of Downe, though only sixteen miles from London Bridge, still retains much of the quiet and countrified character it had in George's childhood. He spent the first eleven years of his life there, with his six surviving brothers and sisters and his parents — the latter playing such an important part in his daily life that they too can be described as his companions. He was a happy and energetic child, 'a boy of one idea', as his mother described him, because he became oblivious of all else when engaged in any pursuit. He kept this faculty of single-minded concentration to the end of his life.

His younger brother Frank wrote a delightful memoir of him for the last volume of George's *Scientific Papers*, published by the Cambridge University Press after his death. In writing of George's early childhood, Frank says that already at the age of seven he showed 'a characteristic interest in current events and the picturesqueness of Natural History', as shown by two entries on a page of his 1852 diary, where he wrote: 'The Duke is dead. Dodos are out of the world.' George's father had evidently been telling him about dodos, the fact of their extinction making as strong an impression on him as had the death of Wellington.

He was still very young when heraldry became his master-passion. 'He retained a love of the science through life', Frank wrote, 'and his copy of Percy's *Reliques* is decorated with coats of arms admirably drawn and painted. In later life he showed a power of neat and accurate draughtsmanship, some of the illustrations in his father's books, e.g. in *Climbing Plants* are by his hand.' Another later interest was the collecting of Lepidoptera — a pursuit he carried on with his customary energy and thoroughness. One of two handsome cabinets in which he kept his collection of butterflies, neatly set out and labelled, remained in his room for the rest of his life.

When he was eleven, he had to leave his much-loved home to seek a better education than could be provided by a governess and a local rector. The eldest son, William, had been sent to Rugby, but his parents so deplored his long absences from home that the younger sons went locally to Clapham Grammar School as boarders. At Clapham, more time was then given to science and mathematics than in public schools, and the headmaster, the Rev. Charles Pritchard, had a special gift for teaching mathematics. Unfortunately for George he left to become Professor of Astronomy at Oxford after George had been his pupil for only three years. This may have accounted for George's failure to get even a Minor Scholarship at St John's, Cambridge, in 1863, or the following year at Trinity, which he entered as a commoner in the autumn of 1864. Two years later, however, he was made a foundation scholar.

Fletcher Moulton, afterwards a Lord of Appeal, was Senior Wrangler when George came second, and later on wrote Frank an interesting letter for his memoir:

My memories of your brother during his undergraduate career correspond closely to your suggestion that his mathematical power developed somewhat slowly and late. Throughout most, if not the whole, of his undergraduate years he was in the same class as myself and Christie, the ex-astronomer Royal, at Routh's. [Routh was the most celebrated mathematical coach of his day.] We all recognized him as one who was certain of being high in the Tripos, but he did not display any of that colossal power of work and taking infinite trouble that characterized him afterwards. On the contrary, he treated his work rather jauntily. At that time his health was excellent and he took his studies lightly so that they did not interfere with his enjoyment of other things. I remember that as the time of the examination came near I used to tell him that he was unfairly handicapped on being in such robust health and such excellent spirits.

Even when he had taken his degree I do not think he realized his innate mathematical power. . . . It has been a standing wonder to me that he developed the patience for making the laborious numerical calculations on which so much of his most original work was necessarily based. He certainly showed no tendency in that direction during his undergraduate years. Indeed he told me more than once in later life that he detested Arithmetic and that these calculations were as tedious and painful to him as they would have been to any other man, but that he realized that they must be done and it was impossible to train anyone else to do them.

In 1868, when George was adjudged Second Wrangler, he was astonished at his own success. His father in his letter of congratulation wrote: 'I always said from your early days that such energy, perseverance and talent as yours, would be sure to succeed; but I never expected such brilliant success as this. Again and again I congratulate you. But you have made my hand tremble so I can hardly write.'

Soon afterwards he won the second of the two Smith's Prizes, the brilliant Fletcher Moulton being awarded the first, and in the autumn he was elected a Fellow of Trinity.

Chief among his many friends at Trinity were the three Balfour brothers—Arthur, Gerald, and Frank. Frank was a brilliant biologist and a singularly lovable and charming man. When he was killed climbing in the Swiss Alps in 1882, Cambridge was stunned by the blow and George was heart-broken. Arthur remained his life-long friend and George often visited him at Whittinghame where he came to know the whole Balfour family well. He had a particular regard for Arthur's eldest sister Eleanor, the wife of Professor Henry Sidgwick and later Principal of Newnham College. It was perhaps the Sidgwicks' interest in psychical research, as well as his friendship with F. W. H. Myers that led George to attend some séances in 1875. He never became a believer and after having detected a medium in fraud he seems to have lost interest in the subject, until in 1899 he was persuaded by Myers to attend some of the celebrated Mrs Piper's séances at Myers's house, but was not converted by her performance.

A younger sister of Arthur's, Evelyn, also married a Fellow of Trinity and friend of George's, John William Strutt, later Lord Rayleigh, the physicist. He was a colleague whom George greatly admired and liked. Yet another link with Arthur Balfour was the Royal Game of Court Tennis, to which George became an addict.

He loved its romance and the old French terms used in the scoring. He continued to play until he was fifty, when a blow from a ball almost destroyed the sight of his left eye and he decided it was too risky to continue playing the game with only one sound eye.

It was not until some years after he had taken his degree that George found his life's work was to lie in the application of mathematics to scientific problems. On leaving Cambridge in 1868 he had intended to make the law his profession and got as far as qualifying as a barrister in 1874. But long before then his health had broken down. According to Frank, what he suffered from was chiefly 'severe digestive troubles, sickness and general discomfort and weakness', but, as in his father's case, it is impossible to determine how much of his ill-health was due to psychological and how much to organic causes. He was always a very highly-strung nervous man, easily upset and worried, a bad sleeper and very thin. Whatever the cause of his ill-health, his suffering, especially in these early years, was very real; no treatment at home or cure abroad seemed to benefit him and he was often sunk in deep depression. His father, sympathising with him in one of these bouts of illness, wrote: 'I know well the feeling of life being objectless and all being vanity of vanities.' Yet between his 'attacks', as George called them, his spirit revived quickly and he was eager to resume the active life he enjoyed so much when his health permitted.

1873 was a particularly bad year for him and wintering at Cannes seemed to aggravate his state. His father urged him to return home to consult Sir Andrew Clark 'whom Huxley thinks so very highly of and who has done him [Huxley] much good by diet in chief part. Huxley considers him a very sensible man. He is an advocate of milk diet to a large extent.' Accordingly he consulted Dr Clark, as Frank records in his memoir, 'who did what was possible to make life more bearable and as time went on his health gradually improved . . . although it remained a serious handicap throughout his life'.

In October 1873, having decided to give up a legal career, he returned to Cambridge and settled down again in Trinity where he had rooms next to the library at G4 in Nevile's Court. During his prolonged ill-health he had begun to occupy himself with writing papers on oddly miscellaneous subjects. In 1872, he published an amusing study in evolution [in *Macmillan's Magazine*] called the

'Development of Dress'. An eugenic paper on 'Beneficial Restrictions to Liberty of Marriage' followed in 1873 in the *Contemporary Review*. Frank records that he was attacked for this 'with gross unfairness and bitterness by the late St George Mivart. He was defended by Huxley, and Charles Darwin formally ceased all intercourse with Mivart'. Some years later his father gave George his views on the conduct of controversy: 'I have always acted on the principle of publishing what I believe to be the truth, without contradicting others, then letting opposed statements fight for existence. But the case is different no doubt with mathematics about which only a few can judge.'

In 1873, he contributed a scientific paper on the Globe to the British Association and the following year he read one on 'Probable Error' to the Mathematical Society. From this time on he was increasingly concerned with mathematical subjects but he retained his wide interest in other topics, reviewing 'Whitney on Language' in 1874, contributing a paper on 'Cousin Marriages' to the Statistical Society in 1875, and writing a 'defence of Jevons' which elicited an appreciative letter of thanks from the economist himself.

Before publishing his papers on non-mathematical subjects he always sent them to his father for his detailed criticism. 'What a man you are for work and new ideas' wrote Charles Darwin on one such occasion and his verdict was generally very favourable, except in October 1873, when George sent him an essay on religion. His father thought it 'clever and interesting' but urged him to pause before publishing it. 'It is a fearfully difficult moral problem about the speaking out on religion and I have never been able to make up my mind.' Nothing more is known of George's paper, so presumably he destroyed it and became too absorbed in his mathematical work to write any further on general subjects.

A packet of over ninety letters from his father was among G.H.D.'s papers at Newnham Grange. Another smaller packet contained George's letters to his father, presumably returned to him after the death of his parents.* This correspondence shows that Charles Darwin was in the habit of asking his son's help in many ways but principally

---

* All of these are now preserved in the Darwin archive at the Cambridge University Library.

over matters in which he thought his son better informed than himself. Even in his undergraduate days George was asked to solve a problem in probability.

Later on came letters enquiring about gravitation, heat and its conduction, and on 'what inclination a polished . . . leaf should hold to the horizon in order to let vertical rain rebound off [it] as completely as possible'. The most important piece of work he did for his father was to correct the proofs of the new edition of *The Descent of Man* in 1873. He was warned it would be a tedious job but he accomplished it much to his father's satisfaction. In 1877, he was asked to investigate worm-castings in Nevile's Court in Trinity College and four years later, when in Madeira on a visit, continued his investigations on worms; but the dry soil of that island proved a far less favourable field for his observations than the damp grass and pavement in the cloisters of Trinity.

In 1878 he was requested to make drawings of pistils in the plant *Thalia*; these drawings enabled his father to understand the mechanism completely, as he wrote gratefully to George. Then there were letters from a German and a Norwegian to translate, for G.H.D. was the family linguist with a good command of French and German and a smattering of out-of-the-way languages. The derivation of words fascinated him and Skeat's *Etymological Dictionary* was always kept in the dining room at Newnham Grange for consultation at meal-times. A task he must have particularly enjoyed was making the genealogical and historical research for the life of Dr Erasmus Darwin which his father was writing in 1879.

Charles Darwin's later letters to his son contain many admiring references to Sir William Thomson (later Lord Kelvin). Sir James Jeans, in his excellent account of G.H.D. in the *Dictionary of National Biography*, explains how George had come to know Sir William Thomson. Thomson had been asked by the Royal Society to report on the suitability for publication of George's paper 'On the Influence of Geological Changes in the Earth's Axis of Rotation',

and out of the ensuing correspondence and conversations, resulted a friendship which terminated only with the death of the older man, as well as a life-long devotion of the younger to problems of the past history of the earth and of the solar system . . . . The object of most of [G.H.D.'s] papers is to put general conjectures to the test of precise numerical calculations.

In October 1878, when George wrote home, presumably about a paper he had just written 'On the Bodily Tides of Viscous and Semi-elastic Spheroids' which Thomson had seen and approved before its publication in the *Philosophical Transactions* of the Royal Society, his father answered:

All of us are delighted, for considering what a man Sir W.T. is it is really grand that you should have staggered him so quickly & that he shd speak of 'your discovery etc' & about the moon's period. I also chuckled greatly about the internal Heat. How this will please the geologists & Evolutionists. That does sound awkward about the heat being bottled up in the middle of the earth. . . . Hurrah for the bowels of the earth & their viscosity & for the moon & for all the Heavenly bodies & for my son George (F.R.S. very soon).

In June of the following year George did become a Fellow of the Royal Society, as his father had prophesied, and four years later, in 1883, he was elected Plumian Professor of Astronomy and Experimental Philosophy at Cambridge. He succeeded Professor Challis who had held the chair since 1836. 'The professorship is not necessarily connected with the Observatory and practical astronomy formed no part of George's duty', Frank wrote in his memoir: 'His lectures being on advanced mathematics usually attracted but few students; in the Long Vacation, however, when he habitually gave one of his courses, there was often a fairly large class.' By the time he became professor he was already well established in academic circles, having served on various university boards and syndicates for some years. His future now fully assured, he could turn his attention to other matters, not that in the excitement of his scientific work he had ever lost his keen interest in the outside world. His health was improving, though he still suffered from occasional attacks of his mysterious malady. He was nearly thirty-eight. Having a warm and affectionate nature, he wished to marry and felt that he should delay no longer.

The story of his engagement and marriage is told at length in a book by Mary Bobbitt, her great-niece, called *With Dearest Love to*

All, the Life and Letters of Lady Jebb. Caroline Jebb was the beautiful and vivacious American widow whom Richard Claverhouse Jebb (1841–1905), Fellow of Trinity, had married in 1874, a year before he was appointed Professor of Greek at Glasgow University. They kept on their house at Cambridge in order to live there during the summers and in the hope that Jebb would ultimately succeed Kennedy in the Chair of Greek, as he did, but not until 1889.

The advertisement of the auction of Patrick Beales's house at Newnham in 1851 mentions a 'picturesque villa residence' about to be built by an architect, opposite the corner of Newnham Road. This was 'Springfield', later on the Jebbs' house, where Mrs Jebb entertained her many friends, most of them Fellows of Trinity, and George Darwin among them. He was in constant attendance and she became not only his friend but his confidante — as she was of almost every man she knew.

In 1883, she invited her niece, Maud Du Puy, to come over from Philadelphia to spend the summer with her in Cambridge. Maud's father was Charles Meredith Du Puy, an American engineer responsible for the design and construction of new railways. He was a good engineer and a clever inventor, but too kind-hearted and a poor man of business. He was really more interested in writing pamphlets on economic matters for the working classes than in making money to support his wife and family of two sons and five daughters. Maud had grown up in a home where there was some difficulty in making ends meet, but the children had been given as good an education as possible. The Du Puys were very proud of their Huguenot ancestry. The founder of the American branch of their family had been a Dr Jean Du Puy who, as a child in 1682, had fled with his father to England to escape persecution in France. He later qualified as a doctor, was appointed His Majesty's Surgeon of the naval fort at Port Royal in Jamaica, and in 1713 migrated to New York where he became a prominent doctor. He died there in 1744 and was buried in Trinity Church where his tombstone and that of his son are still to be seen.

Ellen, Maud's mother, was Caroline Jebb's eldest sister; their father was an English clergyman, John Reynolds, who had emigrated to America in the 1820s.

Early in June 1883, Maud Du Puy arrived at Springfield for her

Maud Du Puy, by Cecilia Beaux, 1879

George Darwin, 1882

Maud Darwin, about 1885

visit. Her aunt lost no time in introducing her to George Darwin. On neither side was it a case of love at first sight; the difference in age was great—she was not yet twenty-two and he was nearly sixteen years her senior. But they soon made friends and were constantly together throughout Maud's idyllic first summer in Cambridge. On leaving the Jebbs early in October, she joined another aunt to spend the winter on the continent as her travelling companion. George was going abroad himself in the new year and encouraged by Mrs Jebb, he sought her out on his way back through Italy. She was delighted to see him again and very soon began to reciprocate his growing affection. At last, in March, her Aunt Cara received the telegram she had been eagerly awaiting from George to say that he had proposed and had been accepted. Maud used to look back on the few weeks she and George had spent together in Italy as the most romantic and blissful of her life. A charming water-colour of Florence, given her as a wedding present by her sister-in-law Mrs Litchfield, always hung in a prominent place in their drawing-room to commemorate those happy days of their courtship.

In her home there must have been misgivings at her engagement. The Du Puys disliked the idea of being separated from Maud by the Atlantic; and, as devoted members of the Episcopalian Church, they did not feel happy at her marrying the son of an 'infidel', as her mother had called Charles Darwin a couple of years before in a letter to her sister Carrie Jebb. Maud had been brought up to observe Sunday strictly—so strictly that, according to her aunt, when she first arrived in England she had 'searched her Bible from cover to cover before she allowed herself to play chess with George on a Sunday', but luckily 'not a line could she find against amusement on the Sabbath as long as the day had begun with going to Church'. 'Chess had grown to be the permitted Sunday game in all country houses', added Aunt Cara. As for George's infidel father, Caroline Jebb had written a firm letter to her sister on the subject in November 1882 when there had been some danger of George's marrying a younger sister of Maud's:

You ask me about George Darwin's religious opinions and I can only say I know nothing about them. If you ask me if he is a man of truth and honour, of good character and life, what he *is*, I can answer. What he believes on a matter so inner as religion is . . . between him and his maker, not a thing to talk about.

But when you call Charles Darwin an infidel, it sounds like a breath out of another century. You can't have read anything written about him in newspaper or magazine for the last twenty years, or any of his own writings. I wonder what you think of Galileo, by the way? He was put in prison for saying that the earth moved, when revealed religion had declared it to be the centre and the sun the thing that rose and set.

Darwin lies buried in Westminster Abbey, where half of the clergymen of England met to do him honour on the day of his funeral. A more lovely life no man ever lived, full of sweetness towards all connected with him. . . .

The Du Puys finally acquiesced in Maud's engagement with a good grace, though not without a battle with Maud over the date of the wedding; her mother wanting to postpone it for a year and a half, to George's despair. He had to remain in Cambridge for the May Term whilst Maud returned to the United States to see her family. When at last Maud succeeded in convincing her mother that they must be allowed to get married that summer, she sent a telegram to George which began with the word 'Victory'.

It happened that the Jebbs were in America that summer, for a lecture engagement at Harvard, so they were able to attend the wedding, on 29 July 1884, at the house of Maud's sister, Mary Spencer, in Erie, Pennsylvania. Mrs Jebb wrote a long and amusing account of the wedding to George's mother:

> after the ceremony, George went about talking to the people and in the interest of conversation, entirely forgot, I suspected, the interesting position he occupied. Never in my life saw I a bride-groom act with such an absence of self-consciousness. He whispered to me that being married made a man ravenously hungry, when did I think they would have supper? He watched the door with perfect singleness of mind and picked up Maud and marched her in with an expression of interest quite independent of the occasion.

Like most good Americans at that time, they began their honey-moon with a visit to Buffalo and Niagara Falls. Soon after this,

George had to let his wife go back to spend two or three weeks with her family before leaving them for good, whilst he travelled about with Jebb to see a little more of America. Then at last the time came for them to set sail for England. George had not much enjoyed being in America; it had been too hot, the food did not suit him, and no doubt there had been far too many dull parties to attend. But now at last they were alone together and on their way home.

CHAPTER SIX

The Making of Newnham Grange

SOON after their return from America, George and Maud spent several weeks at the Grove, staying with George's mother whilst they waited to move into 'Springfield', which the Jebbs were letting them for the winter whilst they house-hunted.

'The Grove' is a large pleasant late-Georgian house of yellow-grey brick bought by Mrs Charles Darwin after her husband's death in 1882, so that she might live part of the year in Cambridge near her sons. The house lies to the south of Huntingdon Road and stands half-hidden by big trees at the further edge of the field in which the Grove cows used to graze. The freehold of what remains of the Grove estate now belongs jointly to Fitzwilliam College and New Hall; it will eventually be divided between them. The house, where Mrs Winifred Armstrong lives as a life-tenant, will go to Fitzwilliam, whilst the land to the south-east of the house will belong to New Hall, which already owns both the land on the north-east side of the drive to the Grove and Grove Lodge, where their gardener lives, beside Huntingdon Road.

There were many links between the Grove and the Darwins, as it was here that Mrs Charles Darwin spent every winter for thirteen years until she died at Down, in October 1896 at the age of eighty-eight. She liked the house and wrote that 'the Grove garden was the very place for an old person, such nooks and corners for shelter and seats'. 'It had old walls and spreading wych-elms which gave it charm and individuality', added her daughter Henrietta.

A link between the Grove and Mrs Darwin's children was that Horace Darwin had built his Huntingdon Road house in an orchard near the Grove. Part of New Hall has been built on the site of Horace's house, and other New Hall buildings stand in what was once the beautiful garden created by Ida Darwin—some of which still abuts on to the kitchen-garden of the Grove.

In 1883-4 Frank Darwin in his turn bought some land to the west of the Grove on which to build his house. He called it 'Wychfield' after the magnificent wych-elm which grew near. (Wychfield is now owned by Trinity Hall; they have built substantial additions to the house to make sets of rooms for undergraduates.) The grounds of Wychfield also adjoin the garden of the Grove. The Frank and Horace Darwin children had free range over all the three gardens and a wonderful playground it made for them.

After Mrs Darwin died, the Grove was sold to Mr Charles Armstrong, the brewer, and his widow still lives there.

Maud had enjoyed her stay at the Grove in this first year of her married life. 'Old Mrs Darwin', as she used to call our grandmother, was the most tactful and perfect mother-in-law to her five daughters-in-law. She had liked and been amused by Maud at first sight, though they had little in common except their love for George, and Maud had responded with real affection and respect.

During their stay at the Grove, George began house-hunting, writing to enquire from the solicitors if he could lease Edward Beales's house at Newnham. Matters moved swiftly and, on 1 October, John Eaden, the Solicitor for Edward's Trustee in Bankruptcy, wrote to ask if Professor Darwin would consider buying the property. This was exactly what he wanted; it would be far better to own a property on which so much would have to be spent. Before committing himself, however, he waited to hear what a former tenant had to say about the house. Dr Bumpsted answered Darwin's enquiries from 'Leighton' (now the Perse Preparatory School) on Trumpington Road, as follows:

> My dear Sir, I am pleased to give you every information I can about the House at Newnham. The House is well-built but has been neglected for many years and requires a great deal of attention. The drainage of all kinds is carried into the river and I never found any inconvenience or anything wrong about the drains. I do not consider the house itself damp.
>
> But the neighbourhood certainly is damp owing to the common in front of the house which is bounded by the Queens Coll. ditch and the river at the back of the house. There is a large cellarage which has much to do with keeping the House dry. Had I been able to obtain a long lease of the place I should have taken it.
>
> I remain very truly yours
> T. Brooke-Bumpsted.

With reference to this simple method of drainage, Maud wrote home later on to say that Cambridge had the reputation of being 'one of the worst drained towns in England but it seems to be healthy'. It appears that the borough had begun installing main drainage, for she added, after describing the new sanitary arrangements in their house, that 'the W.C. will not really be put in until the connection with the drains is made in the future'.

After receiving Dr Bumpsted's favourable report, Professor Darwin put the matter into the capable hands of Mr Charles Bidwell of Ely, whose father, Charles Muriel Bidwell, had founded the well-known Cambridge firm of surveyors and land agents, Bidwell and Sons. Bidwell was asked to value the property and tried to find out privately from John Eaden, the solicitor, what kind of sum they would expect the house to fetch if it were auctioned. 'They, I believe, very much over-estimate the property and from what I could gather your proposal would not draw them.' Four days later he ascertained that the lowest price they would take for the entire property as it stood was £4,600.

Eaden wrote: I tried him at £4,500 but he distinctly states that the Trustee in Bankruptcy and the Committee have decided not to take one fraction less than £4,600, if they sell by private contract, and they think if the property is put up to auction it may probably make more. In my opinion it is a full sum but under all the circumstances if you really like the property I should advise you to give it.

£4,600 was 'a full sum' in those days, but by now G.H.D. had determined to buy the property. His wife was away, so he sent her Bidwell's letter, scribbling on it in pencil: 'I think I will give it. G.H.D.'

In 1871, the Corporation had let the two islands to Edward Beales for twenty-one years at a rent of five guineas. On 21 November 1884, Bidwell wrote that there would be no difficulty about the islands: 'they are leased from the Corporation and John Foster's father is town-clerk'. (The Fosters—father and son—and Lawrence were Darwin's solicitors at 10 Trinity Street.) 'I learnt at their office', Bidwell continued, 'that a transfer of the lease could be got without any trouble and at a nominal expense.'

His next letter referred to the possibility of Darwin's getting 'early possession of the Granaries—but it will depend very much whether Mr Gray the tenant of the house objects. Of course they [the builders] must not do anything which would annoy him. . . . The coal office must not be pulled down until another office can be found in the town.'

No difficulties having arisen, the 10% deposit of £460 was duly paid and, on 1 December 1884, contracts were exchanged with Eaden and Knowles. As Arthur Gray's lease did not end until 25 March 1885, the Indenture conveying the property was not signed until that date. It contains a detailed description of the freehold property, the boundaries of which still correspond exactly to those of the old Armitage site except for some small deviations on the west adjoining Dr Parkinson's house and garden. At the east end of the property, the business premises—from 1851 for a few years the property of the Widow Edelston—are separately des- cribed as still being in the occupation of P. Beales & Co. The leasehold of the two islands is also mentioned. The document ends with the signatures of the seven parties. There are some well-known Cambridge names among them: Robert Bowes, bookseller, William Eaden Lilley, Linendraper and Frederick Warren of St Ives, Coal merchant.

Even before contracts had been exchanged, Darwin had begun the search for an architect. His brother-in-law, Richard Litchfield, strongly recommended a London man, J. J. Stevenson, and by 15 December Stevenson was writing to Litchfield that he would be visiting Cambridge shortly to view the property with Professor Darwin. He wished it to be clearly understood that Darwin would be under no obligation to employ him even if he had begun making some plans of the premises. Mrs Litchfield forwarded this letter to her brother, writing on the back of it: 'I'm sure you will find him ungrabby after the job and interested'. And so Stevenson proved to be.

He was already an architect of some distinction. Born in 1831 at Glasgow, he was educated there and received his professional train- ing in an architect's office at Edinburgh, completing it in London under Sir George Gilbert Scott. After working in a partnership at

Glasgow for nine years and spending a winter of study in Paris, he returned to London for good in 1870. A fellow-student of his in Scott's office, E. R. Robson, had just been appointed architect to the London School Board, and Stevenson joined him there to help with the building of London schools. Together they evolved a simple type of brick design sufficiently in sympathy with early eighteenth-century architecture to be styled Queen Anne. Soon after settling in London, Stevenson built himself the Red House, Bayswater Hill, and it became the meeting-place of friends prominent in literature and art, such as Alfred Ainger, George MacDonald, Sir E. Q. Orchardson, J. H. Middleton (sometime Director of the Fitzwilliam Museum), William Morris, and Professor Robertson Smith. In association with Morris, Stevenson became one of the original members of the committee of the Society for the Protection of Ancient Buildings. When in December 1884 he began work for Professor Darwin, he was already a highly experienced architect, having built churches in Scotland, country houses in England, offices in Newcastle and London, as well as many town houses in South Kensington. Work at Oxford and Cambridge was still to come. At Cambridge he was the architect for new buildings at Christ's in 1886 and again in 1906; they are still called the Stevenson Buildings. In 1889 he built the first University Chemical Laboratory on the corner site of Pembroke Street, St Botolph Lane, and Free School Lane.

In 1880, Macmillan's published his book, *House Architecture*, copiously illustrated partly by his own sketches printed from wood blocks — a method he considered gave 'more satisfactory results than some modern processes'. The first volume, called *Architecture*, begins with the statement that

> to build a house for oneself is an excellent education in architecture. By the time it is finished and the owner has lived in it, he feels how much better a house he could build with the experience he had acquired if he had to do it over again . . . but to go through the experience once in a lifetime is enough for most people.

It is interesting to note that in the index of his book no mention is made of Georgian architecture; it had evidently not become fashionable to admire it by 1880, but luckily for the Darwins he did appreciate its merits, as is shown by his having retained not only all the main features of the Beales's house, but the granaries on the river as well. His love of the Gothic, no doubt strengthened by the time he spent in Sir George Gilbert Scott's office, shows itself in the insertion of the two oriel windows at Newnham Grange, one, the drawing-room bay window and the other, the stone oriel window in the little end room of the outside gallery. Modern architects do not always approve of these un-Georgian additions, nor of his dictum that 'privacy is essential to our comfort', and many no doubt would also deplore the weakness he showed in trying to carry out his clients' wishes whenever possible.

Stevenson's first task was to make plans of all the buildings on the estate (see illustrations preceding title-page). These drawings show the large range of four-storeyed granaries to the east and south-east of the house along the road as well as along the river. Some of them were to be demolished but others might be adapted to provide coach house and stable. The Beales's two big stables on the ground floor of the granaries by the road were not worth saving. The cowhouse alongside them had no adequate window and its only door opened straight on to the road, for the cow evidently spent most of her time grazing on Queens' Green opposite. If the Darwins decided to keep a horse and a cow, new stables for both must be provided.

The house seemed structurally sound and when Mr Stevenson looked over it again, Mrs Darwin said he was 'more and more charmed with it. He examined locks and door-handles and drew George's attention to how good they were, though probably forty or fifty years old.' But it was many years since any repairs or decorations had been undertaken and it would need thorough overhauling, especially the kitchen premises which were dark and hopelessly antiquated, the pantry being the only good room – but that was required for Professor Darwin's study. Sanitary arrangements everywhere were primitive. A new drainage system would have to be installed to connect with the town drains.

The programme before the architect was formidable, but he began making plans at once and, by 30 December, was ready to write to Darwin as follows:

I enclose a plan of your ground at Newnham showing the boundaries and the blocks of buildings. I have marked on the plan where a lawn tennis ground could be got. It would involve pulling down the granaries all but the external walls. I am very anxious to keep something of the present appearance of the buildings towards the river as it seems to me a most characteristic feature of Cambridge, dating probably from a very long time back. I think a wooden gallery of the same sort of construction as the Lucerne bridge on the inside of the wall, with a tile roof, might be both picturesque and useful. It could have windows with some tracery on them inserted in the wall and perhaps a balcony towards the river. . . . I think you would have room between the house and tennis ground for new kitchens and stables.

Luckily his suggestion about the preservation of the outer walls of the two riverside granaries was adopted. In a later letter he stated that their 'old foundations seem excellent and they are, I believe, on piles'. Faint pencil lines on a plan show that the inner wall of the south granary was to be completely demolished and rebuilt at about half the width of the old building; it would form an inner wall for the boathouse, and continue upwards to form the open-sided loggia or gallery which still overlooks the lawn. No tracery was put into the windows opposite, but Mr Stevenson was allowed to build a small balcony over the river. The door on to it is still there but is kept locked, as the balcony railings became unsafe and were removed a few years ago. In this preliminary plan no mention is made of the tea-room, as it was always called, though no one ever had tea there; perhaps Mrs Darwin had later demanded a room for the purpose and so he planned one in the remaining old granary, the north-west corner of which had been demolished to make room for the tennis court. As this floor of the granary was at a higher level than that of the new gallery, the architect had to lead up to it by a short flight of stairs, across a lobby which bridged the passageway to the river below. The door opens on to a small light room with a fireplace in it, now blocked up. One window overlooks the lawn below, the other the river — the latter is the Oriel bay window designed in stone by the architect. It has a certain bizarre charm, though so unsuitably placed in a plain Georgian building. At first Darwin had thought this window too expensive a luxury, but finally relented, perhaps when he saw how much Mr Stevenson's heart was set on it.

On 3 February, the architect wrote to Darwin about his plans for modernising the house:

It is impossible to make the present kitchen a light one and therefore I have made it a Servants' Hall, for which I think it might serve very well, and have shown, on the site of the north granary, new kitchen, pantry larders etc. . . . It would increase the size of the

building and its cost to give a manservant's bedroom. The pantry is large enough for a bed which could be screened off in a corner. . . . Though I have shown the walls of the granary as if they remained with new windows made in them, I think it would likely be cheaper to pull it down and rebuild. There will be no damp course in the old walls and without it it is impossible to secure walls being dry and the granary floors will be quite useless for domestic purposes.

The important decision was therefore taken to demolish the two granaries on the road and erect a new kitchen block from the materials. The Beales's kitchen at the back would then become the pantry and the manservant's bedroom; a new and well-lit servants' hall

would be built on the opposite side of the passage next to the new
kitchen, both rooms overlooking the road.

On 13 February, Mrs Darwin wrote home in triumph to say that
the new plans had arrived at last:

The improvements are chiefly to be made in the kitchen apart-
ment. This is what every English house has in that quarter. Hall or

some small room for servants' sitting-room. Butler's pantry.
Kitchen, with range, no sink. Scullery and smaller kitchen which
has range. A larder, a cupboard or big store-cupboard.

Evidently no such elaborate arrangements were expected in the
United States. Though everything else was provided in the orthodox
English way for Mrs Darwin, she was given no separate scullery or
smaller kitchen. This meant that the sink was in the kitchen, much to
the annoyance of future generations of English cooks.

In due course the demolition of the north granaries took place and
involved everything except part of the outer wall on the road. This
was left standing to a height of about ten feet, no doubt to give privacy
to the tennis court inside. Passers-by sometimes wonder why bricked-

up doors and windows are to be seen in this wall, and do not realise that they mark the sites of the Beales's henhouse and stables. The wall ends at the present back-gate where the cow used to have her doorway to Queens' Green; from this point westwards the rest of the granary was demolished to the ground. It had projected about four feet beyond the main house at an awkward angle, so Stevenson aligned his new building to the north front of the 1793 main house, and on the east brought the wing into line with the outer side of the covered kitchen yard.

Another problem over which he hesitated was at what level the floor of the new building should be—'whether that of the present [i.e. the Beales's] kitchen or that of the present Ground Floor [in the 1793 main house]. The latter is better', he wrote, 'as avoiding steps between the kitchen and Dining room and raising the windows so that the rooms are not looked in on from the street. It would add somewhat to the cost.' In the end he decided to keep to the old level, which was a few inches above that of the courtyard. He probably did not realise at the time how important these few inches of extra height would prove to be in times of flood, when the water rises higher and higher up the back door step till sometimes only half an inch prevents it from flooding the whole of the back premises. The Darwin children never had the excitement of seeing it actually invade the house through the back door, even in what they called a 'really good' flood, but long before that danger was imminent, they knew that the flood was seeping into the cellars and coal would have to be 'rescued' before the coal cellar was too deep under water.

The Beales's larder facing the road must have been very dark, lit as it was only by one low window to the north, but it was light compared with the scullery out of which it led, for the scullery had no window of its own, only borrowed light from a hatch opening into the kitchen. The sink was on the other side of the room and day-light can never have reached it. It is dreadful to think of the mountains of washing-up that must have been done over the years in this dark damp hole of a scullery, by the light of a candle or an oil lamp. It is good to know that it was now to be razed to the ground. Nor can the Beales's kitchen at the back ever have been a light room in spite of its fine large window, for it overlooked the covered backyard. It was made, however, into an excellent pantry with a tolerable bedroom opening out of it for the Swiss manservant, Rittler, whom the Darwins had recently engaged. A year or two later they decided regretfully to part from him, as he was proving not only too attractive to the maids, but on one occasion Mrs Darwin had detected a smell of alcohol in his breath on his return from a party. She found him a good place in Pittsburgh as butler to her brother. He remained much attached to the Darwins and their baby daughter, judging from a couple of letters he wrote them from America. His bedroom became a store-room and they never had a manservant again.

On the first floor of the new wing, the architect made what he called 'a good bedroom' with two windows looking on to Queens' Green. This was soon to become the Darwins' day-nursery, conveniently near to the night nursery in the old building at the back and close to the new sanitary arrangements at the side. He finished the wing with an attic on the top floor surmounted by a small ornamental pinnacle under which the date 1885 is engraved. It can be seen from the road on approaching from the direction of Silver Street Bridge. The date must sometimes puzzle people who know the house to be of Georgian origin; the use of old facing bricks, probably from the demolished south granary, makes it difficult to distinguish the new wing from the older building alongside it.

The next step was to get an estimate for the cost of the complicated building operations involved. Mr Stevenson employed a quantity surveyor from London to make it and, on 10 March 1885, sent Professor Darwin what he called 'the probable estimate', an exact copy of which is given below:

Say for cube of building
for Kitchen etc. 27620 feet.
At 1*d* per foot this would be
£115. I think it would be
safe to put the cost of this
building at 6*d* per cube foot   ———   £690: 0 : 0
Add for internal plumbing
bath, hot water sinks etc.   ———   50: 0 : 0

Continued on next page

Screen to form porch at
Entrance and filling up
arches at side ——— 25: 0 : 0
New flues, air grate and
chimney piece in Hall ——— 150: 0 : 0
Alterations to form W.C. etc.
under stairs and Porch to
Garden ——— 70: 0 : 0
Cost of new chimney pieces
and stoves for Dining Room
Study and Bedroom instead of
that removed to Drawing room
Say ——— 45: 0 : 0
Casements to form double
windows to nine windows on
North front of house with
Quarry glazing, say ——— 70: 0 : 0

1100: 0 : 0
Deduct: Credit old materials 50: 0 : 0

1050: 0 : 0

Stevenson added:

I think this estimate would be safe . . . and I think also that the
old materials of the south granary would more than pay for a
covered gallery such as I proposed. It would be some advantage if
we can make up our minds what to do with this South building so
as to alter it at the same time when you have opportunity of dispos-
ing of the bricks; but all you would get for these bricks is not much
worth considering. The materials are better and worth more to
sell than in the North building. The wooden beams are probably
the most valuable of them, but I doubt if they could be used in the
new buildings.

Bidwell agreed with the architect that the most satisfactory
arrangement would be to sell the demolition material to the builder,
but two of Darwin's Trinity friends, Dr Verrall, the Greek scholar,

and Dr James Ward, the moral philosopher, wanted to buy some of the surplus materials for the houses they were having built in Selwyn Gardens at numbers 5 and 6. The colleges' ban on the marriage of Fellows had been lifted, in 1882, and this had been followed by a spate of university marriages including those of Verrall and Ward. Whether they did in fact buy any demolition material is unknown; their houses are of red brick; no trace of yellow brick is to be seen, but as Stevenson had said that 'the tiles are sure to be good and there should be about enough for the three houses', perhaps some of the tiles on their roofs did come from the Beales's granaries.

Mr Stevenson sent Mr Gandy, the surveyor, to Cambridge to find a builder. A Mr William Saint was recommended as a more active builder than Mr Bell who had been so slow over the building of Frank and Horace Darwin's houses. Mr Gandy asked both Saint and Bell to submit estimates for the work. Rather to Darwin's relief, Saint's was the lower of the two, so he was engaged. He proved an excellent choice and soon became a family institution. 'Send for Mr Saint' was the well-known cry in domestic crises. He would appear, a short bulky man with a pointed brown beard looking like a smaller version of the Prince of Wales (later Edward VII), and soon things would be put to rights. To Mrs Darwin in particular he became a kind of oracle and his pronouncements were quoted as sacred.

After this, matters moved with remarkable rapidity. Mr Saint intended to begin work on the morning of 30 March, before he had signed the contract, 'which is irregular', Mr Stevenson wrote, 'but practical and can do no harm'.

Four days earlier, Mrs Darwin had written home in great excitement, Mr Gray's lease having just expired: 'We have our house at last and the builders go in on Monday 30 March. They promise to finish it by the first of May in a month's time! and by the first of October the rest is to be built.' Two days later she wrote: 'They are getting on with our house splendidly now. The North granary roof is nearly off and they are working in the inside of the house too. Our side-board has been unpacked and it is very beautiful. Unfortunately two carved heads that formed the handles have been broken off and lost on the way.' This refers to the enormous, elaborately carved black-oak side-board they had bought when on holiday at Nice in January. It was most unsuitable for an English Georgian house, but Mrs Darwin never ceased to admire the four pieces of furniture they had made out of it. Most important of all was the grand mantelpiece, supported by carved figures at each end, which stood in the dining room for nearly eighty years until it had become so riddled with worm that Darwin College had to have it removed and burnt. But the side-board, partly constructed out of some of the same carved wood, still remains intact in the recess, and is part of Darwin College library. One of the cupboards lacks a handle; this was the carved head lost on the journey to England, as Mrs Darwin related in her letter. An elaborate two-tiered table, on top of which a large blue oriental plate for the visiting cards of callers was always kept, was made for the inner hall and is still in the College. More of the black oak was used by Mr Stevenson to construct a mantelpiece for the new fireplace in the hall, and is still there.

'For keeping the house warm', Stevenson wrote on 3 February 1885, 'I feel pretty sure that an air-grate in the hall will be sufficient when the cold air is prevented by the Porch with swing door . . . facing the entrance. I have shewn another flue beside it from the basement which will cost a trifling sum extra to build and which . . . would enable you to have a furnace in the cellar should you find it necessary which I don't think you will.' But Mrs Darwin did not agree that a furnace was an unnecessary luxury, for later that month, she wrote rather wistfully to her mother: 'Mr Stevenson and George are both so opposed to a furnace that I believe I shall have to give it up. . . . You do freeze in houses over here but somehow you do not catch cold. I have not had a cold the whole winter and I never feel really warm.' She was right in thinking that the primitive form of central heating provided by the hall-fire, even though heaped with unlimited coal at £1 a ton, was not enough to keep the house warm, in spite of the flues provided in it to carry the hot air up to the landing; but the blazing fire did make a wonderfully cheerful picture on a cold winter's day and gave some warmth to the main body of the house, even if 'the Porch with swing door' by no means excluded all the multifarious draughts. The architect's estimate for the cost of this new chimney and fireplace with its flues and air-gratings was £150.

At last the house was to receive a name. On 5 April, Mrs Darwin wrote home that it was to be called Newnham Grange. Her aunt Cara had looked up *Granaries* in the dictionary and found that another word meaning the same thing was Grange.

The workmen are in quantities and work kept going splendidly. The garden door has been cut open, the chimney partially built in the hall, half the granaries are down, a door cut through from my room into my dressing room . . . some of the rooms have received first coats of paint and are ready for paper. George's study altered. They even think they can get the pantry and man's bed-room done. . . . It is great fun to go over and interview the foreman every day and see the progress that is made. I was horrified to hear him say it would cost £200–£300 to put the little cottage [i.e. the counting house] in order. It is a dear little house with four rooms in it, it is on the river and looks fairly well, only some ivy has grown into some windows and then has broken its way through the roof, which makes it picturesque but uninhabitable. . . . The men are waiting for the papers and paint to be chosen. . . . I was in despair, when a happy thought struck me, why not have Mr Leach? Mr Leach is a man who has a great deal of taste and people send all over England for him to do their houses. So now he is a person in whom I shall have confidence and who is experienced. He lives in Cambridge.

This was Frederick William Leach, whose 'Art Warehouse' was at 3 St Mary's Passage. He was indeed a man of taste, having worked previously with William Morris who often recommended him to his clients. The artistic tradition was strongly represented in his family and today Messrs W. Perry Leach and Son's decorating and furnish-ing shop at 18 King's Parade is owned by one of his grandsons.

On 1 May, Mrs Darwin described the great shopping expedition to London she made with her cousin, Ella Du Puy, who had come from America to help her settle into the house. £750 had been set aside to cover the cost of furnishing. 'Yesterday we bought eight bedsteads and all the bedding. My bedstead is a four-foot brass one, the others are all iron with brass knobs on them, excepting the servants' which are iron. All but the latter have the best spiral and hair mattresses and oh! how they cost! $30 for the mattress and $15 for the springs!' Nor was it any longer necessary to call upon Mr

Leach for his advice since her cousin was an artist with strong views about interior decoration and furniture. They proceeded to buy a 'lovely Wilton staircarpet' and a Morris rug for her husband's bedroom, but 'matting is awfully dear, 2/6d a yard for the best quality'. This was needed for a dado in the smoking-room. She continued two days later: 'I wish you could see how lovely our house is. The rooms are all such a nice shape, so well-proportioned and it is all so lovely now. The fruit trees are all in blossom, the lilac and wistaria out and the river so nice. There is a lovely beech tree with iron steps down to the river, it is the most romantic place possible.' Her letter to a sister-in-law on 15 May is proudly headed *Newnham Grange*:

Next week with or without doors I am going down to live there. With Rittler [the Swiss manservant] in the distance and an unloaded revolver nearby I will defy robbers. . . . I know that being on the premises will hurry the workmen. . . . If I can get the smoking-room in order there will be a sitting-room and then I will be on the premises to give orders to the people about the blinds, carpets, etc.

But after all, she had to wait another fortnight before they made the move into the house. This finally took place on Friday 29 May. Three days later, she and her cousin found time to row down the river with the inexperienced but delighted Rittler at the oars, to pick up her husband at Trinity and bring him back 'to explore our islands':

We found both islands lovely, the one just opposite the house simply a mass of blossom and nettles. Peonies, laburnum, lilacs, cherries, currants and gooseberries. It was much larger than I thought too and so pretty. . . . When you come to England I am sure you will be enthusiastic about our house and garden and river. It is all so lovely, though on the front side of the house it is noisy with carriages and carts driving by, on the other side you would think you were away off in the country, the common extends so far.

The noise was considered so bad even in those days that Professor Darwin had double windows made for all the rooms which faced the road in the main part of the house and later on for his bedroom overlooking the river to the south as well.

The Darwins named the island opposite the house the 'Little Island' to distinguish it from the 'Big Island' farther upstream. Hitherto the only means of access to the islands must have been by boat; so Professor Darwin asked the Corporation for permission to build bridges to them. To further this plan he surrendered the short remainder of his lease of the islands, and obtained a new one for twenty-one years at an annual rent of five guineas. Provisional leave to build two bridges was given on 12 June. He asked an engineer of his acquaintance, a Mr F. H. Anson of 15 Dean's Yard, Westminster, to design a bridge to span the river from the mainland to the Little Island. Mr Anson sent him a sketch for the bridge, writing:

My present idea is to make it of oak and like a 'Queen post truss' roof with the ridge cut away. . . . Oak need not be painted. An arched bridge such as 'the Mathematical Bridge' [at Queens'] would I think be rather more costly as it would want better abutments but it would be prettier. Iron would be the cheapest material for the job, I think, and would last longer, but it would need painting and would not look so picturesque. I hardly know what to charge you for 'professional services'. . . . I think however that five guineas would be about a fair charge and cost of journey if any.

Contemporary photographs show that Mr Anson's preliminary design for a Queen post bridge was rejected in favour of one with a single central King post, as in the present bridge. The Corporation stipulated that sufficient headroom must be left for the passage of boats underneath. Eight foot was allowed for this. The necessary height above the river was obtained by the use of a short flight of steps up to the bridge. These four steps also ensured that the former tow-path below would not be entirely blocked, though henceforward an adult had to bend double or a child would sometimes go on all fours to use the path where it passed under the abutments of the bridge. As the Little Island opposite lies more than a foot below the level of the tow-path, a stairway of ten steps down from the bridge had to be made on the island side.

Professor Darwin wrote to the Corporation stating that the sketch of the proposed bridge was 'unsatisfactory as regards the engineering' and would be modified. This seems an odd result of having engaged an engineer especially to design it. Mr Stevenson was perhaps disappointed at not having been commissioned to build the bridge, and he wrote with excessive humility to Professor Darwin soon afterwards:

Might I see the drawing of the bridge before it is executed; I should not presume to make any suggestions as to its strength or structure, but I feel interested in the external appearance of the house and premises, and though engineers' designs generally look best without ornament it is just possible I might be able to make a suggestion which might help the appearance.

It is tempting to believe that his letter resulted in his having been permitted to design the wooden balls which surmount the King posts; they look like his work. No further letter from the engineer has been found but presumably he made a second design which satisfied both Professor Darwin and the Corporation. It has remained as the proto-type of the bridge to this day. Though presumably made of oak like its successors, it was painted; the painting added an extra pound to the £12.10s. that Saint charged for building the bridge.

The second bridge which was to lead from the Little Island to the Big Island was apparently designed by Mr Saint on the instructions of Professor Darwin and cost £7.10s. with an extra 7s. 6d. for painting. It was to be a 'Plank Bridge 50 feet span as sketch with 4 hemp ropes each 60 ft. long as handrails and $4\frac{5}{8}''$ iron tension rods each about 13 ft. long with heads'. Two years later it was widened and provided with sides of 'rustic work with sawn fir poles', forming a kind of large-scale lattice-work. These sides must have been far more effective in preventing children from falling into the river than the 'hemp ropes and handrails' can ever have been. The elongated trestle bridge proved very frail, as it was submerged in times of flood; it also became a favourite pastime of undergraduates in canoes or punts to hang on to the tension rods and swing themselves violently to and fro under-neath the low bridge.

Both bridges have served their purpose well for the last eighty years, though they had often to be repaired and even practically re-built on two or three occasions, but the original design was always copied in essentials. Some twelve years or more ago when the plank bridge to the Big Island was rebuilt, the tension rods, having nearly rusted away, had to be removed altogether and the bridge strength-ened instead by the use of stouter planks and by bedding the support-ing posts in concrete foundations in the river. The bridge from the mainland to the Little Island was rebuilt some years ago with cranked iron girders substituted for the structural oak beams, as these had decayed; but as the girders were painted green like the bridge, they did not change its outward appearance or alter the engineer's design.

CHAPTER SEVEN

Innovations at Newnham Grange

IN one of the solicitor's letters to Mr Darwin occurs the following message under the heading *Telephone*: 'The Manager is getting way-leaves to lay this on to your house and Springfield at once. We presumed he will call on you to see exactly where you want it placed.' It can hardly be the present custom of Telephone Managers to call on their would-be subscribers in person, but these were the very early days of the telephone company at Cambridge and the Darwins must have been among the earliest of its clients, for George Darwin was given 10 for the Newnham Grange number and his brothers Horace and Frank 17 and 18 for their houses in Huntingdon Road. The Grange proudly retained 10 as its number until, in 1935, four-figure numbers superseded all the two-figure numbers and the manual telephone exchange in Alexandra Street was replaced by a new automatic exchange and switch-board at the present head post-office in St Andrew's Street.* In November 1885 the telephone was still such a novelty in Cambridge that the Darwins used it at one of their dinner parties to entertain their guests, among whom were Charles Villiers Stanford, the composer and later Professor of Music in the University, and his wife. 'We amused them', wrote Mrs Darwin, 'by talking to Ida [Mrs Horace Darwin] on the telephone. They had never seen one. Mrs Stanford was very curious about the house. Everyone is, though, and the way people call is a caution.'

---

* According to some notes kept by Miss Porter of the Folk Museum, there were at first in the early eighties two telephone exchanges — one dealing with local calls and the other with the trunk line system. After some years they were taken over by the National Telephone Company. In the 1895 *Directory*, the latter's address is given as 12 Market Hill, above The Shades public-house, where its subscribers were connected to the 500-line exchange. Like its predecessors, the National Telephone Company was also a private company, but after gradually absorbing all the small companies in the country, it created a monopoly of the entire system, though it was not until its licence from the Post Office had expired in 1911, that the company was nationalised and the telephone was run by the Post Office as a public service.

Meanwhile the work on the house had been proceeding at a great pace. By 4 July 1885, Mrs Darwin wrote home that the roof of the new wing was on and a promise made that in two weeks' time the kitchen would be in use. She enclosed a small photograph taken by A. G. Dew Smith, friend and a noted photographer, 'from the steps of our piazza looking up the river to the mill pond. It is our lovely copper beech you see.' The verandah, or piazza as she called it, formerly extended along almost the whole south wall of the drawing-room until, in 1889, the architect was recalled to enlarge the room by incorporating the greater part of the verandah into it. In this he made what he characteristically called an Oriel, but was more usually called a bow-window. The original lead roof of the verandah covers it and the addition gives greater depth to what had been a severely oblong and rather narrow room. The bow-window, though hardly Georgian in type, provides an enchanting vista of shining water, as one looks through it up the river to Newnham Millpool. According to Saint's estimate, the cost would be £132 10s. and the work completed in under six weeks.

On 9 July she continued the letter with an account of a call from Sidney Colvin. He had recently resigned from the Fitzwilliam to become Keeper of the Prints and Drawings at the British Museum, and praise from him on aesthetic matters was much valued. 'Mr Colvin came in and spent a long time with us. It was most amusing to see the way his admiration grew about the house. As he came into the smoking-room [now the Senior Combination Room] he exclaimed at its beauty and then went round the room taking in things. When he went away he said we had the nicest house in Cambridge.' In a less triumphant vein she added: 'Will the house ever be fixed? A leakage in the gas at last found in the spare bedroom in the floor—someone had pounded a nail into the pipe. Board and plaster have to come up and the carpet of course.'

It was fifty-two years since gas had first been brought to Cambridge. Cooper states in his *Annals* under 1823 that 'This year the Town was lit by Gas. Oil gas was at first used, but a few years afterwards coal gas was substituted.' By 1834, gas was evidently well established in the borough, for the Cambridge Gas Company

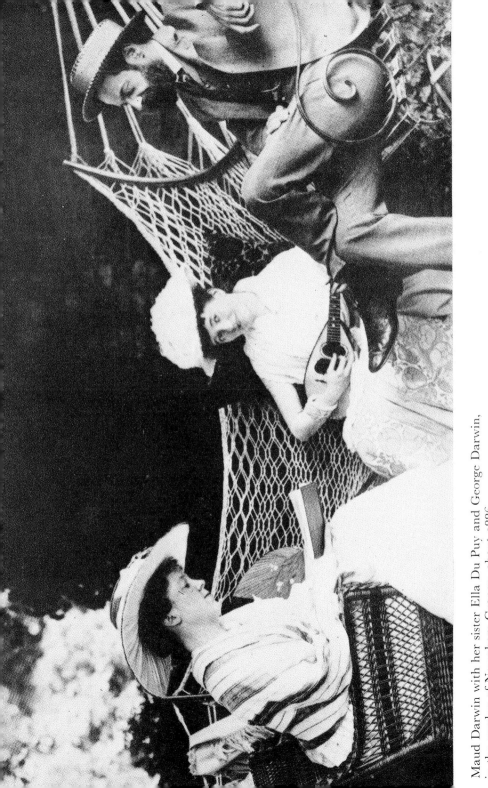

Maud Darwin with her sister Ella Du Puy and George Darwin, in the garden of Newnham Grange, about 1886

The Study (above) and the Drawing-room

was incorporated by Parliament in that year. So it seems highly probable that the Darwins inherited the gas installation from their predecessors, but they may have been responsible for some innovations in its use, such as fitting on incandescent gas-mantles with pilot-lights to some of the gas-burners in the back premises. These gave a much better and whiter light but were not considered elegant enough for the main part of the house, where all the sitting-rooms (except the dining room which had one burner near the hatch) still depended on oil-lamps and candles for their illumination. Writing home in November 1886, Mrs Darwin said: 'If you want to save your gas bills you ought to put on a gas regulator. . . . Our bill is about 19/– a quarter for the summer. . . . The gas is 3/2 a 1000 ft. We have five burners going in full tilt, from dark until 10.30 in the passage alone, besides that there is the pantry, kitchen, servants' hall, dining room and nursery.' Patent reflecting candles were sometimes used for reading in bed; they were, however, mainly kept to take away on holidays. A gas ring for boiling kettles or heating flat-irons was in constant use in the new housemaid's cupboard, but years had to pass before the huge Eagle coal range, on which all the cooking was done in the kitchen, was supplemented, though not superseded, by a gas-stove, and a coke-boiler was installed to take over the heating of the bath-water from the range. One or two of the bedrooms were given gas-fires, yet open coal-fires remained the principal form of heating on both floors until well into the twentieth century. Then a coke-burning stove was fitted into the hall fireplace. Years later, gas took the place of coal in the dining-room and study fireplaces, as well as in some of the bedrooms. Hitherto a fire in the bedroom had been regarded as a justifiable luxury for visitors and a necessity for others only in time of illness.

It was not until after Lady (Maud) Darwin's death in 1947 that oil central heating was installed in the house by her son Charles. This entailed blocking the drawing-room fireplace and chimney, up which most of the heat used to disappear, however much coal was heaped upon the fire; it was a pity the fireplace had to go, as the basket grate, with its rounded brass front surmounted by shining balls and standing on claw-footed bow legs, was a handsome object, and a focal point in the room. It may have been to replace some mahogany monstrosity that the Darwins bought this grate and 'the old Adams-style chimney-piece', as Mrs Darwin called it. In a letter that September she described the new replica chimney-piece with its mirror over it as 'really lovely and so much prettier than any structural thing going up to the ceiling'. Her cousin, Ella Du Puy, had designed the 'mirror arrangement'. 'It is all gilded and lincrusta Walton [sic] inlaid, the background of which is painted white. You cannot tell the lincrusta from the wood-carving of the chimney-piece. The mirror is divided by gilded wood . . . and on one side is a tiny shelf.' This and the 'Adams-style' white chimney-piece remain in the drawing-room, now the Parlour of the College.

In 1888, Professor Darwin was in touch with an engineer of the Electric Power Storage Company in London about a supply for Cambridge, though nothing seems to have resulted from this negotiation. He may have been encouraged in this endeavour by Lord Kelvin who had celebrated the 600th anniversary of the foundation of Peterhouse in 1884 by giving his old college its electric light installation. He probably also designed it himself, according to Dr Hinton, the present domestic bursar, who states that 'all the equipment has disappeared now . . . and the chimney must have come down at the time the bath-house was built in the 1930s'. The generation of electricity at Peterhouse was not welcomed by the women who dried their linen on Coe Fen close to the great wall of the College, and they soon made a vigorous protest against the way soot blew over from the chimney and spoilt their washing, but there is no record that any attention was paid to their complaint.

Electricity did not reach the rest of Cambridge until about 1892, when the building of the Cambridge Electric Supply Company's chimney and the two Lancashire boilers was begun in Thompson's Lane on the river beyond Magdalene bridge. The chimney was only pulled down in 1967, after the works had been removed elsewhere. Cambridge was one of the first three places to use the steam turbines invented by Sir Charles Parsons, and he sat on the board of the Cambridge Electricity Company for many years. For the first two years, the electricity was only supplied for lighting during the hours of darkness, but when the demand increased, a twenty-four-hour supply was provided and larger machinery was installed in Thompson's Lane.

It was in 1895, apparently the first year of the public supply, that Professor Darwin at last had his house wired and electricity took the place of gas in lighting the house. Not all the burners were dismantled, however: the one in Mrs Darwin's bedroom was kept in working order to heat her curling-tongs.

It was as well that the builder, urged on by the architect, had made such rapid progress with the alterations and building of the new wing, for Mrs Darwin was expecting the birth of her first child in August. Though the work on the gallery and the clearing-up of the premises outside had not yet been finished, inside the house all was ready when Gwendolen Mary Darwin was born on 26 August 1885.

A few days after this event, her mother wrote home to say that she had moved temporarily 'into the white room, as it is away from the noise of building'. This move was probably to the room in the south-west corner of the house; if so, later on it became her permanent bedroom. She continued: 'I can see over the common for three-quarters of a mile. The village boys have cut down some trees and shrubs and made a path over the ditch to our big island; it was most amusing to see them scamper when they saw George coming to them as they [her husband and the gardener] were burning a wasps' nest on the island.' This way of trespassing on to the island is still a common practice among the young, but they are bolder and more aggressive than the local boys used to be.

CHAPTER EIGHT

The River

THE noise of building which disturbed Mrs Darwin came from the thirty to fifty workmen who, she calculated, must have been employed on the site for the whole of the spring and summer. They were still busy on what the architect called the River buildings, where the boathouse and the gallery above it were being constructed from the bricks of the demolished inner walls of the granary, the river wall having been left standing. The Horse mill and the Engine room, once part of Patrick Beales's Brewhouse, were completely pulled down except for a few feet of the Horse mill, which was left intact to form the corner of the present back yard and the tennis-court fence. Its rounded end is a reminder of the way the mill-horse used to plod round and round grinding barley in the old Horse mill. The present boathouse stands about two feet above the river, and when there is a flood it fills with water. Then the boat inside floats up and bumps about against the walls, sometimes damaging itself, and after the flood subsides an aftermath of mud and wrecked boat-paraphernalia has to be cleared up.

The boathouse ends in a brick wall partitioning off a small dark room or cellar used at first as a tool shed. This shed opens on to the passage to the river door at right-angles. On the opposite side of the passage, higher up, but with its floor well below the level of the lawn, is another ill-lit room once part of the ground floor of the second granary. In March 1887, Mrs Darwin called this shed 'the mushroom house which was really made for a cowhouse if we ever wanted a cow'. Here it was, in April of that year, that her first mushroom bed was made and the spawn sown. The only evidence that the Darwins did ever keep a cow comes from a letter Mrs Darwin wrote in January 1888 to say that she had been feeding her second baby on 'the milk from our cow' but it did not suit him. Perhaps it was this failure that caused them to give up having a cow and to convert her stable into the potting and tool shed. The former toolhouse by the river door was then used for growing mushrooms; it was still called the Mushroom House for years after they were no longer grown there.

A flight of five steps now leads down to it and the river door, but in the 1885 plans only one step was needed. Much levelling of the south-east side of the former yard was required to create the tennis court, with the consequence that a short but steep staircase had later to be made in the passage-way leading down to the river. The water on to which the big door opens used to be eight or ten feet deep and provided a pleasant bathe for those who could swim and enjoyed hanging on to the boughs of the great plane tree diagonally opposite, where they sweep into the water at the corner of the Little Island.

Bathing is no longer possible here, as the river has silted up what was once a deep pool. This must be partly due to the 1947 reconstruction of the flood gates between the upper river, or Granta, as it should be called, and the lower river, or Cam. The new arrangement of the gates appears to have altered the direction of the current, so that now the river erodes the bank of the Lammas land and washes away the corner of Laundress Green even faster than before.* In my youth, the water lapped right up against the wooden embankment of the kitchen garden, but now mud has been swept down by the current to form a foreshore along it almost as far as to Silver Street Bridge and people can walk where once they rowed in a boat. My own garden as a child was at the entrance to the kitchen garden. I used to garden its edge, where I planted nasturtiums to hang into the river six or more feet below, from a ladder standing in the river itself. The present shallowness of what was once our bathing pool had, however, another cause: in the 1950s, when the walls of the gallery and the Old Granary were found to be weak, my brother had them shored up with loads of brick-rubble dumped in the river at their base.

* Laundress Green is the small triangular piece of common-land seen from Silver Street Bridge to the right of the Mill pool. The name presumably originated in the Green's use as a drying-ground for a number of University laundries and for washer-women living in the two parishes of St Botolph and St Mary the Less. On Mondays and Tuesdays the ground was free from grazing animals, so that women from Granta Place and Mill Lane could safely hang out their laundry there to dry. For this privilege they probably had to pay a shilling a year to the Corporation and put up their own posts, as they did for a similar use of Coe Fen near by. In Victorian and Edwardian days, the Green used to be gay with washing fluttering and dancing in the breeze but the custom has long since died out. During spring-cleaning, however, until more recent times, carpets and mats were still brought there for beating; probably the use of vacuum cleaners put an end to this custom too.

The big door under its round arch is clearly depicted in the architect's 1884 drawing of the river buildings. The granaries on either
side of the river door he labels 'Coal Stores', but Mr Bailey of Austin
Beales and Co. [now Charringtons] doubts if the barges would have
used this entry as a commercial dumping place for their coal. Coal
was always conveyed loose in the barges, never in sacks, and the
doorway is hardly wide enough to allow it to be easily barrowed up
and dumped on the ground floor of the granaries on either side.
Probably the barges would have unloaded their cargoes on the wharf
between the old granaries and Silver Street Bridge, for it was at one
time hired by Patrick Beales from the Corporation; or they would
have been sent further upstream to his wharf near Newnham Millpool. Coal in quantity is generally kept out of doors as it does not
suffer from being wet, and the granaries were built for the storage of
corn, not coal. It was possibly only after Patrick Beales had ceased to
be a corn-merchant, or to brew beer on the premises, that he used the
empty ground floor for the storage of his own domestic coal. This may
indeed have been unloaded from a barge through the river-door, but
more probably it was brought in by his coal carts from the railway.
Lavishly as domestic coal was used in those days, it is difficult to
believe that the bottom floors of the huge granaries can ever have
been as much as half-filled with coal even after stocking-up in the
summer months.

By November 1885, the boathouse was presumably finished and
Mr Saint sent Professor Darwin an estimate of £3 2s. for laying' two
timber planks at a width of about four feet from river's edge to Boathouse with rollers'. To lay two more such timber planks from end to
end in the centre of the boathouse would cost another £1 4s., so now
the time had come to commission the boat. In April 1886, Mr Darwin obtained estimates from two boat-builders: Mr J. M. Logan of
Victoria House, Chesterton Road, and the University Boathouse. As
Logan's estimate was for £23 and the University Boathouse only
asked £17 12s. and included more extras, it seems safe to assume that
the latter's estimate was accepted. It reads as follows:

The dinghy, spruce built, seventeen feet long, with mahogany
gunwhales fittings and seats, with 2 pairs of sculls and seats, and a
pair of oars, paddle boathook, *copper fastened* & made from the *best*

materials & of the *best workmanship*, a chain to [be] fixed at bows as a 'painter'. An ordinary back rail, & a cushion for coxwain's seat with 2 rowing mats included £17.12s. And I agree also to lend you a boat whilst your own is being completed.

When the boat arrived it was named the *Griffin* and the family crest was painted on the blades of the sculls and oars. Many years later Mr Darwin bought his children a Canadian canoe for £16, after they had themselves succeeded in saving half the amount required and could swim. It was named the *Escallop* from the Scallop shells in the Darwin coat of arms. It shared the boathouse with the *Griffin* but has long since disappeared, worn out. The *Griffin* still survives and can be used, though in the course of eighty years it has grown steadily heavier owing to the increasing number of its patches. Some years ago outriggers were fitted on it, in place of the old leather-bound rowlocks, in an attempt to make it easier to row, but they proved of little benefit.

The great days of the May Races are long since over, or so think some of their older spectators; the advent of the motor car has made access to the lower river, where the college races are held, far too easy. Up to and during Edwardian times those entertaining May Week visitors were almost obliged to hire a boat and row their guests down to the races, unless the latter had been invited to join a party on one of the few barges moored up-stream near the end of the race; or they preferred to remain on dry land, driving down in a 'fly' or hansom-cab to Ditton Paddock to join other privileged spectators at that favoured spot. The tow-path on the opposite side of the river was left, as it still is, for the swarms of Town and Gown coming via Chesterton or conveyed across the Cam by chain-ferries from Cambridge. Rowing coaches, on horse-back in earlier days but more recently on bicycles, wove their perilous way along the bank of the river through the crowds, exhorting the crews through cardboard megaphones to further effort, their shouting drowned by the din of wooden rattles and the bawling of excited onlookers.

The Darwins of course did not have to hire a boat unless the party they were entertaining was too numerous to be packed into the *Griffin*, when a second boat was hired to take the overflow. On family occasions, if the *Griffin* sufficed, a couple of undergraduates would be invited to help with the rowing. The distance from Newnham Grange to Fen Ditton is under three miles, but to impatient children the leisurely row down seemed an eternity, even though it was enlivened by the thrilling descent to the lower river through Jesus Lock. When at last Ditton Paddock was reached, the boat was turned to face up-stream to ensure a quick get-away and then moored to the bank. If, as was probable, no space was left by the Paddock, the *Griffin* had to be squeezed into the serried ranks of the innumerable other boats and canoes already assembled. It was secured by means of oars rammed upright into the muddy bed of the river.

Ditton Paddock is the big grass meadow sloping down to the river below Fen Ditton Church. The fine old tower can be seen behind the wall and the trees separating the Paddock from the garden of the former Rectory. A few years ago, Jesus College bought the field because it provides the best view of the boat races, and they wished to preserve it as an open space. During May Week the college lets the rear of it as a parking place for cars and the front portion forms a sort of natural Grand Stand for spectators who pay a small fee for the privilege. But sixty or seventy years ago, when the Paddock still belonged to the Rectory, it presented a scene of far greater animation and elegance. Then it was thronged by parties of girls in flowing summer frocks and large flowery hats, accompanied by their inevitable chaperones dressed in more sober array, and by their hosts in college blazers and straw hats or boaters. The May Week parties assembled there, not only to watch the races, but also to partake of strawberries and cream, or unripe cherries, and the excellent teas provided by the Rector in two large hired marquees. It was said that he added a considerable sum to his stipend by this enterprise. As the present Rector said to me of the former occupant of his benefice: 'One can imagine the poor man praying for a dry and sunny race-week.' Many of the parties in the boats used to land to take tea in the Paddock during the hour which elapsed between the rowing of the two divisions. It was not until 1920 that a third division was added. By 1966 there were eight divisions and 129 crews taking part, and the numbers continue to grow.

The Darwins generally brought a picnic tea with them to eat in the boat after the first race, whilst they watched the eights of the first division paddle past to take up their places for the second race. It used to be a particularly pretty sight because those boats which had made bumps on the previous afternoon flew their college flags proudly in the stern, and the coxes in their blazers wore their boaters decorated with wreaths of flowers made up in their college colours, as did some of the crews. This display was probably a survival from the Boat Procession along the Backs on the final day of the races. The last of these evening processions took place in 1892.

It was thrilling to wait at Ditton Paddock, after the starting gun had fired, for the first sight of the boats sweeping round Grassy Corner in the distance and there was always a good hope that bumps would be made as the eights passed by the Paddock, On one memorable occasion, Trinity Hall II, after being bumped opposite the *Griffin*, sank with all aboard and the crew had to swim or wade to the shore.

The instant that the last (or Sandwich) boat had passed and the race was over, a mad scramble began among the moored boats to start on the unofficial, but to many participants, the far more exciting, race back to be among the first boats to reach Jesus Lock. There were no rules, and unshipping a neighbour's rudder was regarded as fair game. The cautious used to wire on their rudders, or a nervous don would sit in the stern seat so that he could hold on to the rudder against enemy attacks. Occasionally an undergraduate might even be seen sitting precariously on top of his rudder, steering it by hand or seat. At the beginning of the race home, the river was so jammed with boats that hardly any room was left in it for rowing. Then a child, squatting in the prow, could render valiant service by pushing away the boats which impeded the progress of the *Griffin* and by so doing give an impetus to the forward movement of his or her own boat; or sometimes one of the oarsmen would stand up and use his oar as a punt pole. When at last a short stretch of open water appeared the two oarsmen would pull furiously at their oars, making the boat bound forward at each stroke until again its path was blocked, and the slow progress would have to be resumed. On one occasion an undergraduate, infuriated by the obstruction of a boat along-side, leapt to his feet and, leaning over the offending boat, seized an elderly gentleman, sitting in the steering seat, by his tie and proceeded to choke him by pulling the noose. Happily, his companion in the boat intervened in the nick of time and forced him to relinquish his hold on the tie, and so saved the poor gentleman's life. Sometimes canoes capsized, but no one was ever drowned.

the *Griffin* received many a bump and blow, but she never upset, not even when a member of her crew was that wild Irishman, Horace de Vere Cole, afterwards famed for the part he played in the Sultan of Zanzibar* and other hoaxes. The unofficial race was over and the lock safely entered, when suddenly Horace Cole stood up and, throwing the lock-keeper a sixpence, snatched hold of his boat hook. Then, standing almost on the gunnel, he was about to use it to knock the boater off the head of a stranger in a boat in front of us, when Professor Darwin seized Cole by the tail of his blazer and pulled him backwards into the boat—thus saving the stranger's hat and the *Griffin* from capsizing. The Darwins did not consider it really good form to knock people's straw hats into the river, especially when the race was over and the haven of Jesus Lock had been reached.

Besides the *Griffin*, there was always, and still is, a garden punt generally kept moored near the landing stage. In the summer months it was frequently needed to rescue balls hit into the river from the lawn above; this was always the hazard of tennis as played at Newnham Grange. The punt was also used as a kind of water-borne cart or floating wheel-barrow in the shallow waters between the house and the islands, or as a vessel from which river weeds could be cut by scythe. It was frequently water-logged and needed constant baling-out. The two flat ends might be used as seats, but except for

* This was a hoax perpetrated by five undergraduates on the civic authorities of Cambridge during the visit of the Sultan of Zanzibar to Great Britain in 1905. Horace Cole was its chief instigator. He took the part of the uncle of the Sultan, the Sultan himself not being represented. The other actors in it were Adrian Stephen, brother of Virginia Woolf, Bowen Colthurst, Leland Buxton, and an Oxford undergraduate called 'Drummer' Howard, who acted as the white interpreter. The Town Clerk met them at the station and conducted them to the Guildhall to be introduced to the Mayor. After attending a charity bazaar, at which the Sultan's uncle spent lavishly at the stalls, they were shown the principal colleges and the tour ended with the Town Clerk escorting them back to the station. Here, instead of catching the train, they bolted out of the station and, jumping into two hansoms, drove off into the country to change into their own clothes and dine at the house of some friends.

having a flat bottom it bore little resemblance to the elegant slim punt of today. It was not until after the turn of the century that Cambridge began to have pleasure-punts. It was believed, erroneously, that the bed of the river was too muddy to allow of punting: no doubt this was a theory originating in Oxford, the home of punts. It was only in Edwardian times that the punt was established as an institution at Cambridge and began to take the place of the Rob Roys, the Canadian canoes, and even the rowing boats.

Before this era an extraordinary little craft, a kind of water tricycle on floats, painted Cambridge blue, was on rare occasions to be seen on the river. For some unknown reason, unless it were that it always seemed to arrive during luncheon-time, the Darwin children called it the Rice Pudding Boat. The owner, or inventor, used to sit in its middle to propel it by means of pedals attached to cranks. Its approach to Newnham Grange was heralded by a great noise of splashing and clattering of machinery, as the intrepid navigator toiled upstream, pedalling away for dear life, to turn in Newnham Millpool and return past the house. It must have been a very early model, if indeed not the prototype of the pedalloes now to be seen on the Riviera coast. Perhaps some mechanically-minded don had heard the story of the water velocipede, and this had put it into his head to invent one. The story was this: on 26 May 1822, a notice had been posted about the town of Cambridge to announce that 'Zachariah Whitmore of Philadelphia, North America, begs to inform the inhabitants of Cambridge that he intends starting from Lynn on his Water Velocipede at 12 o'clock and will arrive at Cambridge between 6 and 8 o'clock in the evening of Whit Monday next.' Accordingly, about two thousand people are reported to have turned up to see Zachariah arrive, but after waiting several hours, they found it was all a hoax!

It was during his second year at Newnham Grange that Professor Darwin heard of the Corporation's plan to commemorate the Queen's Jubilee in 1887 by erecting public bath-houses on Laundress Green opposite the Old Granary. He was roused at once. The draft of his protest to the Corporation has survived. It must have been written in 1887.

Gentlemen,

I believe that one of the plans which has been suggested for the Queen's Jubilee is the erection of public baths. I wish to call your attention to serious objections to one of the sites which have been proposed, namely on the small piece of common adjoining the King's Mill. If you contemplate adopting this plan you will no doubt be advised as to any legal difficulties which may attend the enclosure of a portion of commonland, and to that I need not refer further. It must be the opinion of every inhabitant of Cambridge that the river from Magdalene Bridge to the Newnham Mill possesses quite a unique beauty and that it should be our pride to preserve and embellish it. One of the most interesting varieties in the scene is when, on coming out into the King's Millpool, the cutivated gardens and park-like meadows of the Colleges are exchanged for an extensive view over Sheep's Green with its old pollard willows. The erection of the baths at the proposed site would absolutely ruin this view, as it would be cut off by a palisade of hoardings which cannot but be repulsively ugly.

During the first year in which I lived in this house no very large proportion of pleasure-seekers in boats came up beyond the King's Millpool to the Newnham Mill. I have however at considerable expense converted the old gloomy granaries into a picturesque gallery, have thrown a pretty bridge over the river and have reduced the two islands (which I hold on lease from the Corporation) from a desert of nettles, docks and brambles to pretty gardens. These things I have of course done for my own interest, but I submit that the public has gained largely thereby and that another quarter of a mile has been added to the beauty of the Backs. In proof of this I may remark that during the boating season the boats now come up in swarms past my house. If the baths are placed as proposed the boats will certainly revert to their old custom and will turn back at Queens' Bridge, thus missing the reaches of the river up to Newnham. The proposed public baths would be in full view of my garden. I am convinced that any Surveyor would, if the proposed plan be carried out, appraise the depreciation of my property at £1000 to £1500. I personally should regard such a sum as an absolutely inadequate compensation and the damage to me cannot be represented in money.

If your Committee should agree with me, as to the beauty of this last reach, and I cannot but think that they will do so, I am convinced that they will not adopt a plan which thus mutilates the beauty of the Backs or will inflict so severe a loss upon one who may claim with truth to have contributed to some considerable extent to the charms of our river.

He wrote at the same time to obtain the support of the President of Queens'. This draft ends: 'I hope therefore that your College may feel itself so affected by the scheme as to enter a vigorous protest against it. There has been a good deal of correspondence in the Camb. papers on the subject.'

Whether it was Professor Darwin's grand protest or opposition from the general public that prevailed upon the Corporation to drop their scheme, dropped it was. It was not until 1929, after at least one more abortive attempt had been made to get public bath-houses, that the borough at last opened its first one on a site at the corner of Mill Road and Gwydir Street, where they still are. This seems a surprisingly long time to have to wait for the supply of such a social need, but perhaps it was argued that, as the Colleges existed without bathrooms, none were really needed in the town.

The call for public bath-houses was no doubt influenced by the hot dry 'Queen's Weather' of 1887 and the consequent lowness of the river, but by 1888 the Darwins had discovered that there was a grave disadvantage in living on their branch of the Cam. When the water gates at Newnham Mill were closed, a most offensive smell rose from the temporarily stagnating river. By February 1888, Professor Darwin could endure it no longer: he was never a man to suffer in silence what he believed to be a remediable evil. Indeed, such was his known capacity for expressing himself lucidly in vigorous, if sometimes rather over-formal, language, that on university and scientific committees the task of formulating reports or writing important letters was generally handed over to him, and he would take endless trouble over drafting the papers. Mr Charles Foster, the owner of both mills, was a cousin of Darwin's solicitor. He was privately approached by the solicitor, and asked what steps could be taken to increase the flow of water past the house. The solicitor reported that Mr Charles Foster 'is quite ready to consider any proposition which you like to make to him as to the passing of water thro' Newnham Mill. He tells us that owing to the scarcity of water he is not running the mill at all now but runs his surplus water thro' there on Sundays as he agreed to do.' Professor Darwin replied, asking to be allowed to have some waste water from the mill for an hour or two on week-days and undertook to recoup Mr Foster for his loss of power and for his trouble. 'When the water runs to waste there is a certain loss of horse-power to you and as you rely principally on steam I understand that you can make good the loss by your engines. The question then is to value a horse-power and to estimate the number of horse-powers in the Newnham wheel.'

This was a problem after Professor Darwin's own heart, and he proceeded to make a series of elaborate calculations such as must have astonished Mr Foster by their erudition and complexity. The final conclusion was that an hour's waste water was worth three farthings to Mr Foster; so Darwin offered to pay the mill owner £1 for an hour's waste water on 313 working days and added, as a further inducement, that he would double this amount to £2 a year for one hour's waste *during the middle of the day* . . . . 'If I write much about what to you is a small matter I must beg you to believe that to me it is of the highest importance as being a matter of daily and hourly comfort.'

But Mr Foster refused. 'I have given your application', he wrote, 'my careful consideration and regret I am unable to see my way to giving you any control over the water passing through the Newnham Mill. A season similar to 1887, when no doubt you would especially value the privilege, might equally cause us to regret our having sanctioned any waste.'

It is not known if Mr Foster subsequently relented. Cambridge had 'the reputation of being the worst drained town in England', as Mrs Darwin had written in an earlier letter, but after the drains had ceased to discharge into the river it did become much cleaner and, 'waste water' running through it or not, it gradually lost the smell which had so distressed the Darwins during their first years at Newnham Grange.

CHAPTER NINE

Darwin Family Affairs and the River Again

JUBILEE Year ended triumphantly for the Darwins with the birth of their eldest son on 19 December 1887. He was named Charles Galton, his second name being given him after his father's cousin Francis Galton, grandson of Dr Erasmus Darwin. Professor Darwin greatly admired and liked Galton and was delighted when he agreed to become Charles's titular godfather, stipulating only that he would not actually take the baptismal vows. The other godfather was Lord Kelvin, so no doubt it was a great satisfaction to all parties when at an early age Charles showed a strong bent towards science.

The letters which Mrs Darwin wrote home before and after the birth of her son show how different the pre-natal and post-natal treatment of mothers was in those days. Nearly two months before his birth she wrote: 'People are shocked if I go out, for some reason they think a woman should lie on the sofa and do nothing. I hate to do nothing, but I find that people are so horrified to see me about that I must begin now and give up dinner parties.' Walking up or down stairs seems to have been regarded as a particularly dangerous activity. Three weeks after the birth of Charles, she wrote:

I am getting on very well. I am carried downstairs every morning now and lie on the drawing room sofa all day. We have had three of the most balmy spring days. So yesterday with George's help I walked as far as our first bridge and back to the drawing room. [After Gwen's birth it was nearly four weeks before she was allowed to begin walking.] It was so nice to feel the fresh air again. The baby had his first walk too. [He was carried of course in the nurse's arms; perambulators were kept for older babies.] He is three weeks and a day old and is beginning to be nice. He looks very wise and not so red.

Her son did not thrive on her milk, so, as she reports, he was tried on Nestlé's condensed milk, then on milk from our cow, and now the Milkmaid's brand of condensed milk which so far is satisfactory. Tomorrow if we find it does not do we are to try the Aylesbury artificial mother's food. We weigh him every two days. He weighs now 8 lb 15 oz. and weighed 8 lb 1 oz. at birth. He ought to weigh at least two pounds more.

Mrs Darwin, like all mothers in those days, did not realize the danger of feeding babies only on proprietary foods.

In 1878 Dr W. B. Cheadle had differentiated infantile scurvy from rickets in babies. Dr (later Sir) Thomas Barlow, Physician to Queen Victoria, eventually became such an authority on the subject that the condition was named 'Barlow's Disease' after him. In his 1894 Bradshaw Lecture on infantile scurvy, he stated that the babies of people who could afford to bring them up on proprietary foods suffered far more from infantile scurvy than the children of the poor who gave them a mixed diet from an early age. He therefore advocated feeding babies by the eighth month with what he called 'living food' — sieved potatoes and gravy, together with the juice of fresh fruit, the classic remedy for scurvy. Luckily Charles survived being fed on proprietary food without the addition of any 'living food'. When he was older, he was probably given a daily spoonful of Kepler's Malt Extract which perhaps did contain some vitamins; it was regarded in those days as a valuable tonic or food for children. They loved it on account of its sweetness, but later on when it was mixed with cod-liver oil it lost much of its popularity with children if not with the doctors.

In 1887, the Corporation refused to sell Professor Darwin 'the wharves lying between his house "the Grange", Newnham, and the Small Bridges'. It is interesting to note that the Corporation still referred to Silver Street Bridge as the Small Bridges, though the second bridge had been removed as long ago as 1756. The Corporation did not wish to upset the tenants, Watts and Son, timber, slate and coal merchants, who were renting it at £15 a year, but by 1887 they were making such little use of their wharf that it had become very dilapidated and a public eye-sore.

It was probably in the winter or spring of 1888 that Darwin was asked by the Corporation to take a lease of the site, on condition that it should be used only as a garden, and in order to secure the

Maud Darwin, with Gwen as a baby

MARGARET DARWIN. 189

Margaret Darwin, dressed as the Infanta Margarita by Velazquez

removal of the unsightly tile wharf. In consequence of this he took the lease, and adorned the top of the wall next to the road with a series of brick flower boxes.

Some months before, Watts had tried to rent from Darwin the small oblong strip of freehold land at the east end of the old granary and the adjoining Counting House, or Lodge as it was now called, as he urgently needed more storage room for his tiles. In return for the use of this small piece of land, Watts said he would surrender the lease of the wharf. Darwin politely refused. The fact was that if the Darwins decided to convert the Lodge into a dwelling-house, this small piece of freehold land at the back would be needed; or, if the strip was not used for the Lodge, it would form part of the garden the Darwins were hoping to make on the site of the wharf. In fact, the staircase and entrance to the Old Granary were later built on this piece of land.

In the spring of 1888, Watts at last gave up his lease, and it was probably then that the Corporation sent a deputation to ask Professor Darwin if he would take it over. However on 10 May 1888, when he applied for it he was refused, on the ground this time that the rent of £5 he offered was too small. Some time later the Council agreed to let Professor Darwin the wharf 'for a term of 17 years from Michaelmas next (so that the tenancy will be co-terminous with that of the two islands now held by [him] under the Corporation) at the rate of £10 per annum subject to the condition that the same be used as a garden only'.

Now that he had possession of the land, G.H.D. was faced with the problem of how to get to it. The Lodge and the old granary blocked the way completely: access to it was only possible by the road or the river. Mr Stevenson apparently suggested the construction of a Rustic Bridge Gangway to be attached to the river wall of the granary, hanging over the water. There are faint pencil indications of this on his plan of the river buildings. Saint was asked to estimate the cost. The problem was whether to reach this gangway through the wood cellar (later the College bicycle store) or from the river door. Mr Holmes, the gardener, remembers Sir Charles Darwin telling him that there used to be a gangway starting at the river door and running to the kitchen-garden, so it is clear that the plan of the longer gangway was chosen. It was supported over the river 'on three strong cast-iron cantilevers built into the old wall', and ended at the corner of the new garden. The rent required by the Corporation was only a shilling a year. When, a few years later, the ground floor of the Counting House was required for a coach-house (now the garage), the floor had to be lowered by some two or three feet to bring it down to ground level. When this was done, easy access to the kitchen-garden through the coach-house became possible and rendered the gangway unnecessary. It was therefore removed and no trace of it is left.

When the wall separating Professor Darwin's new leasehold plot of land from his strip of freehold was removed, a stone engraved 'G.H.D. 1888' was built into the wall by the road to mark the boundary between his freehold and leasehold properties. The stone can still be seen, though it is almost hidden by the bicycle shed adjoining the entrance to the Old Granary.

The brick wall separating the wharf from the road was too low to give privacy, or to allow fruit trees to be trained on it, so Saint was asked to raise the height of the wall by $2\frac{1}{2}$ feet. In this new wall he incorporated nine or ten square cement flower boxes at intervals on top. These were eventually used as beds for a variety of tall dark purple cabbage or kale much admired by Mrs Darwin for its decorative quality, which gave a slightly sombre aspect to the wall, reminding passers-by of the plumes worn by black horses in the funeral processions of those days. However, their gloomy effect was counteracted by the gay sight of the yellow alyssum, the marigolds, the wall-flowers, and the snapdragons growing on the top of the old wall nearer Newnham Grange.

Saint estimated the cost of making the garden on the wharf as:

100 loads Earth	2. 10. 0
100 loads Carting	6. 5. 0.
50 loads Rubbish etc. carted back	1. 17. 6.

but perhaps less than 100 loads would be required as this would cover the whole surface about 9 inches thick.

Thus the untidy old wharf was made into a neat, though very narrow, kitchen garden, roughly 140 feet long by 33 feet at the widest point. A wire fence along the river bank later on acted as the support for a row of espalier quince, pear, and apple trees, and by 1892 the end wall, facing Silver Street Bridge, sheltered a couple of what the vendor called his 'A.1.' second-hand wooden beehives, a yellow straw skep sometimes standing amongst them, for in those days skeps were still in use. The elderly gardener, Charles Sexton, an experienced bee-keeper, was put in charge of them. Here the bees and their descendants flourished for the next twenty years until they came to a terrible end. One bitterly cold winter night someone got into the garden, removed the roofs and left the bees inside their hives to freeze to death. No clue as to the perpetrator of the crime or his motive was ever discovered but this was the end of bee-keeping at Newnham Grange.

'Old Secky', as Sexton was affectionately called behind his back by the Darwin children, had another avocation, that of fishing for eels. His method was simple. He stood an ordinary watering can on the bed of the river, usually near the landing-stage where it was well covered by the water and yet within reach of the land. With luck an unwary eel would stop to investigate the can and enter it, to remain there, trapped, until such time as Secky hauled out the can with a rake by its top-handle. Then he would take the eel home to his cottage in Newnham High Street and feast on it—with the invariable result that he was unable to resume work next day, as eels were too rich a delicacy for him. Another talent he had was for losing his spectacles when at work by pushing them up on to his forehead. On occasion, even two pairs were thus mislaid, one above the other, and as he searched in vain for them in the potting shed he would be overheard muttering: 'Drat them pesky children, they've been and gone and taken them again.'

Water for drinking was often filtered in those days, as untreated water from the main was not yet regarded as quite pure and safe. J. H. Middleton, Director of the Fitzwilliam Museum, wrote Professor Darwin a postcard in November 1886, recommending him: 'One of Doulton's Manganous Carbon Filters (Dr Bernays' patent). The 4 gal. one costs 25/-, the 7 gal. one costs 40/-. They are of stoneware and stand on a table.' Professor Darwin presumably did get one, for a large stoneware filter remained in the storeroom, collecting dust, for years.

Life as lived in an old house seldom lacks variety, but the site of Newnham Grange created far more worries than those associated with the upkeep of a house not standing on a river. There exists a letter from the South Level Drainage, Superintendent's Office, Ely, written on 30 December 1889, in answer to an enquiry from the Professor asking if the man then engaged 'in cleansing the River' could afterwards clean out Darwin's ditch. The answer was in the affirmative. The Superintendent calculated the ditch to be ten or eleven chains long and the cost of cleansing it would be £5.0.0. He assumed that Professor Darwin would have no objection if part of the 'sullage'—presumably the mud dredged out of the ditch—was put on his land. Permission would be obtained from the Town Clerk to put the rest on their property, 'the Green'.

Having had the Little Island ditch 'cleansed and stanked' (that is, the earth piled up at the sides), Professor Darwin then approached the Corporation with the request that they would now repair the bank for him. The Town Clerk replied that according to the lease it was Professor Darwin who was responsible for all repairs. The Professor, however, soon established that though he had covenanted to 'stank', there was no mention in the lease of the islands of his obligation to 'pile' or 'plank with land-tiles'. He agreed that these words were included in the lease of the wharf, and had accordingly carried out the whole repair of the wharf bank himself, without asking the Corporation for help. The Corporation thereupon compromised and asked whether Darwin would be prepared to carry out the work at the cost estimated by Mr Saint, namely £49, if the Corporation made a contribution of £30 towards such expense. The work was accordingly done. But three years later, seventy yards of the bank of the Big Island required extensive repair at a cost of £56. Professor Darwin wrote once more to the Town Clerk to say that he wished

to call the attention of the Corporation to the state of the bank of the upper of the two islands of which I am the lessee. The bank has never been piled and it is obvious that it was once of considerably wider extent. My long bridge has as one of its supports the stump of a tree which is now 6 feet from shore & there is another stump standing in the water several feet out. The banks

are now crumbling away considerably & every flood detaches some
portions. I have this year been compelled to cut down two trees
whose roots were undermined.

The Town Clerk replied that he would lay the matter before the
Sub-Committee of the Lease Committee. The further correspondence is missing but it can be presumed that once again the Corporation paid a good proportion of the estimated cost.

Then, some inexplicable trouble occurred about the height of the
bridge to the Little Island near the house. There is no clue as to why
Professor Darwin wished to lower it by three feet. Saint undertook a
little private research on the matter and, on 12 August 1893, wrote
to the Professor:

I found that all the bridges at the back of the Colleges had a
greater height in the centre spans than we have so I called at the
Surveyor's Office to see if they had any bye-law dealing with it.
The Surveyor said they have none but as the height of the present
bridge was sanctioned by the 'Lease Committee' they would
strongly object to any alteration being made without leave being
first obtained from them and he does not at all think they would
agree to the alteration being made.

However, the Borough Surveyor was wrong in this surmise, for on
26 October, the General Purposes Committee granted permission
for the lowering of the bridge, 'upon condition that in the event of
its proving an obstruction to the navigation of that part of the river
you would undertake to alter or remove it. . . . At the same time the
Committee thought it would be advisable if you were to remove the
three projections under the bridge.'

Weeds in the river were apt to be another cause of trouble.
When Professor Darwin reported to the Cam Conservators that the
weeds in the stretch of the river opposite his islands and Newnham
Grange were blocking the stream, they would agree that cutting was
necessary, but sometimes the Borough Surveyor was so long in
sending his men to do it for the Conservancy that my father got his
gardener to cut the weeds instead. The gardener would stand on the
end of our garden punt and, plunging his scythe as deep as he could

into the river, dragged it along, while the garden boy punted him
slowly up and down; the severed long green ribbon-like weed
surfaced, smelling deliciously of the Cam, floating there so thickly
that sometimes the river looked like a miniature, but green, log-
jam in Canada. It is many years since I last noticed any sign of
weed-cutting in the Granta or Cam, nor have I seen the long green
weed rippling in the current by the Big Island as in my childhood it
used to do. Its disappearance has not been explained.

The 1890s were marked by three family events. On 22 March
1890, I was born at Newnham Grange. We were staying at Down
House with my grandmother when I was christened Margaret
Elizabeth in the neighbouring village of Keston, chosen instead of
Downe as the parson was a friend of the family. My aunt Elizabeth
(Bessy) Darwin was my godmother. Seventy years later, my brother
Charles told me he remembered the christening and his horror when
I disappeared from view under the voluminous folds of Aunt Bessy's
long black cloak as I was passed to her to hold by the font. It seems
rather a remarkable example of early memory, as he was barely two
and a half years old at the time.

On 22 August 1894, my younger brother Billy was born at
Marlborough. A house had been taken there for the summer
holidays, partly because of the interest and beauty of the surrounding
country but still more because of Dr J. B. R. Maurice's reputation
as an obstetrician. He was father of ten sons, some of whom became
doctors and succeeded to the family practice, a dynasty which has
reigned over Marlborough for five generations. The baby was
christened William Robert, both traditional Darwin names, but he
was generally called Billy. Soon after his birth he developed severe
jaundice, and perhaps it was due to Dr Maurice that he survived.
A curious result of his illness was that two of his first teeth came
through green in colour. This was a source of pride to his brother
and sisters, but luckily all his second teeth were white.

Five years later, the Darwins' fifth and last child, born at Newnham Grange, died of this same disease, to the great disappointment
and grief of the family.

CHAPTER TEN

The Granaries and the Counting House

In 1895, the Counting House and part of the remaining granary were converted into an unusual and charming living-house and named The Old Granary. It is impossible to discover with certainty when either the Counting House or any of the granaries was built.

The granary and stables on the north, facing the road, were pulled down in 1885 to make room for the new tennis court and kitchen wing of Newnham Grange, though part of one wall was left as the outer wall to the garden. This demolished granary, or perhaps an even earlier one on the site, is partly shown in the plan attached to the 1790 indenture of nine hundred and ninety-nine years made between Patrick Beales and the Corporation, but only the beginnings of the east and west sides are drawn, as in the case of the 'Dwelling House', and there is no indication in the plan of the existence of the Counting House or of the riverside granaries. The indenture permitted Beales to take down any buildings now 'erected and built on the premises' and erect any kind of building he might later want on the site.

Cooper categorically states in his *Memorials of Cambridge* (1866) that Samuel Pickering Beales, to whom the whole property had passed on the death of his brother Patrick in 1792, 'erected thereon a substantial mansion and *mercantile premises*'. Unfortunately, no map of this area has been found between Loggan's map of 1688 and Custance's of 1798.*

Loggan, in 1688, shows Causeway House and a smaller building to the east of it, but not adjoining it. There are no other buildings anywhere in the vicinity. Custance, in 1798, shows the new 'substantial mansion', superseding the much smaller old 'Dwelling House', and the granary adjoining the house, in much greater detail than in the 1790 indenture plan. And here for the first time

---

* J. W. Clark, in Willis and Clark's *Architectural History of the University of Cambridge* (1886), says that Loggan's survey, though the scale is small, 'is so accurately drawn and so clearly engraved, as to be of the greatest service'. Custance's plan, he adds, is copied from Loggan's on the same scale, but 'the details have been carefully corrected to date'.

appears the curved line of the granaries on the river, but as yet there is no Counting House at their north end.

Large old beams are still to be seen in the lower floors of the present riverside granary, as well as in some of the sitting-rooms and passages above (where the pine beams were cased in oak in 1895). These have caused some people, J. J. Stevenson among them, to surmise that the riverside granaries are very old. But Mr H. G. Hughes, an architect who restored a Norfolk windmill dated 1816, has pointed out that all the beams in that building are of about the same size and are of pine, a wood preferred to oak on account of its superior length and the straightness of its grain. And Mr R. C. Lambeth, Rural District Organizer until 1968, says that in his experience almost all the old granaries and malthouses surviving in Cambridge are of Napoleonic date and the riverside granaries bear them a strong resemblance in many ways, especially in having the same kind of pine beams. These probably came from the Baltic, where they would have been logged and roughly shaped by adze into 12-inch-square timber in the forests. Having arrived at King's Lynn by ship, they were either transferred to barges or floated up the Ouse through Denver Sluice to Cambridge.

Many beams for industrial buildings were also imported from Nova Scotia, after having been similarly prepared in the forests, but as they were imported through Liverpool, Mr Lambeth thinks that those in the east of England probably did not come from Nova Scotia but from the Baltic. The schooners bringing over the timber from Nova Scotia were built there, up to 3000 tons displacement, and loaded through the stern solid with the square timbers, some of which might have been as much as 40 to 60 feet in length. The blue-nosed ships, as they were called from the colour of their bows, often sailed across the Atlantic with remarkable speed; but after their cargo of timber was unloaded at Liverpool, the shells of the ships were broken up and sold as wood, so that each time a load of timber was imported from Nova Scotia, another blue-nosed ship had to be built to bring it over.

Grain in storage expands very much, so the walls of granary buildings containing it are usually strengthened by horizontal iron rods or ties. In the Newnham Grange granary, the rods are mostly recent with hexagon bolts, but there is still one of the old type to be

seen on the north-west wall. The end of the straps resemble twin
serpents (or eels?), being given heads and tails, and the rods are held
with thin large square nuts.

If it may be assumed there are no omissions in Loggan's map, the
granaries must have been built after 1688. They are not shown in the
indenture plan of 1790: this is, however, in itself, inconclusive
evidence that they were not in existence by then. However, there are
grounds for thinking that they were built some time between 1790
and 1798, when they appear unmistakably in Custance's map.
They resemble other Cambridge granaries of only slightly later date.
Another reason is Cooper's assertion that S. P. Beales erected, not
only a substantial mansion on the site, but mercantile premises as
well, which seems to imply some important buildings, such as the
big four-storey granaries on the river.

There is no evidence to show that any of the previous owners of
Causeway House were corn merchants. Simeon Lord, for example,
who lived there from 1747 for many years, is known to have been a
china merchant with a shop near Great St. Mary's and the Merchant's Yard at Small Bridges. It is impossible to discover why he,
or Patrick Beales, years later, rented this yard from Queens' College.
It must have been of some importance to Beales in his business or he
would not have advertised its acquisition in the *Cambridge Chronicle*
in 1780, or been willing to pay rates on it for £12, a considerable
ratable value in those days. Perhaps he wanted it as a yard for his
wagons, or as a coal dump near the road and river. Yet in Custance's
map, made only a few years after Patrick Beales's death, and the
subsequent renunciation of its lease by his brother Samuel, the
Merchant's Yard appears to be nothing more than a triangular
walled garden, divided by paths into three neat flower or vegetable
beds. There are no buildings or evidence of commercial activities
on it whatever. The western half did eventually become a builder's
yard, but this was later on.

By 1785, Patrick Beales's business had evidently expanded so
greatly that he needed much more space and accordingly he rented
the Armitage and the Waste Ground from the Corporation, although
judging from the entries in the parochial rate-books, he does not
appear actually to have lived on the premises or in Causeway
House. In 1790, he surrendered his 40 years' lease for the one of 999

years, probably in order to get complete security for the buildings he was planning to erect. But as he died two years later, it was his brother who carried out the work and built the riverside granaries and the other mercantile premises.

In 1797, an artist called Richard Harraden came to Cambridge to make water-colour drawings of the colleges and university buildings for publication as prints. Number 7, the last of the series, drawn in May 1798, shows Queens' College and Silver Street Bridge as viewed from the top of Laundress Green. On the right of the picture opposite is the corner of King's Mill (pulled down in 1928) and on the extreme left is the corner of the old granary rising out of the river. There are three square latticed windows in the wall, one above the other, which are presumably an imaginative rendering, for they differ from the real ones which were long, low, and slightly arched with closer lattice work in them than he depicts. One of these original latticed windows is still to be seen in the west wall of the Old Granary. Harraden has also placed the window rather too near the corner of the wall and has not drawn the roof in correct perspective; viewed from where he must have stood when he made his drawing, he should have continued the line of the corner wall straight upwards to show the edge of the roof, instead of slanting it at an angle. His vision could not have embraced both sides of his very wide picture simultaneously, and he probably put in the corner of the granary more as a balance to the King's Mill on the opposite side of his drawing than to make an accurate record of a mercantile building in which he had no interest. What is of interest to us is that he shows the brick tunnel, already described on page 2, into which the Newnham branch of the river was channelled in 1756, a few yards from what is now the road frontage of the Old Granary. Its arched top can be faintly, but clearly, seen behind the bows of a sailing barge lying partly in front of the granary. Above and behind the tunnel are the wooden railings along the road; on the farther side is a high, solidly built brick wall surrounding two sides of what must be the triangular Merchant's Yard. The third side is hidden; it was formed by part of the Queens' Ditch.

The picture by Harraden is a further proof that the granaries were in existence before May 1798, when Custance's map was published and Harraden's drawing was made.

Harraden's view of Queens' College (1798) showing the old bridge with the Beales's granary on the extreme left

The date of the Counting House is also uncertain. The building is not shown in Custance's map; in its place, a small tongue of river extends right round the north end of the granary to the road. As the old branch of the river used to form the boundary between Small Bridges and the Armitage, so the tunnel, which channelled the river, still to this day forms the eastern boundary of the Armitage. Its invisible presence accounts for the odd little strip of freehold land to the north-east of the Old Granary, and Professor Darwin placed two engraved stones, one in the wall of his kitchen-garden and the other on the edge of the river bank, to mark not only the end of his freehold, but the west side of the tunnel.

If Custance's map is to be believed, and he was generally accurate, the Counting House must have been built later on land made by filling in the protrusion of the river he shows. The house has no cellars, and the fact that its entrance floor was built more than two feet above ground level seems to indicate that this was necessary to keep the house dry, as well as to raise the floor above flood level.

It is not known when this filling-in of the marshy land round the end of the granary was done, but it must have been completed before 1830 when Richard Gray Baker drew his map of Cambridge, for he shows the granary tapering to the road, with what may have been an out-building attached to it on its eastern side. Mr Hughes sees no sign of the present square and formal Counting House in the 1830 map to suggest that it had been built by this time; indeed, judging from its design, it seems to belong to a rather later date. It had some pretensions to style with its stone string coursing, its blind relieving arches and rounded brick arches over the windows, now partly blocked up, and its pretty little porch at the front door. (See rear endpaper). Its roughly triangular south-east end is neatly fitted on to the old granary, in spite of the awkward angle at which the two buildings met, and it is carefully aligned to the road at the other end. It may have been built by one of the Bealeses as a house for his manager and only later turned into the Counting House or offices for the business. We are forced to leave the original purpose of the building and its exact date uncertain, but since it is mentioned as the Counting House in the 1851 advertisement of the auction sale of Patrick Beales's premises, we can rest assured that it was an early Victorian building.

Gray Baker's map also shows that by 1830 much work had been done to confine the river downstream to a straight bank, probably by some stanking and piling. Land behind it and round the north-east end of the extended granary had been made up and probably levelled, for a large gated opening in the middle of the straight wall that still divides the garden from the road suggests that it may already have become by then the Corporation Wharf, leased at one time to Patrick Beales II and finally to Mr Watts, the tile-maker (see pages 80-1). Paths are not marked on Gray Baker's map but it shows that, on the opposite side of the road, building had taken place in the east end of the Merchant's Yard. Whether this building represents Numbers 1 and 2, Newnham, the two prim little yellow brick houses that used to stand there, is uncertain. If it does, they remained there for over a century, until they were demolished in 1935 to make room for the Fisher Building of Queens'. The house nearest Silver Street Bridge had a quaint little garden at its side, probably made to fit the blunted tip of the otherwise triangular Merchant's Yard. A long narrow building at the back of the western half of the Yard also appears in Gray Baker's map, perhaps the forerunner of the shed in the builder's yard it was later to become; for in 1881, Queens' let No. 2 at £35, and the yard at £20, to Mr Flack, a builder. It was known as Flack's Yard for many years until he retired in 1925 and soon after died, when Queens' let the yard to Coulson & Sons, the Cambridge builders. They only stayed there for ten years; in 1935, they gave back the lease to the College when it wanted the site for Fisher Building. Queen's however to this day continues to pay a small ground-rent to the Corporation for the 'Messuage' of Nos. 1 and 2 and the Yard.

The road on its north side from Queens' Green to Silver Street Bridge must have remained almost unchanged in appearance from 1841, when the path was widened at the bend and presumably the iron railings painted fawn-colour were put up to shield the foot passengers from the dangerous traffic of those days, and the cattle being driven to market. Probably the railings, like the cast-iron bridge, were made in Swann Hurrell's Foundry in Thompson's Lane.

When she first saw the small building which was still used by the Bealeses as their office, Mrs Darwin described it as 'a dear little house'.

Instead of having its entrance on the road, its door opened down five steps into the old cobbled yard, still surrounded by granaries and stables. Many and ingenious, if impracticable, were the plans she made for the use of this cottage. In 1885, the architect had been consulted about its repair; a photograph taken a year later shows that the ivy smothering it had been stripped off and the roof repaired, but there is no evidence that any inside work had as yet been undertaken.

On 6 September 1886, Mrs Darwin wrote home that 'we are really going to keep chickens, not chickens straggling over the garden but in the space by the cottage and they are to have the whole of the second floor of the granary for themselves'. (By this she meant what we in England call the first floor.) 'It is low down so it will be all right. Next year I hope to have a cow and then I am going to try growing mushrooms in the upper floors of the granary and sell them, but that is in the future.'

Readers of *Period Piece* may remember Gwen Raverat's description of 'the hens' hole' in the granary wall. Though long since bricked up, its outline can still be seen almost above the entrance to the woodcellar, or the bicycle storehouse as it had become. For some years, after the chickens were removed to new quarters on the Big Island, this hole continued to provide a private entrance to the lofts above for such children as were still small enough to squirm through it. Larger children and adults had to enter the loft by the conventional way through a trap-door in the floor, reached by climbing up a ladder from the woodcellar below. Eventually, a steep iron staircase was built against the wall outside with a door at the top to enable the Newnham Grange maids to use the loft as a drying place for the washing, and the tenants in the Granary as a refuge in case of fire. To escape they had but to open a trap-door in the floor of their dining-room and drop down a few feet into the darkness of the loft below, unless they preferred to use the vertical ladder fixed to the wall. The trap-door is still there but the graduates living in the Old Granary are now supposed to use the lift as a means of escape. In order to make room for this lift, built for my sister after she had a stroke, the outside iron staircase and the door at the top were removed, and the only means of access to the loft, long since become a lumber room for Newnham Grange, is now by means of the lift and a door in the lift shaft.

In the spring of 1888, Miss Mary Reynolds came over from America to visit her sister, Mrs Jebb, at Springfield. Her niece, Maud Darwin, in the hope of persuading her aunt to stay on in Cambridge after the Jebbs' return to Glasgow in the autumn, offered to lend her the Counting House as a residence, but unluckily this idea did not meet with her Aunt's approval. 'We have all been over to the cottage to see if it is possible that it can be made habitable for Aunt Mary', Mrs Darwin wrote home in July. 'The cottage has only four rooms in it, two of them very small and so narrow a winding staircase between the walls that she says if she grows any fatter she could not get up or down. We are going to send for the builder to see what it will cost to get it [the cottage] into repair.'

Mr Saint estimated the *Alterations to Lodge* would cost £207, but 'if the present Drawingroom is made into kitchen and new Drawing-room is made in old Granary as alternative plan and the floor lowered to the level of the present floors of Lodge with additional window the cost will be . . . £212'. Professor Darwin has pencilled underneath: 'No allowance for new bedroom.' One of the many difficulties in making a living-house out of these two separate, but adjoining, buildings was the different levels of the floors. This difference accounts for the many steps and short staircases in the Old Granary. However, Aunt Mary returned to America in due course and the plans for making the cottage habitable lapsed until 1895 when Mrs Darwin's dream house at last came into being.

Unfortunately, two of my father's letter-files are missing at this point; they cover the sixteen months from May 1894 to September 1895, during which time the plans for the new house were made and the building was begun. Mr Stevenson was of course called upon to take charge of what he later described as 'that most interesting work'. The plans were on a much grander scale than those envisaged for Aunt Mary's 'little cottage'. A coach-house, stable, and harness-room for Newnham Grange were to be provided, with a passage through the coach-house to the kitchen-garden. This involved lowering the floor of the Counting House by a couple of feet to ground level and replacing the door, its porch, and the big window in the west wall, by a side door and a pair of coach-house doors wide enough to admit a carriage. A covered staircase built against the east wall from the road led up to the first floor of the

Counting House where the entrance to the new house was to be. My mother in consequence generally called the Old Granary 'the Flat', though it was anything but flat inside; but, as it had no ground floor nor access to the garden on either side, in her eyes it was, and remained, a flat.

Stevenson's plans survive to show how the first floor of the Counting House and the top two floors of the granary were converted into a living-house by some additional building and the use of the existing chimney. Very few alterations to these plans have taken place since his day. He made the kitchen quarters and the entrance hall out of the top floor of the Counting House, lowering the floors to correspond with the bottom level of the coach-house floor. This accounts for the odd-looking partial blocking of the windows as seen from the road. The small hall, with its window overlooking the river to the south-east, is nearly triangular in shape; this is because the Counting House was built against the end wall of the granary at a sharp angle. My sister used this hall as her dining-room, as the kitchen opened conveniently out of it, but when the College made the Old Granary into rooms for six postgraduate students, the kitchen was no longer needed, and has been turned into one of the bed-sitting-rooms. The scullery, pantry, and larder formerly opening out of it have been walled off and made into a pantry and utility room for the common use of the students. A second storey was built by Stevenson above the kitchen and hall to provide three small bedrooms and a lavatory.

The top two floors of the granary provided the rest of the accommodation. In 1885, the size of the granary had been reduced to make room for the tennis court, the west corner being demolished and the wall rebuilt farther back in two recesses to the river passage-way. For the entry into the former granary, Stevenson had to make a staircase of eight steps up from the hall. The levels here are most confusing; it should be remembered that underneath the sitting-rooms lie two floors—the Newnham Grange lumber-room and below that the bicycle store.

Two sitting-rooms were made on the third floor of the granary; both opened on to a long balcony over the river. The second of these rooms was intended for the dining-room and as such it was used for many years, perhaps even until my sister's time. I remember it long ago as a rather gloomy room, lit only by a single window and a glass door to the covered end of the balcony. No doubt the gloom was accentuated by the deep red of the wall-paper, for in those days it was an established convention that all dining-rooms should have such papers, though very occasionally a dark green was

permissible. It was not till late-Edwardian times that the aesthetically-minded began to make use of plain light-brown paper on the walls of their dining-rooms, as less light-absorbing and a better background for pictures. When, however, my sister came to live in the Granary in 1946 and wished to use the dining-room as her sitting-room, the other room being her studio, she was allowed to put in a large window on the west. Previous tenants had not been permitted to overlook the tennis court except, unavoidably, through the small bathroom window on the top floor.

The study, a necessity in all Cambridge houses inhabited by University people, was ingeniously contrived by being built on the top of the tea-room. It may be remembered that the architect made this tea-room at the south-east end of the gallery in the remaining granary, in 1885. The new study was at a different level from the dining-room, so that four steps had to be put to reach it from this, its only point of access.

On the top floor are the two best bedrooms, lit by big dormer windows in the roof, with a narrow dressing-room between. The passage—its window overlooking the road—and the bathroom complete the lay-out of the top floor.

An attic was made above the bedrooms with a trap-door into it in the ceiling of the passage. The roof had to be extensively repaired, if not actually rebuilt, but I am sure the old tiles were used for it, as far as possible. The beams and rafters are intact and it looks much as it did in 1895, when I was last up there as a very small girl. I remember the laborious climb up through what seemed to be endless trap-doors, our undergraduate cousin Ralph Wedgwood in charge of us and the ladder. When at last we reached the top, we sat blissfully on the dusty floor under the rafters, lit by chinks of light coming through the holes in the roof, to be regaled by Ralph with dried prunes begged from the cook, tasting more of his pocket than of prunes, but very delicious all the same.

The letter-file which covers the completion of the Old Granary is luckily still in existence. My mother wrote to the long-suffering architect on 4 September 1895:

Dear Mr Stevenson,
I have come home for a night to see how things are getting on generally. I have seen Mr Saint and we both agree that the cottage roof looks very bald by the road, and seems to need an eave. Mr Saint says there is time to put one on now, if you consent. You may think that it is not in keeping with the granary, and if so, I give up my opinion. The flat piece of wall of the granary by the tea-room, looks well, because it is broken by the chimney, which runs up to a great height, and because of the sloping roof of the tearoom. [Later on, when the study was built on top of it, this sloping roof of course disappeared, but traces of it can still be seen above the tea-room window overlooking

the lawn.] I was very sorry to see that you had forgotten to give the order to have the addition to the cottage [i.e. the Counting House] made in flat tiles. It would have been so great an improvement. . . . I find that I have so much oak from the sideboard left over that I really believe there will be enough carving to use in a chimney piece for the dining-room in the flat.

Mr Stevenson answered her letter with admirable patience:

There would have been some difficulty in adding to the height of the cottage walls and gables otherwise than in brick. These walls had to carry the roof, and wood framing covered with tiles would not have been a good support for the weight and thrust of the roof and I rather think it would not have been permissible by the building regulations of Cambridge. But the eaves at the gable to the road might project, and, if the tiles are not put on the cottage roof, this can be done yet so as to give some shadow there. . . . I shall be glad to see when I get back what can be done with the carving left over from the sideboard. It is a pity it could not have been included in your own dining-room chimney piece.

Whilst he was on holiday in Scotland, Stevenson had put his junior partner, Harry Redfern, in charge of the work. Accordingly the next letter comes from him. On 10 September he wrote to Professor Darwin to say that he had sent a drawing to Saint 'showing how to improve the mean appearance which the new gable towards the road is said to have'. He also enclosed a drawing to show how the study might

be improved by carrying up the walls vertically till they reach the ceiling. This of course would very greatly increase the room's book-holding capacity. I have drawn a flat roof for the study now. It has every advantage that a tiled one would possess and is less obtrusive, wh. I suppose is a recommendation under the circumstances. It will shew but little from Newnham Grange and does not compete unfavourably with the big roof of the Old Granary, as seen from the river. If you approve of the arrangement suggested upon the enclosed drawing I will at once make details for Saint and give him the necessary instructions. . . .

Two days later he wrote again to say that, as Professor Darwin was desirous of increasing the floor space in the study, he had prepared another sketch:

The change presents no difficulty since we have Saint's word that the old walls are strong enough to take the new weight added to them by this arrangement. Now the Study becomes a very quaint room. I have supposed a writing-table wd occupy the recess; so there is a single window at that point to light it.

By 9 October Stevenson was back at work and he wrote the following letter:

[Saint] tells me you wish the end of the balcony, I presume next the stone oriel, closed with glass. If so the glass should be leaded glass like that in the staircase [and] I suppose clear, so as not to shut out the view.

He asked:

if the coach house . . . is to be finished in 'granolithic' at 1/6 per yard extra over the concrete floor provided. Granolithic is harder and better-looking, but I don't know that it will resist damp any better than concrete, which I though practically sufficient. For full imperviousness to damp a layer of asphalte would probably be necessary under the finished surface of concrete or granolithic.

A fortnight later he wrote again to say that he had at last got the internal stair at the flat to work satisfactorily:

It has been one of the most interesting puzzles in that most interesting work, to get it in between the old beams. Though one was cut away, the beam below it came in the way. It is better than in the first drawings without I think more cost, and will I

believe look well. I have found a place on it for the carved post
from the Italian cabinet. I suppose you will not object to the
stair being stained a rich brown colour to match.

It occurred to me that the lower part of the oak covered beams
in the dining-room and drawing-room might be stained somewhat
darker than their cornice, which continues the cornice of the
room, which was the reason for its being the size it is. The beams
would not then look so large. . . . I shall now get the drawings
done for the cupboard above the sideboard. I think I can work
the carved face into it.

So at last every scrap of Mrs Darwin's beloved Italian carved
cabinet was used. The cupboard made to hang above the sideboard
in the Old Granary dining-room has disappeared, but the carved
post Mr Stevenson managed to incorporate so cleverly in the inside
stair is still there. It is no longer 'a rich brown colour', however,
as the College has had it painted white to match the stairs. This
my mother would have regarded as a desecration of what she,
probably erroneously, believed to be a fine example of Renaissance
carving.

Meanwhile W. J. Crampton & Co. of 40 St Andrew's Street,
electrical engineers, were beginning to wire the house for electricity;
the estimate they gave for this work in June 1895 was £12. 3s. This
was considerably lower than the £38. 10s. Professor Darwin paid
for the installation of nineteen lights in Newnham Grange, but then
the Grange was a much bigger house, and Professor Darwin had
employed a London firm. The work at Newnham Grange seems
to have gone without a hitch and was finished by the late autumn.
But Crampton's installation in the Granary was not finished and
connected with the mains by the Cambridge Electric Supply
Company until February 1896, though the work was begun at
about the same time as that in Newnham Grange.

CHAPTER ELEVEN

Tenants of the Old Granary

In August 1895 the Old Granary, although far from ready for occupation, was put into the hands of the estate agent, Arthur Rutter, of 63 Sidney Street, to let at a rent of £90, free of taxes 'except for water and gas'. On 23 August, Mr Rutter sent Professor Darwin an angry letter that he had just received from a Captain Robinson written after hearing from his wife that she had decided to take 'Mr Darwin's flat at Newnham'. 'I think it better I should let you know *myself*', wrote the Captain, 'that I cannot afford such a rent for any house in Cambridge.' Mr Rutter's wry comment on the back of this letter was: 'I think that Capt. Robinson has not conferred with Mrs Robinson whose idea is that although paying a higher rent for the flat, she would save it in the cost for service.' I fear that poor Mrs Robinson's subsequent conference with her husband must have been an unhappy one.

No further correspondence about the renting of the Old Granary occurs until the end of the year when a letter came, this time not from the estate agent, but from the Darwins' friend, J. D. Duff, Fellow and Tutor of Trinity, Lecturer in Classics, and later known for his excellent translation from the Russian of Aksakoff's *Years of Childhood*. He had been in constant attendance at Newnham Grange for the last eight or nine years and his round and rosy presence was a familiar sight to the older children of whom he was a great favourite. Mrs Darwin was also fond of him and had even indulged in a little mild match-making on his behalf when her younger sister Carrie spent a year at Cambridge with them in 1887. It had nevertheless proved a thankless task. Mrs Darwin wrote home that Duffy, as she called him, had

> never given her [Carrie] a thing — oh yes, he brought some choco-lates on one occasion and then when she seemed to enjoy them, he told her to take them home. Carrie isn't a grain in love with him. My experience of English lovers is that if they mean anything

they come straight to the point and make it evident. But if not, they are just as friendly as they can be without the least idea of anything more, and just as Mr Duff told Nellie [another of her younger sisters] it was quite proper for her to go out rowing with himself and H.B. [Smith], when I was away one day, without having the least idea it was unusual, I think he only enjoys being with us all because he is friendly and likes us.

Now, however, Mr Duff had made a match for himself in Ulster where, on 28 December 1895, he had married Miss Laura Lenox-Conyngham. On his engagement, Mrs Darwin must have suggested that the Old Granary would suit them admirably for their first home in Cambridge; and in due course they decided to take it. Professor Darwin wrote to them at Ventnor, whither they had now gone for Mr Duff to recuperate from a breakdown in health. After giving them details as to a drain, the cleaning of windows, and the installation of electric lights, etc., he offered to have fires lit in the flat to dry out the plaster in the new ceilings. The Duffs would not be technically his tenants until March quarter day, but they gladly authorized him to do this and the end of March saw them safely installed in their new, and presumably dry, home, where they were to remain for the next two years.

The Duffs were succeeded at the Old Granary by another Trinity man, also a friend of the Darwins. This was Arthur Hugh Clough, son of the poet, and nephew of Miss Anne Jemina Clough, the first Principal of Newnham. He was also the brother of Miss B. A. (Thena) Clough, who came up to Newnham in 1884 and remained there working in various capacities until she retired from being Principal in 1923, dying years later at the age of ninety-nine.

Arthur Clough was an interesting and unusual man. A Foundation Scholar of Trinity, he got Firsts in Classics and Moral Sciences. He entered the Education Department of the Civil Service as an examiner, but disliked being a civil servant so much that, in 1898, he resigned to become his own master again and farm the property he had acquired at Burley, near Ringwood in the New Forest. He had a deep love of the country and a philanthropic wish to increase the number of small-holders living on it, so he bought up possible farming land wherever he could find it, in Sussex, Hampshire, Wiltshire, and Dorset, in order to settle suitable men on the small-holdings he made out of his purchases. He often had to build farm-houses for his tenants and this directed his attention to the deplorable state of rural housing. Early in the 1900s, he wrote a pamphlet on land valuations; arguing that much good agricultural land on large estates was being wasted, and small-holders were needed to develop it. I remember hearing about his plans for rural housing: a local small builder was to be employed, if possible; the little square houses must be built round a central chimney-stack, so that no heat would be wasted on outer walls, and — this was before the First World War — he claimed that they could be built for the remarkably small sum of £100.* It should be remembered what a small part wages played in building costs then, especially in the country where agricultural labourers were still often paid only twelve shillings a week. His small-holders' houses must have been stoutly built in spite of their cheapness, for I am told by his nephew that they are still in use.

In 1892, Arthur Clough had married Eleanor, eldest daughter of Douglas Freshfield, the mountaineer, and it may have been partly to please her that in 1898 he took a lease of the Old Granary with the view of spending the winter there and sub-letting it for the rest of the year. However, as time passed, he became so involved in his farming and rural housing projects that, in 1903, he regretfully gave up the flat, since they could make so little use of it. As so often happens, a little difficulty then arose over dilapidations. Clough was usually the most generous of men over money affairs, but now he strongly objected to paying for some internal decorations to be done again. Only two years before, he had rejected Mr Saint's

---

* Richard Butler, a nephew of Arthur Clough, tells me that it was Clough who gave his cousin Mr Clough Williams-Ellis his first chances as an architect, by employing him to develop his (Clough's) Sussex property, with the help of an excellent local builder. Later on, he acted as clerk-of-works on a cottage Clough had entered for a competition at Letchworth, where it won the first prize 'for value'. Mr Williams-Ellis adds that he won 'a similar competition initiated by St. Loe Strachey of the *Spectator* in 1914 by building a country cottage complete with drains and water supply for precisely £101'. It was probably this achievement that A. H. Clough had in mind when he told us that hundred-pound cottages were a real possibility.

estimate for the job as preposterously large and had brought up
his own man from Hampshire to do the painting at a minimal cost.
Saint had been annoyed at this procedure and, after the Cloughs
had left in March 1903, he wrote Professor Darwin an outraged
letter:

> I do not think your late Tenant has treated you well, or even
> fairly, in the way he has treated inside work. . . . If it had been
> a barn it could not have been done worse; in my estimate of cost
> I of course allowed for it to be done as it was at first under
> Mr Stevenson. I am quite sure he would not have approved of
> the very unsatisfactory way Mr Clough allowed it to be done. . . .
> I will promise you I shall not allow my men to copy that done
> previously. I would take care that £20 should be spent satis-
> factorily.

Mr Clough's offer to pay the new tenant a lump sum down for
the dilapidations was, I believe, accepted and my parents and the
Cloughs parted the best of friends, but I am sure Mr Clough always
remained anathema to Mr Saint, a view fully reciprocated by the
former.

The next tenant of the Old Granary was Arthur Christopher
Benson, son of the Archbishop of Canterbury and elder brother of
E. F. Benson, the novelist, and Father Hugh the Catholic writer
and apologist. A Scholar of Eton and King's, A. C. Benson obtained
a First in classics and returned to Eton to teach. In 1892, he was
made a house master and 'was soon justly considered to be one of
the best ever known at Eton', according to his biographer in the
Dictionary of National Biography; but, ten years later, anxious to devote
himself entirely to writing, he decided to retire to Cambridge.
About this time — his aunt, Mrs Henry Sidgwick, having told him
that A. H. Clough would be vacating the Old Granary the following
spring — he wrote to ask if he might be considered as a future tenant,
adding that he felt sure he would give very little trouble. Invariably
polite and anxious to please, the many letters from him found in
my father's file, however, show him to have been fussy and

indecisive. Having 'run over' to Cambridge to see the house, in the parlance of the day—my father and his friends seem constantly to have been 'running up' to London—he wrote that he was disposed to take it. Its only defect was that it was just one room too small. He suggested that a slice might be taken out of the drying room underneath to form another room, and at the same time could not the cellar be made bigger to hold his large stock of wine? Professor Darwin agreed to lengthen the cellar but could not consent to the making of the room, as his builder refused to 'meddle with' the river-wall by putting a window in it. Mr Benson wanted this extra room in order to keep a third maid. This Mrs Darwin thought to be totally unnecessary. Later on, he graciously admitted that two maids were quite sufficient to run his house and she had been 'practical and wise' in her advice.

Then there was the question of the stable below. 'Do you keep horses underneath the house?' enquired Mr Benson. 'I should like to feel secure on that point—it would be difficult to avoid smell in that case.' Professor Darwin agreed not to use the stable during a short lease but could not enter on such a covenant for a long lease, 'as it would distinctly diminish the market value of this house [Newnham Grange] to have a stable which could not be used as such', adding reassuringly: 'There is only a stable for one horse.'

Then in the early spring of 1903, Mrs Darwin had a broody hen put to sit on eggs in the drying-room. This might have caused difficulty, but Mr Benson magnanimously instructed his solicitors to write to Professor Darwin saying that he did 'not at all object to the sitting hen, but would not care to have the place made into an extensive fowl run'. Did he perhaps know that it had formerly been used for this purpose?

On 17 November 1902, some months before the little matter of the nesting hen had arisen, Mr Benson wrote that he would take the house on a seven-year lease at a rent of £85, with leave to sublet subject to Professor Darwin's approval. The lease was duly signed on 26 February 1903. Benson was to have possession on Lady Day but, on 9 March, he asked for permission to let the house to M. S. Dimsdale and his wife. 'They are ready', he added, 'to take it subject to a short notice, to give it up when required, which is what suits me exactly.' Permission was willingly given and the

Dimsdales moved in with their servants and furniture at the end of March.

Marcus Dimsdale had been a Scholar and contemporary of Benson's at Eton. He was now a Classical Fellow and Lecturer at King's. He had recently married Miss Elspeth Philipps and had bought the old house facing Hobson's Conduit at the corner of Lensfield Road and Trumpington Street for their permanent home. Much rebuilding and restoration was needed to make it into the attractive Corner House it now is, and no doubt they were glad not to be turned out of the Old Granary until the end of November when at last Mr Benson was ready to leave Windsor and settle down in Cambridge. However, after all these preparations he only lived in the Old Granary for a year or two, as he was made a Fellow of Magdalene in October 1904. During his ten years as Master (1915–1925), he saw 'Magdalene rise from comparative insignificance to the position of one of the best and most sought-after among the smaller Cambridge colleges' — to quote from the *D.N.B.* once more.

We were told later on that he had written his book, *Beside Still Waters*, whilst living in the Old Granary. This we children regarded as an insult to our beloved Cam, more especially as under his balcony the river flowed with a perceptible current, but, as he wrote so many books, his published works amounting to over one hundred volumes, perhaps he had difficulty in finding titles for them all and should be forgiven. In *A Christmas Garland* (1912), Max Beerbohm had a brilliant, if cruel, parody of some of Benson's mild and platitudinous books, entitling it 'Out of Harm's Way. Chapter XLII: Christmas'. Mr Wilmarth S. Lewis, an American friend of Max Beerbohm, told me the sad sequel to this parody, and later on put it in writing for me:

This is the way I remember Max's story about A. C. Benson. When I asked him if any of the writers he parodied in *A Christmas Garland* were wounded, he said 'Yes, Benson. I did not send him a copy of it, but Heinemann's did by mistake. He thanked me for it and then wrote: "I'm afraid I read only the first paragraph because I could not bear to see myself made a greater fool of than I know I am." ' When I said 'He had the last word, didn't he?' Max agreed and added that the parody was 'very cruel'. As I wrote this down immediately after our day with him I think it is accurate.

Benson may have let the Old Granary to the Bertrand Russells for a few months, when he moved into Magdalene in 1905; or perhaps it was earlier that they rented it from Arthur Clough. Lord Russell did not remember exactly when it was and had no

'What had happened? I shall never know.'

papers in which to look up the matter. In a letter to my sister after the publication of *Period Piece* in 1952 he told her that they had at one time rented the Old Granary and believed he knew the sequel to an incident which she describes in her book. One evening returning along Silver Street, when she was passing the Anchor, Gwen suddenly saw a small gang of rather disreputable undergraduates running towards her from the other side of the road. They were carrying the body of a woman who seemed to be dead, possibly drowned in the river. Under her depiction of the scene on page 171, her caption runs: 'What had happened? I shall never know.'

Readers of her book will be glad to learn that Lord Russell supplied her with the answer to this question, and kindly allowed me to print his letter here in full:

31 December 1952
41 Queen's Rd.,
Richmond,
Surrey.

Dear Mrs. Raverat,

I have been reading your 'Period Piece' with the very greatest delight. I think you have done the characters with most remarkable charm and skill. You have probably forgotten that I used to come to your parents' house when you were a girl, and at one time rented the Old Granary, so that the environment you describe is not unfamiliar to me.

I am writing to you, however, not only to convey my appreciation, but also because I think I know the sequel to an incident which you describe. You mention a number of undergraduates fishing a girl out of the river. At just the date concerned some undergraduates came to Mrs Whitehead* telling her that they had pulled out of the river a pregnant young woman who was attempting suicide. They were naturally embarrassed and wanted to unload her as soon as possible on some philanthropic lady. Mrs Whitehead applied to us and we took her on as a maid. She got engaged to be married but at the last moment, her fiancé got cold feet and I had to give him five pounds to go through with the ceremony. She tried to steal everything small and valuable in our house, but we discovered the attempt and thwarted it without saying anything. After her marriage we lost sight of her and I hope she lived happy ever after — though I rather doubt it. I don't think there can be much doubt that she is the same woman of whom you write.

Yours sincerely,
Russell.

* Mrs (Evelyn) Whitehead was the wife of Alfred North Whitehead, mathematician and philosopher. The Whiteheads were great friends of the Russells; and Whitehead collaborated with him in *Principia Mathematica*, the first volume of which was published in 1910.

Lady Corbett, the widow of Admiral Sir John Corbett, K.G.B., was the next person to take the Old Granary. This was probably at the instigation of Mrs Darwin, for history had been neatly repeating itself. Lady Corbett's youngest son, George, was engaged to be married to Mrs Darwin's niece, Maud Spencer, who had come over from Erie, Pennsylvania, in 1900 to visit her aunt Maud, just as her aunt Maud had come over from Philadelphia in 1883, to visit her aunt, Caroline Jebb. Now, this second Maud was also going to marry a man called George.

George Corbett was at this time a pre-clinical undergraduate at King's. As it did not occur to professional men in those days to marry until they could afford to support a wife, Maud and George had to wait seven years, till George had qualified at St Mary's Hospital, London, and had got a post as assistant to a doctor at Ealing before they could celebrate their marriage at St Botolph's in March 1907. There was no Health Service then to help him to a practice, so when the following year he was ready to set up as a fully trained doctor, he had to borrow £2000 from his mother to buy a partnership in the practice before he could establish himself as a general practitioner in Steyning, Sussex.

After her husband's death in 1893, Lady Corbett moved from London to Cambridge to live near her eldest son William. He was a Fellow and Lecturer at King's 'whose extraordinary knowledge of English topographical history had made him an authority on Doomsday Book' — to quote from his obituary in the King's College Annual Report. His mother had been living in a house on Grange Road until, early in 1906, she decided to take the Old Granary from Mr Benson. She was assigned the remainder of his seven years' lease and by the time it expired four years later she was so well-established in the Old Granary and the Darwins were so attached to her that no further agreement was considered necessary. She remained in occupation for the rest of her life, dying there in 1918. Her son kept on the flat, probably sub-letting it for a time, for a mysterious Geoffrey Holloway's name appears in the 1920 and 1921 directories as occupant. In 1921, having married Jane Borrett, the widow of a distant connection, William Corbett moved into the Old Granary to live there until 1924, when he retired from King's and settled down in Norfolk at Horstead House, his father's old home on the Broads. But he did not live to enjoy his retirement for long, as he died the following year at the age of fifty-nine, after a short illness.

The Corbett family continued in possession of the Old Granary until 1926 or 1927, according to the evidence of the directories. They were succeeded by Louis Colville Grey Clarke, then Curator of the University Museum of Archaeology and Ethnology, whose home the Granary remained for the next eleven or twelve years. Like A. C. Benson, earlier, and Henry Morris afterwards, Louis Clarke was a bachelor. The house suited him admirably, situated within easy reach of the Museum and providing him with a peculiarly sympathetic setting for the fine furniture and works of art with which he filled it. Unluckily, I have no family records to help me give a more personal account of his tenancy, but I know that it gave my mother pleasure to have such a distinguished and charming man as her tenant and neighbour, though she did not see much of him.

As an undergraduate at Trinity Hall, of which he later became a much-loved Fellow, ample means had already allowed him to travel widely in Europe, and after taking his degree in history in 1903, he made lengthy journeys to Central America, Mexico, Chile, Peru, and Ethiopia, thus developing his strong archaeological, anthropological, and aesthetic interests. During the First World War he served with the Army in France but before long he was invalided out. In 1919, he went to Oxford to take the Diploma in Anthropology and did valuable work in the Pitt Rivers Museum. In 1922, he became Curator of the Museum of Archaeology and Ethnology in Cambridge, in succession to Baron Anatole von Hügel. Whilst Curator he took part in important excavations in New Mexico.

Louis Clarke was living at the Old Granary when, in 1937, he was appointed to follow Sir Sydney Cockerell as Director of the Fitzwilliam Museum; the Second World War limited him severely in what he might have achieved there, though he kept the Museum alive during the war by organizing temporary exhibitions to take the place of the collections moved away for safety. On his retirement in 1946 he became Honorary Keeper of the Prints, and continued his ceaseless stream of gifts to the Museum, to which he bequeathed a collection of works of art that is among the greatest benefactions the Fitzwilliam has ever received.

In 1938, whilst still Director of the Museum, Louis Clarke gave up his tenancy of the Old Granary to live at the former home of F. W. H. Myers, Leckhampton House, off the Grange Road. Here he spent the remainder of his long life, deeply interested in his beautiful garden, entertaining his many friends and still in his old age taking an active part in archaeological and anthropological studies. He died in 1960. The house is now used by its owners, Corpus Christi College, as part of a residential centre for their research students.

The next tenant of the Old Granary in 1938 was a man as distinguished in his own way as Louis Clarke was in his. Henry Morris was the son of a plumber in Manchester. When the First World War began, he was still an undergraduate at Exeter College, but left Oxford in 1914 to serve as an officer in the R.A.S.C., spending the last two years of the War in France and Italy. In 1919, he came up to King's to read Moral Science and in 1920 obtained a second class in Part 1 of the Tripos. He then began his life work as an educational administrator, first as Assistant Secretary to the Kent Education Committee and later on in the same capacity in Cambridgeshire where he was soon promoted to the post of Chief Education Officer. He remained at the Shire Hall for the next thirty-two years.

He regarded his essential function to be that of an initiator and by 1924 was ready to open his campaign for the creation of Village Colleges. This was to be his great contribution to educational history and his title to fame. His achievement as a practical idealist is best described in his obituary in the King's College Annual Report:

he envisaged a number of centres at strategic points throughout the country, each of which, while including a senior school [now usually called a secondary school], would be a community centre . . . providing cultural, adult-educational and social facilities for a group of neighbouring villages. Thus the country-side could be civilized without being urbanized. Morris's practical idealism convinced the County Council, and in 1930 the First Village College was opened at Sawston. Morris, and indeed the

Education Committee, had encountered great difficulties: the Board of Education had declined to sanction expenditure on building for 'Further Education' or even on an assembly hall for the school, and Morris had had personally to persuade several charitable trusts and others to have sufficient faith in the project to contribute over £10,000 for the buildings.

The immediate success of the Sawston experiment led to the network of Village Colleges which now covers Cambridgeshire. Five were built during Morris's tenure of office and . . . he was able to open the ninth a year before his death. [There are now (1967) twelve.] These Village Colleges have become world famous; . . . Morris's achievement in realising his Village College idea — in his words, 'giving the countryside a centre of reference arousing the affection and loyalty of the country child and country people, and conferring significance on their way of life' — may well be regarded . . . as comparable with Grundtvig's achievement in starting 'folk high schools' in Denmark.

Morris was insistent that Village Colleges must be things of beauty, both without and within; and Gropius and Maxwell Fry were commissioned to build Impington [described by Pevsner as 'one of the best buildings of its date (1939) in England, if not the best']. The style of Impington has had great influence upon the design of schools built since the war. . . .

Morris was also much concerned with the furnishing and interior decoration of the schools, abominating what he called 'County Council green' and 'Municipal brown', and delighting in seeing flowers, properly arranged in vases, standing in the class-rooms and corridors. He encouraged the practice of music, the enjoyment of the arts, including what he called 'the edible art', and the Crafts of Rural Science, in his schools, but 'like all men of vision he was often thwarted'. He 'was a temperamental man, with many facets to his personality; he would alternately charm and exasperate, but would never bore. . . . It was those who worked with him daily who admired him most.'

In 1944, my mother gave him notice, as she wanted to have the Old Granary back as a home for her daughter Gwen; Morris, however, held that he was a protected tenant, although the Rent

Acts, of which the 1939 Act forms part, contain a provision that the landlord, by applying to the Court, could always obtain possession of his house if he wanted it for himself or his immediate family. Gwen Raverat was seen emerging from the family solicitor's office one morning, laughing, because after she had received much good advice from the solicitor he had been interrupted by his clerk reminding him in a whisper that he had already been engaged by Mr Morris. The solicitor begged Mrs Raverat to forget all he had told her. A long and acrimonious correspondence followed, but Mr G. D. Edwards, Morris's successor as Chief Education Officer, informed me that as the result of a legal argument, his tenancy was extended twelve months beyond the period of notice required by the original agreement, so that he was not required to go until some time in 1946. He was heart-broken at the idea of leaving, and remarked that people should really not be *allowed* to get so fond of their houses. Mr Edwards says he frequently visited him in the Old Granary and he always felt 'how vividly the two rooms overlooking the river, so elegantly and exquisitely furnished, reflected his personality, his love of all things beautiful — above all, his concept of "gracious living" '. It was during this 'year of grace' that he was offered, and immediately accepted, the tenancy of 15 Fitzwilliam Street, owned by Peterhouse, where he continued living 'happily and elegantly'. But he often told Mr Edwards how much he missed his exquisite view of the river which he had so long enjoyed at the Old Granary, and on leaving it he was seen shaking his fist in the direction of Lady Darwin.

He retired in 1954 but characteristically continued with some pioneering work at Welwyn Garden City, where he initiated a scheme to provide studios for artists, and at Hatfield New Town built 'a new venture in Public Houses'. Eventually his health gave way and he died in 1961 after a long illness.

CHAPTER TWELVE

Gwen Raverat: 1885–1957

THE last private occupant of the Old Granary was my sister, Gwen Raverat, who lived there from 1946 until she died in 1957. She has described her early life so fully in *Period Piece* that no more need be said about it. Determined to be an artist, she drew and painted with passion all through her childhood. What was perhaps unusual at that age was that she constantly drew real objects, not fancies out of her head like most children. I remember the little sketchbook that she brought back full of sketches of Rembrandt's son Titus when she returned from a trip abroad with my father; they had been to a great exhibition of Rembrandt, I think at Amsterdam. She was about ten or eleven at the time.

However, it was not until she was twenty-three that her wish to become a student at the Slade was fulfilled. Meanwhile, her uncongenial life as an Edwardian young lady had been transfromed by the friendship she made with a group of university students. For the celebration of Milton's Tercentenary, in July 1908, Dr Shipley (soon to be Master of Christ's) summoned Justin and Rupert Brooke, Francis Cornford, Jane Harrison, Frances and Gwen Darwin, and others to produce *Comus*. Francis Cornford, then a young Classics don at Trinity, and in spite of 'his great age of thirty-three', was persuaded to act the part of Comus and gave a most memorable performance. (A few months later he was engaged to be married to Frances Darwin.) Gwen thus became involved in the dramatic activities of a circle of lively and gifted Newnham students and undergraduates,* of whom Rupert Brooke was the magnetic central figure. She soon made a deep and lasting friendship with him and

---

* In my youth undergraduates were never referred to as students; that name was reserved for girls at Girton and Newnham. They could not properly be termed undergraduates until they were allowed the B.A. degree (in 1949).

some of the others and then, for a time, 'to be young was very Heaven'.

It was not until the following year that she met her future husband. Jacques Raverat was born in 1885 at Le Havre. His father, M. Georges Raverat, was a French business-man of high standing, serving on many public boards, who took a great interest in education and, having read both Edmond Demolin's books on the *Superiorité des Anglo-Saxons* and *L'École Nouvelle*, he sent his son to Bedales in 1898. During most of his three or four years there, Jacques enjoyed idyllic happiness. Three years of working at the Sorbonne for his '*licence de mathématiques*' followed; then, having obtained it and done his military service for the one year required of students, he realized his ambition of going to Cambridge, and was admitted by Emmanuel as an advanced student in Mathematics in October 1906. At the end of his first year, however, his health broke down and he was unable to return from France to finish his course. He spent the following year recovering from his still undiagnosed illness and, in the late spring of 1909, came to London hoping to complete his cure under the care of a London physician, Dr Bramwell, who treated him with auto-suggestion and advocated his taking up some handwork. Accordingly, he was admitted to the Ashendene Press to learn fine printing under St John Hornby.* Through most of the fine hot summer of 1909, he spent as much time as he could at Cambridge with Rupert Brooke and his other friends, among whom was now numbered Gwen Darwin. He saw much of her too in London that autumn and when, in 1910, he decided to give up printing and become a painter, he joined her at the Slade.

In 1909, Augustus John came to Cambridge to paint Jane Harrison, the well-known Newnham Classical don and friend of Gilbert Murray. Gwen had by then been for some time at the Slade where Augustus John was the great figure. It was our cousin Ruth Darwin who had suggested to the Newnham Committee through D. S. MacColl that John was the right man to paint her. I remember happening to look out of an upstairs window at Newnham Grange and seeing his caravan pass on his way to camp at

---

* The only remaining evidence of his time at the Ashendene Press is a not very accurate edition of Blake's *Marriage of Heaven and Hell* dated 1910; twenty-four copies were printed on handmade paper with the Press watermark.

Grantchester. The horse-drawn caravan had some little boys running after it with a tall woman in gypsy-looking clothes, I suppose Dorelia.

Gwen decided she ought to do something about entertaining Mr John and my parents agreed to ask him to tea one Sunday. We were all sitting under the copper beech on a fine summer afternoon awaiting him — Gwen, Charles, and I feeling very dashing and Bohemian at the prospect of entertaining such a famous painter, when the parlourmaid showed him through the side door into the garden. He was advancing down the path towards us looking very neat and correctly dressed, when my dog Jack, a mild mongrel of Irish terrier breed, suddenly made a rush at him and bit him in the leg. Luckily no damage was done except for a small tear in his trousers. He behaved with admirable sang-froid and laughed it off; but I of course made matters worse by exclaiming truthfully: 'That's the first time Jack's ever done that!' It should have broken the ice but I fear it did not.

In September 1910, Gwen and Jacques announced their engagement and in June 1911 they were married at a London registry office. It was an unusually perfect marriage. Both had powerful brains and shared their main interests on the same level. Frances Darwin (by this time Mrs F. C. Cornford), writing to Rupert Brooke about their engagement, said that 'to find two people who answer each other from the top to the bottom of the piano like Gwen and Jacques is the rarest and most splendid thing'. For his English friends his being French added a special quality to his charm, though to them, except for his brown eyes, Roman nose and wavy black hair, he did not quite look the part, on account of his being a tall heavily-built man. He was very French, however, in his attitude to many things, especially to gastronomy, scorning anyone who did not take food seriously. He showed much sensitivity to the arts and to his friends, though his sympathy might be marred by absurd Bellocian prejudices. He had a delightful, if earthy, sense of humour and capacity for making silly jokes, when not plunged in an occasional black mood of depression.

After a prolonged honeymoon at his father's seventeenth-century chateau in Burgundy and a few months in London, Jacques and Gwen rented a small house at Croydon-cum-Clopton, about ten miles south-west of Cambridge. It had no road to it but the wonderful view down to Royston compensated for the isolation. Here they lived for the next two years, painting most of the time, though Gwen also did much wood-engraving. She had virtually taught herself the art of wood-engraving when a student, as there was no teacher of this at the Slade. She had bought her own tools and begun with soft pear-wood as was the custom, before turning to hard box-wood for her finer work. She soon became one of the pioneers in the revived art of wood-cutting. Her work is considered remarkable for its control of light – sunlight, moonlight, candle-light, light reflected on water. Her themes were frequently taken from ballads, often romantic and passionate. She illustrated several books with woodcuts, notably *Daphnis & Chloe* for the Ashendene Press, and in later years began to experiment with coloured blocks, though she once said that the hardest task she had ever completed were the lines of floating cloud behind a row of thin poplars – it was so hard to prevent the lines from damaging the poplars. Many of her smaller landscapes recall her adored Bewick.

Had Jacques lived longer, there is no telling where his talents in painting, and in writing too, might have taken him. His health had deteriorated since his marriage and disseminated sclerosis was now diagnosed, so not surprisingly, on the outbreak of the 1914 War, all his frantic efforts to be taken as an interpreter in the French army were in vain. Early in 1915 they moved into a more convenient house at Weston, near Baldock, and lived there for the next five years, returning to Newnham Grange for the birth of their elder daughter, Elisabeth, in 1916 and again for that of their younger daughter, Sophie, in 1919.

The War over, they went to live in France, Jacques now an invalid in a wheel-chair. They took a villa at Vence in the Alpes-Maritimes behind Nice. Infatuated with the beauty of the place and its scope for painting, they enjoyed a few years of happiness there before Jacques became so ill that Gwen had to nurse him night and day. He died at last in March 1925 and she returned home with the children, utterly exhausted, to live in London for the next three years. She then decided to move to the country again, and found the perfect house to suit her in the Old Rectory at Harlton, six miles from Cambridge. The girls were in reach of the Perse School and her house soon became a meeting place for Cambridge friends and relations or visitors from London. Here she also found time to do much of her best work in book illustration.

While in London she had valuable experience in designing sets and costumes for the ballet, or 'Masque for Dancing', devised by my husband, Geoffrey Keynes, and herself from Blake's engraved *Illustrations of the Book of Job*; this was first performed by the Camargo Society at the Cambridge Theatre in London on 5 July 1931 with choreography by Ninette de Valois and music by our cousin, Ralph Vaughan Williams. Gwen had even painted the first of the back scenes herself almost unaided in the Old Vic workshops. The ballet, known as *Job*, has been part of the repertory of the Royal Ballet at Covent Garden Opera House until the present time; Gwen's designs being used until 1940 when they had become dilapidated and were replaced by revised sets and costumes by John Piper. Her original watercolours are now preserved in Cambridge at the Fitzwilliam Museum.

In the 1930s, the Cambridge University Music Society was producing Handel operas, and Gwen was several times called upon to design the sets and costumes. So at Harlton she lived a full life once more and recovered a measure of happiness; she retained a sombre view of life to the end—yet coloured by her dramatic and passionate nature.

During the Second World War, with both her daughters married,* Gwen took up war work as a factory hand at the Cambridge Scientific Instrument Company (founded in 1881 by her uncle Horace Darwin). To be nearer her work she let the Old Rectory, furnished, in 1941 and moved into a rented room near her cousin Frances Cornford's house, Conduit Head, off the Madingley Road.

Not long after this she was offered a post far more in keeping with her talents, as a draughtsman in the Naval Intelligence Division's office installed temporarily at the Scott Polar Institute in Lensfield Road. They were compiling handbooks designed to provide

---

* Elisabeth Raverat married a Norwegian international lawyer, Edvard Hambro, in 1940, recently President of the United Nations at New York. Sophie Raverat married, also in 1940, a zoologist and Fellow of Trinity, Mark Pryor, Senior Tutor of the College until 1964. He had a car accident in 1967 from which he did not recover consciousness, and died in 1970.

information about countries which the services, but particularly the Navy, might be called upon 'to visit'. Her job was to make the block diagrams. For this work she sometimes had no help from any photographs or books, and had to invent her own method of showing what the terrain would look like, by a close study of the contours on the map. This involved her in elaborate calculations but the resulting diagrams seem to have pleased Naval Intelligence, or rather the dons employed in compiling the handbooks; and at the end of the war she was rewarded by a formal letter of thanks from the Admiralty and the presentation of three of the volumes to which she had contributed. The work had been fascinating, but concentrated and tiring, and when the time came she was glad to give it up and return to Harlton. She lived there until Mr Morris vacated the Old Granary in 1946. Then the Harlton Old Rectory, of which she was only a tenant, was sold at auction and Gwen moved into her new home.

She made the Old Granary both comfortable and pleasant, but it was never again as beautifully furnished as in the days of Louis Clarke or Henry Morris. She was free from artistic snobbery; elegance and period furnishing were never her aim. She was content with her old furniture, much of it inherited from uncles and aunts. However, her walls were adorned with her own and Jacques' landscape paintings, and some of 'Cookham' Stanley Spencer's early pictures. He had joined the Slade before they left; they had taken him under their wing, and he remained a lifelong friend.

Gwen made the sitting-room into her studio. She loved the Old Granary with its associations and familiar surroundings, especially her view of the Millpool and Silver Street Bridge, and above all she loved living by the river again within sound of the mill race and the water coming through the floodgates. It is noticeable how frequently water and willow trees appear in her wood-cuts and pictures; by moving into the Old Granary she had come home to them again.

It was some time after our mother's death, early in 1947, that Gwen conceived the idea of making drawings from memory of family incidents and asked Mr Richard de la Mare of Faber's if he would like to publish such a book, with explanatory text added to it by herself. He accepted her proposal with enthusiasm and *Period*

Piece, intended originally as a picture book, became a book to be read in its own right, the illustrations adding much to its authenticity and charm. Those who know the people in it can testify to the likeness of her portraits, always excepting those of herself, but then Gwen never saw herself, except occasionally when she looked disapprovingly at her round face in the looking glass. What little experience of authorship she had was mostly obtained from her work as an art critic for *Time and Tide* from 1928 to 1939. In his interesting introduction to her book of engravings, published after her death, Mr Reynolds Stone notes that her reviews were always free of jargon. This unaffected style holds good for the way she wrote *Period Piece*. She had read widely all manner of books, especially on anthropology and was familiar with most English standard novels, having read such authors as Defoe, Fielding, Scott, Jane Austen and Trollope aloud by the hour to her husband during his long illness. Among French novels, they particularly enjoyed Stendhal and Proust. She was fond of poetry, especially of Milton, and she went to the length of once teaching herself enough Greek to read Homer in the original—she and Jacques had a passion for the Iliad and the Odyssey at the time—but of normal literary training she had none. Perhaps it was the lack of this that gave her prose its incisive freshness and colloquial turn of phrase.

It was luckily not until after Gwen had finished the writing of her book and drawn all but two or three of the pictures, that she suffered the stroke which paralysed her right side. Her brain was not affected and she fought heroically against her disabilities, but she made a poor recovery and could hardly walk a few steps without help. *Period Piece* was published in 1952; its unexpectedly great success gave her much pleasure, and her fan-mail much entertainment. When her book was published in America, she was amused to hear that in the *New York Times* list of best-sellers, *Period Piece* had taken seventh place between the Kinsey Report on the Male and the new version of the Holy Bible.

After her stroke she was unable to continue wood-engraving, and line-drawing she found too exacting; the great mercy was that she was still able to paint, and the moment she could she took up her brushes again. This occupation, more than anything else, helped her to endure the frustrations of her life and the constant nagging pain in her paralysed arm. Her helplessness was a kind of slow torture to someone who had always been so active and impatient of restraint. She had to have an attendant within call most of the time and was fortunate in finding a series of Swiss nurses who wanted to come over and live with a family to learn English. Above all, there was always her devoted housekeeper Nan, from Harlton, in the background to help when needed.

The Old Granary became a centre for her innumerable friends. With her devastating honesty and intensity of feeling, coupled with what Christopher Cornford called her 'irrational ferocity', she could be formidable, but she was generally such good company, so fundamentally generous and sympathetic, so original and humorous, that her house was constantly thronged by people, many of them young men. Sometimes they came just for the pleasure of being with her, or perhaps it was her much-loved son-in-law, Mark Pryor, bringing her some tasty piece of news, the more scandalous the better. One of them tells me of the extraordinary impression made by her presence, as of a person who knew deeply about passion, and made life seem marvellous.

In these last years of her life she became a well-known sight in the neighbourhood, slumped in her wheel-chair, wrapped in an old rug and black cloak, with a clergyman's hat rammed on her head. This hat was her comfort, it fitted her so well, and also her pride, as she had been told it was the last of its kind when she bought it from Almond's University and Clerical Tailors. These wide-brimmed, shallow-crowned hats are hardly ever seen now, but in Victorian days most clergymen wore 'Shovel hats' as they were called. (I am told that the last one to be observed in Cambridge was on the head of Monsignor Gilbey of Trinity.) Thus equipped, Gwen would be taken to some place from which she wished to make a painting. Her Swiss nurse, having seen that everything needed for her work was within reach, would be sent away with instructions when to return and fetch her home. And there Gwen would sit hour after hour, oblivious of the weather, absorbed in her painting. She looked so like a poor old beggar that once an Italian working-class woman, murmuring '*Poveretta*', stopped to give her sixpence in alms. Gwen accepted the offering gratefully, lest she might hurt the kind woman's feelings. At another time a lady stopped and asked her

'Do you mind my looking at your painting?' 'No', replied Gwen, 'no more than if you were reading my private letters.'

Everybody called her Gwen, even the people who hardly knew her. A few years ago I had occasion to call on her butcher in Silver Street, wanting some bones for my dog, and, to make an excuse for the smallness of my purchase, introduced myself to Mr Haslop as Mrs Raverat's sister. He paused a moment to reflect and then said: 'Mrs Raverat?' — a pause — 'Gwen. . . . Yes, of course, . . . I read her book.'

As the years passed, she grew more and more helpless and longed for death, of which she never had the slightest fear. When at last she died, on 11 February 1957, it was at the Old Granary, close to Newnham Grange, her birthplace in 1885.

After her death, my brother Charles let the Old Granary to New Hall to house five of its students and a Fellow, until such time as the College could move out of the Hermitage into its permanent home on the Huntingdon Road. Then, when they left in 1965, Darwin College took final possession of the Old Granary and made it into rooms for seven of their graduate students.

CHAPTER THIRTEEN

Laundress Green and Lammas Land: 1895–1912

THE Old Granary was nearly ready for letting to its first occupants when Professor Darwin had occasion to address another of his eloquently worded protests to the Corporation. This time it was against 'the erection of bathing sheds for women on the portion of Sheep's Green known as Laundress Common'. It is not clear where the women were meant to bathe. The leat, or millstream, might have been made into a secluded and also a safe bathing place, as long as the millers kept their sluice gates shut, but what if they decided to do some grinding and needed power for the mill? With the opening of the sluice gates, the poor ladies would have been swept into the mill-race and drowned against the grid. This cannot have been the Corporation's intention. They must have meant the ladies to bathe in the Cam below Laundress Green. It is odd, however, that the protest makes no reference to the shallowness of the river there, nor to the undesirable publicity of the site, where people crossing Silver Street Bridge, rowing up to Newnham in boats, or walking along the public path past the King's Mill to Sheep's Green, would have had a fine view of the ladies disporting themselves in the water. Professor Darwin protested on 5 December 1895:

> The very short time [three days] which has elapsed since the nature of the proposal has become known to us has rendered it impossible to circulate the protest widely, but I am confident that there would be found a very wide spread sympathy with the tenour of the protest amongst the inhabitants of our town — I beg you will notice that the memorial expresses the desire that provision be made for women to bathe. The protest is only directed against the suggested site.
>
> I would especially draw your attention to the signature of Mrs Sidgwick, the Misses Kennedy, Miss Clough, Mrs Archer-Hind [and] Mrs [James] Ward who are all interested or concerned in Newnham College. . . .

It will be seen that many of the gentlemen who sign are well-known for their public spirit and interest in the welfare of all classes in our town.

I have signed the protest myself because I agree with it, but I do not seek to disguise that I have other and more cogent reasons for the strongest objection to the selection of this site. It will, I think, be acknowledged that I have done something to render the stretch of river from the King's Mill Pool to Newnham Mill more attractive than it was formerly. What I have done has no doubt been done on my own premises and on those which I hold on lease from the Corporation, but I claim that I have also had in view the embellishment of the place for the public. In the summer this stretch of river is visited by swarms of pleasure boats. I had one day the curiosity to count them and I observed twelve in view at one moment from my drawing-room window. I think that nine out of ten boating parties at the Backs of the Colleges also row past my house.

The greater part of the Sheds which it is proposed to erect would be visible from my windows, and the whole would be immediately under the windows of the dwelling-house which I have just constructed out of the old granary at the end of my garden. It is difficult for me to estimate the amount of detriment I should suffer by the proposed establishment, but hundreds of pounds.

He then reminds the Corporation that it was they who persuaded him to take a lease of their unsightly Tile Wharf in 1888 and make it into a garden. (See page 81.)

I would ask the Committee to consider whether it would be consistent on the part of the Corporation or fair to me to erect immediately opposite this garden a row of wooden sheds? In conclusion I beg leave to urge on its Committee that the selection of a site for the bathing establishment be reconsidered and that one be chosen which shall leave the beauty of the river scenery intact, shall be convenient for the ladies for whose use it is intended and shall not injuriously affect any private person.

A copy of the list of participants has been preserved with the draft of the protest. It shows what a small society Cambridge was in those days that I either remember, or know about, most of the hundred and sixteen signatories. In the first column of the list come the names of twenty-six ladies connected with the University, including those of the six 'concerned in' Newnham College. The second column covers nine Masters of colleges and eight Professors with my father's name among the latter. The rest of the signatories are alphabetically arranged in two columns: they consist mostly of University people but include some well-known shop-keepers, such as Munsey and Thurlbourn. No doubt the protest would have had many more signatures to it if Professor Darwin had been afforded a longer time in which to collect them.

In the list of Masters of colleges, the name of Dr Montagu Butler does not appear. He himself in a letter to my father gives the reason for the omission of Trinity — a letter so characteristic both of the man and the time, that I give it in full:

Trinity Lodge
Cambridge

Dec. 5 1895

My dear Darwin,

I am greatly ashamed of myself for having inadvertently proved false to you. *Yesterday* I quite remembered my promise to visit the threatened spot, but our Divident Meeting at 2.15, followed by the 'General Board', 4–6.15, occupied all the afternoon. Again early this morning I remembered my promise, but from 10.30 to 1.30 I gave myself up to a Sermon, which — must I confess it? — so demoralised me as to make me forget everything else. The consequence was that when I went out a walk with Miss Ramsey, my Wife's cousin who is now staying with us, instead of going straight to Queens' Bridge, *I never thought of it*, and went instead along the Madingley Road. Duty has only *just* flown back to my memory, 5.15 p.m. Pray try to forgive me. I am always making similar blunders. I do not like to sign your paper, while knowing so little of the movement *for* and of, the site, but you might if you could, say to anyone that you know I should prefer that the sheds should be further down the river. A 'lame and impotent conclusion' alas! but all that is possible!

Most truly yours,
H. Montagu Butler

Professor Darwin did not have to wait long before hearing that his protest had not been made in vain. Mr Arthur Deck, 'Pharmaceutical and Analytical Chymist to H.R.H. the Prince of Wales', as he proudly styled himself on his 'Memorandum' King's Parade note-paper, was on the Town Council Commons' Committee and a most valuable ally of Professor Darwin. After the meeting on 6 December, he hastened to write the following breathless letter, marked *Confidential* to 'G. H. Darwin Esq.' to say:

Dear Sir
I think we have settled about Laundress Green *there will not be any bathing place* (n)or will it be interfered with at all so you may enjoy your look out as usual I raised a great many objections to it which I will explain at a future time I told them I never was in favour of Laundress Green and the bathing place will be in the upper stream on the Coe Fen side — about where I first proposed.

Yours faithfully
Arthur Deck

On Christmas Eve, the Town Clerk, Mr J. E. L. Whitehead, wrote to my father officially to tell him that the Commons' Committee 'have practically decided to abandon the scheme and therefore do not consider it necessary to reply to the objections raised by the Memorialists'. There was, however, an ironical conclusion to the matter. Three days later, the Town Clerk wrote to him again, heading his letter 'Re Wharf at Newnham' to say that he (Professor Darwin) was 'clearly liable' for repairs to the banks of the Wharf. Mr Whitehead continued: 'At the same meeting a suggestion was made that the Wharf would make a possible site for the proposed Ladies Bathing Place. Would you care to surrender the Lease if the Corporation were willing to take it off your hands?' My father's reply can be imagined, but apparently the Corporation would not take No for an answer, for six weeks later they sent him a copy of a Resolution they had passed on 6 February 1896:

Agreed that Professor Darwin be informed that the Committee do not think that any great expenditure is necessary at present to maintain the Wharf in proper repair but that if he finds an amount necessary is greater than he cares to spend the Committee have important purposes to which they can apply the site.

Of course the 'important purposes' may not have been for building Ladies' Bathing Sheds on the Wharf but it seems possible that it was what the Corporation still had in mind.

It was largely owing to Alderman Deck that a few years later, the Ladies Bathing-place was sited on the upper river, though not on the Coe Fen side, but opposite, with the back of the sheds turned towards Coe Fen. Here the Granta, or upper river, forks into two branches to form leats for the Mills, a quarter of a mile downstream; and it was in the Newnham branch, called Snobs' Stream, that the women's bathing-place was made. It had its proper setting of grass lawns and willow trees, but some of its romance for children must have vanished in 1910, when the footbridge to it was built. Until then the only means of reaching the bathing place was by a chain ferry from Coe Fen, the paths to it along Sheep's Green being taboo to women owing to the dangerous proximity of the men's and boys' bathing-places. The grumpy old man who worked the ferry charged a half-penny, but, on one occasion in his absence I ventured to pull myself across, dragging the chain up out of the water, dripping through my hands, whilst I savoured 'the thrilling sweet and rotten . . . river smell' with a shiver of anticipation at the chilly bathe awaiting me.

The fact is that the river at this point was never deep enough for a really good bathing-place, but after the First World War, when mixed bathing had become acceptable to the general public, strong swimmers were allowed by the custodian, Miss Hardy, to swim in the main river, in full view of the onlookers from Coe Fen bridge. In May 1966, to cut expenses, the men's bathing-place was converted to mixed bathing and the women's bathing-place was turned into a most attractive enclosed site for picnics. This can still be reached by the Coe Fen bridge, or from Barton Road and Newnham by a wooden footbridge over Snobs' Stream.*

* I am indebted to Mr Jack Overhill for most of these facts. He must easily be the greatest living authority on the Granta, as he has been bathing in it from Sheep's Green since 1907 (every day all the year round since 1922) — this, with complete impunity, in spite of recent fears as to the pollution of the river.

In 1899, Professor Darwin rounded off his freehold and leasehold estate by buying the Lammas land to the south of Newnham Grange. A rumour had reached him that someone wanted to purchase its freehold in order to make tennis-courts on it for hire during the summer months. This does not seem to have been a very practical scheme, as the meadow is low-lying and the grass risked damage from the mud and debris left behind by floods, nor would it be possible to prevent the commoners' animals from ruining the courts in the autumn by their trampling and grazing. For the essence of Lammas land is that it must be left open for the use of commoners from old Lammas Day (12 August) until the following 6 April. It is not surprising that my father should wish to save Newnham Grange from such a disturbance to its peace. I am sure too that the idea of owning a piece of land with the ancient rights of Lammas must have appealed to him.

The origin of the name *Lammas* is indeed ancient. According to the *Oxford English Dictionary*, it comes from an old English compound word, *hlaf*, meaning loaf or bread, and *Maesse* (mass). 'The 1st of August . . . in the early English church [was] observed as a harvest festival, at which loaves of bread were consecrated, made from the first ripe corn.' In a later passage, the *Dictionary* quotes Lubbock as writing in 1870 that 'our Lammas Lands were so-called because they were private property until Lammas Day (August 1st) after which period they were subject to common rights of pasturage till the spring'. The change in the calendar made in 1752 meant that Lammas Day, on 1 August, fell eleven days earlier in the progress of the seasons than hitherto. Therefore to allow time for the gathering of the hay, 12 August (Old Lammas Day) generally remained the operative date for the opening of the land to the commoners, and 6 April (Old Lady Day) for its closure.

Cambridge formerly had a number of Lammas lands but there are none left now still in use according to their customary rights. Most, like my father's Lammas land, have become part of a neighbouring common, open to the public all the year round; others, like Christ's Pieces, have been turned into municipal gardens, though probably an act of Parliament was needed to extinguish their rights of Lammas. Such an act was passed in 1801 when Downing College was built on St Thomas's Leys, for it was Lammas land.

The Lammas land

The Mill Pasture, Nutter's or Foster's Close, as it was and still is indiscriminately called, is an island of about one and a half acres, surrounded by ditches and the river. A small causeway joins it to Sheep's Green below the path along the upper river near the flood-gates. The ditch between it and the Little Island (re-named Darwin Island by the College) is still navigable; as used to be the ditch dividing the Lammas land from the Big Island on the west, until it became so overgrown with trees and bushes and so silted-up that a canoe could not now force its way through, even if steel bars with chains across to bar the passage at both ends had not been put in by my mother. As for the ditches separating the meadow from Sheep's Green, they appear to consist mostly of liquid mud, the surface of which is just capable of supporting the weight of a duck. I watched one recently conducting her large family of tiny ducklings safely over it to Sheep's Green from the end of the Big Island.

In 1915 my mother wrote to Arthur Gray, the Master of Jesus, for advice about her tenancy of the Lammas land. (Mr Gray, from whose book I have already quoted, was the authority on the history of Cambridge.) In his fascinating reply he wrote that his 'answers must be muddled and muddling. [Even] Maitland confesses that the mediaeval mind had never made itself up about common rights [of which Lammas rights are an adjunct]. It is a question of usage, not law and the usage differed in various places', especially in Cambridge

Her first question was: is Lammas land when commonable open to commoners for cows and sheep only? No doubt she was thinking of her land in relation to Sheep's Green. Mr Gray replied that

in earliest days Sheep's Green was reserved for sheep, as Coe Fen [Cow Fen] for cows. . . . Later these orders were modified and within limits *horses* and cows were allowed to be pastured on commons. . . . Sheep's Green adjoins the Newnham Lammas land and probably . . . the conditions of one apply to the other.

My mother had a copy of the Corporation's *Register of Stock to be turned on Commons* for the year 1914. Opposite Sheep's Green under the heading Rights of Commons it reads: 'For sheep of butchers (freemen) all the year; for cows of St Botolph and St Mary the Less all the year on Sundays, Wednesdays and Fridays, from sunrise to sunset.' There is no mention of horses. By 1956, forty-two years later, the entry opposite Sheep's Green in the list of Common lands within the city merely states: 'For dairy stock all the year, by day and night.' Thus, the common has forfeited its right to be called by its old name since sheep are no longer admitted.

Six Lammas lands are listed in the 1914 Register of Stock, Nutter's or Foster's Close coming last. Its Rights of Common are given as extending from 12 August to 6 April and its 'Remaining Rights' as 'vested in the Trustees of the late Professor Sir G. H. Darwin', but nothing is said about what animals were allowed on it or on any of the other five Lammas lands named. Mr Gray suggested that my father's Lammas land 'may be regarded as an extension of the pasture of Sheep's Green' but, in so doing, he appears to have forgotten the existence of Laundress Green, the piece of Common land only separated from what was our Lammas land by the short branch of river below the flood gates. Here 'horses, mares, geldings and cows of St Botolph and St Mary the Less' were permitted all the year on the same three days as cows on Sheep's Green. I therefore have the temerity to disagree with him and believe that the Lammas land should be regarded rather as an extension of the pasture of Laundress Green than of Sheep's Green, where horses are still banned to this day.

My father, exercising his freehold rights, could graze horses on his Lammas land between 6 April and 12 August and constantly did so, padlocking the gate to keep them in. I picture cattle on it too, but they were probably Mr James Mott's dairy cows exercising their rights of Common during the autumn and winter months on Wednesdays, Fridays, and Sundays. I believe that the commoners were allowed to graze horses as well as cows on our Lammas land, because the 1956 list of stock allowed on common lands within the city, reads opposite Nutter's Close: 'For cows, geldings and mares from Ap 1 to 30 November.' Thus, by 1956 the old right of Lammas had lapsed and commoners' horses and cows were allowed on what had been our Lammas land, though horses were not permitted on Sheep's Green, a regulation which still holds good.

In the 1956 list, the entry for Laundress Green has obviously been copied verbatim from the 1914 Register of Stock. Horses are restricted to the same days, or rather nights, as cows, since both animals are nominally admitted only from 'Sunset to Sunrise', not from 'Sunrise to Sunset' like the Sheep's Green cows. Laundress Green, enclosed on all sides by water except for the path to Sheep's Green, across which there used to be a barrier at the flood gates, was a very suitable place in which to pen beasts at night. But the 1914 rules for Laundress Green had lapsed long before they were reprinted in the 1956 list, as my sister's housekeeper Nan, who lived in the Old Granary opposite the Green from 1946 to 1956, can bear witness. She says that horses and cows seemed to be there night and day at any time of the year. It was only laundresses who were no longer to be seen even on washing-day Mondays.

The second question my mother put to Mr Gray concerned Mr Mott, the Newnham dairy-man. She asked if he were entitled to bar her gate when she had left it open (in commonable times). 'This floors me', replied the Master of Jesus, but nevertheless he tried to answer her question with a disquisition on Christ's Pieces when they were still Lammas land in 1870 and he was a freshman lodging opposite them. However, as he did not know when their gates were opened or shut this did not help him. 'At Newnham', he says, 'the Lammas may be regarded as merely an extension of the *pasture* of Sheep's Green and therefore open to it at all times when the Commoners entered on the Lammas land. I am afraid that my knowledge is here quite at fault.'

My mother had also consulted the Town Clerk on the same point and he had come to a different conclusion. He maintained that there was 'no need for the gate of the Lammas land to be left open, and in fact, it would not be desirable to do so'. I expect my mother acquiesced in this view and thus avoided quarrelling with Mr Mott over his possible infringements of the rights of common. After all, he would have to re-open the gate in the afternoon to allow his cows to troop home to their sheds in Newnham Road to be milked. It was these cows we used to watch from the drawing-room window fording the river at Newnham Millpool.

The third question she put to Mr Gray was: 'Who are the people who have the right to use Lammas land?' He replied: 'Presumably (though I am not certain and Maitland doesn't say) the commoners.' After a long argument as to who the commoners are, he continued:

I imagine that the rights of the free commoners are now extin-
guished as far as *commons* are concerned, and that people who use the
commons nowadays have to pay for the privilege. The Town Clerk
no doubt can inform you. . . .* Mr Mott's contentions may be
based on bad historical grounds (1) that he has rights of common
(2) that he has a right to use Lammas land as a parishioner of
St Botolph's. I doubt if he could establish either point. It would be
a delightful and horribly expensive and uncertain thing for either
party to contest the matter at law.

One of the names by which the Lammas land was known in the
past was that of the Mill Pasture. This suggests that its freehold was
regarded as a perquisite of the millers of King's Mill for their cart-
horses. My belief that this was so is strengthened by the fact that it is
generally called Nutter's Close in the maps of Cambridge and in the
books of the Corporation, and the Nutters ran the King's Mill for
many years.† In 1842, they disposed of it to the Fosters, after which it
began to be called Foster's Close though it never lost its former name.
It was from the Fosters that my father bought the Lammas land in
1899. He wrote about the possibility of buying it to Mr C. F. Foster,
the mill owner who in 1888 had refused to sell him any of the waste
water from Newnham mill. He was referred to C. F. Foster's brother,
Ebenezer Bird Foster, as the owner of the freehold. The transaction

* Taking the advice that the Master of Jesus gave my mother in 1915, I enquired at
the Town Clerk's office what the owner has to pay to pasture his animals on the commons. The answer is: nothing at all for the grazing but all animals have to be registered
under the general bye-laws. The licence costs four shillings, is paid on 1 December, and
covers all the animals the owner may want to put on the commons for the coming year.
Owing to over-grazing, Coe Fen is now only open for grazing from 1 April to 30
November, but Sheep's Green can be used 'for dairy stock all the year by day and night',
though only by 'attested or Tuberculin Attested cattle', according to the notices on Fen
Causeway gate.

† Mr Jack Overhill helped me with this note by calling on Miss Winifred Nutter of
Hills Road, Cambridge, to find out if she could tell him more about the Nutter family.
She said that her great grandfather 'worked the mill at the bottom of Mill Lane', i.e.
the King's Mill, and that William and James Nutter, who ran Grantchester Mill, were
her cousins. My mother bought the light-brown stone-ground flour from 'Mr Nutter of
Grantchester' for the delicious home-made bread we always ate at Newnham Grange,
until the mill was burnt down in 1928 and the flour was no longer obtainable. Since the
owners, Merton College, did not think Grantchester Mill was worth rebuilding as a
flour mill, the Nutter brothers moved their business to the modern mill by Fulbourn
railway station.

went through smoothly. Though there was no reference to the land being subject to Lammas rights in the title deeds, Mr E. B. Foster's solicitors, Ginn and Matthew, assured Professor Darwin that 'there is no doubt whatever of the existence of these rights', and he was satisfied on this score. The price asked and promptly paid was £200 and, by 1 September 1899, the land was his. As by then it was commonable until the following spring, there was no hurry about letting it.

It was our old friend, Mr William Saint, the builder, who became the yearly tenant. Saint was to pay £6 for the use of the Lammas land till 12 August: 'he not to object to fowls, not to turn in calf-less cows, not to remove manure'. So my mother's hens were once more in the picture and their right confirmed to cross the ditch by their Bridge of Sighs, as I called the bridge to myself on account of its arched wire-netting covering. It was no doubt she who also claimed the manure for the garden, though this was an unnecessary stipulation as the droppings always belong to the owner of the Lammas land. I see my father's hand, however, in the clause about the calf-less cows: he was anticipating the possibility of sleepless nights from the miserable lowing of a cow deprived of her calf. However, I think Saint never had any cows and always used the field for his cart horses. I have no memory of the later lettings, unless it be that after Mr Saint died, Mr Sindall the well-known builder took the Lammas land for his cart horses, but I do recall vividly that two mares with their foals were there in 1915 when my future husband, Geoffrey Keynes, was home on leave from France and came to see me. At the time my mother was making a home for the two youngest children of my cousin Colonel Josiah Wedgwood, and thinking to amuse the younger child of five or six, we took her over on to the Lammas land to see the foals. One of the gigantic mares near us was peacefully engaged cropping the grass when suddenly she turned and lashed out in the direction of the little girl. Mercifully Geoffrey had seen what she intended to do in time to snatch the child up and throw her clear of the enormous fetlocked hoof. Gloria was furious at the ignominy she had suffered but never realised how close to death or terrible injury she had been.

It was all very well to own the Lammas land but we could make little use of it until my father had devised some means of getting there

from the Little Island. This was the kind of problem which delighted
him and he solved it as ingeniously as he had done the puzzle of how
to get to the Wharf in 1888. On the Big Island we had long had a
plank drawbridge by which to cross the ditch to Sheep's Green. This
was a true drawbridge, raised or lowered by a rope and pulley nailed
on to a conveniently placed elm tree. The means my father provided
for reaching the Lammas land was a more elegant arrangement. It
was a swing bridge. By grasping a wooden handle fixed to the near
end of a heavy plank, even a child could move it across to the other
side of the ditch, so well was its weight balanced and so smoothly did
it rotate on a sort of turntable fixed to the wooden landing stage at
the edge of the island. This bridge, with occasional renewals, remained in use for over forty years, but by the time my brother Charles
took over Newnham Grange it was in such a bad state that he had it
removed and put up a drawbridge in its place, like the one on the
Big Island.

My mother continued letting the Lammas land till her death in
1947; latterly it was as pasture for cows since by then there were few,
if any, cart horses left to be put out to grass. Her last tenant was
Mr Bull,* the dairy-man in Hills Road. He renewed his tenancy
with my brother, as Mr Holmes the gardener well remembered, for
he had often to come to Mr Bull's rescue when boys or dogs were
harrying the cattle, or hooligan intruders were threatening to
damage the fences opposite Sheep's Green and had to be turned off.
On one occasion, Mr Bull encountered a would-be trespasser from
Barton Road in the very act of driving his cows on to the Lammas
land through the temporarily open gate. An argument ensued, no
doubt the poacher maintaining that he had rights of common to
pasture his cows on the field, and ridiculing Mr Bull's assertion that
he had hired the field for grazing his cows during the summer months
when it was protected by rights of Lammas. The altercation grew
so loud and angry that Mr Holmes came hurrying over to see what
was happening and arrived just in time to prevent the men from
coming to blows, my brother Charles keeping watch prudently in
the background.

* His name is a reminder of the saying that Cambridge is the only town in England
where one can buy milk from a Bull and ink from a Heffer.

By this time, the Lammas land had become nothing but a liability to its owner, what with the increase of hooliganism and the fact that no further tenant could be found to succeed Mr Bull when he gave up hiring the field. So the gates were left permanently open. My brother made no further attempt to enforce his rights and, in 1951, decided to give up the Lammas land altogether. I am not sure if he knew or remembered that in 1919 the Corporation had approached his mother with the suggestion that she should sell them the freehold, when the lease of the islands was about to fall in, and she was faced with the problem of having to make extensive repairs to the banks. Nothing however came of this suggestion, and when she had carried out some repairs to the banks of the islands, she had been granted a new lease of them.

Now it was my brother's turn to approach the Corporation with the request that they would take over the Lammas land from him. This ended in a remarkably neat barter transaction with no money passing on either side. In exchange for the freehold of the Lammas land, the Corporation gave him the freeholds of the Little Island and of the kitchen-garden, both of which he had hitherto held on lease. It was a satisfactory if also rather a sad ending to the fifty years my family had held the freehold of the Lammas land, for it involved the extinction of the rights of Lammas over the last piece of Lammas land left in Cambridge.

During my father's last years it had been a great asset to him, as he had taken up archery as a hobby and could use the field for his target practice. From a safe distance, it was pleasant to watch him shooting. I believe he became a proficient archer; and of course, being a mathematician, he always kept a careful record of his score. I too spent much time on the Lammas land as a child, wandering blissfully about it, especially on a fine winter's day, to the accompaniment of the roar of the river as it rushed through the flood gates in white turbulence. In the early spring there would be the loud cawing of the rooks nesting in their rookery on the Big Island elms, and later on the meadow would become a sea of buttercups. On hot days I paddled in the river from the bank opposite Laundress Green, where the water was not too deep or muddy, once finding myself an involuntary 'Leech-gatherer'. I doubt if the pool still exists because the erection in 1948 of a different type of flood gate has so altered the flow of the river that it has eroded the bank to a considerable extent; the Lammas land is smaller than it used to be and no longer measures the 1.565 acres which my father bought in 1899.

A few incidents concerning trees remain to be recorded. Three letters addressed to Professor Darwin by the Town Clerk, J. E. L. Whitehead, are extant. The first is an answer to his enquiry as to whether he had the right to fell a tree on the Big Island. 'It seems doubtful whether you have any such right', replied the Town Clerk on 7 February 1899. 'I shall not be able to get the matter finally settled until I can arrange for the Committee to view the tree which you wish to remove. In the meantime it will help me if you will kindly let me know what sort of tree it is.' The answer was, an ash. Three weeks later, the Committee presumably having viewed the tree, the Town Clerk granted his permission to cut it down, 'on condition that the Corporation have the wood', and added that the tree 'might be felled so as to leave a stump not exceeding two feet above the level of the surface of the ground'.

The third letter, written in 1903, is also on the subject of trees, though in an opposite sense. Professor Darwin was informed that the Commons' Committee had granted his request to plant some trees on Sheep's Green. 'Of course you will be aware', wrote Mr Whitehead, 'that the trees once planted will become the property of the Corporation and will be pruned and removed as occasion may require.' For 'pruned' he might have written 'pollarded', for all the trees in question were willows.

According to an entry I made in one of the diaries I kept from the age of eleven for a few years, the dozen trees ordered by my father arrived on 13 March 1903, and were planted the same afternoon 'on the Common near the Lammas' by Jim the garden boy, Ranson the gardener, and Billy, my younger brother, then aged eight and a half. He had dressed himself carefully for the occasion. His coat was 'dreadfully disreputable', I wrote.

An enormous tear down the back all jagged and *filthy* in front as were his hands and face, feet, legs and knickerbockers. He *was* a sight. Of course crowds of lookers-on collected and it was splendid to see Billy swaggering over the tiny children . . . He shovelled in a most professional manner. The men kept making jokes about him, such as: 'He'll soon be a head gardener' and 'He'll soon be drinking his pint pot'.

We used to call this part of Sheep's Green the Fen, because it was so marshy. The larger of the ancient river beds in it has been cleared out of late years to act as an overflow for the upper river, so there is always some water in it now to join the Cam at Newnham Millpool. The shorter bed is dry, except in rainy seasons when it fills and floods over its banks into the ditches round the Lammas land and the Big Island. It was by this dry bed that the twelve trees were planted. If any of the willows still growing there look as if they were over sixty years old, then they are the survivors of those trees we planted that March day in 1903.

I have a vivid recollection of some more tree-planting we undertook, though I do not remember in which year it occurred. It was on an exquisitely beautiful winter day; the river was sparkling in the mild sunshine and the grass was emerald green when my father emerged from his study to superintend the planting of four Lombardy poplars on the Lammas land. For this, as freeholder, he needed no permision from the Commons' Committee but of course they were only to be planted on the edge of the field, not to interfere with the commoners' pasturage. Three of the trees were for ornamenting the bank facing the willows on the Fen. My sister Gwen was chosen to plant the central one.

We then moved over to the opposite side of the Lammas land to plant the remaining poplar on the bank of the river facing Laundress Green. At this moment Jim (later Sir James) Butler appeared by chance: he was probably on his way home to Trinity from St Faith's where he and his two younger brothers, like my two brothers, were, or had been, at school, for Charles by then had left to go to Marlborough. So to Jim was assigned the honour of planting the last tree — an honour I regret to say he has completely forgotten, though for years after we used to refer to the tree as 'Jim's poplar'. There was some joking and laughter when Ranson produced a large dead rat and solemnly dropped it into the hole so that it could be interred under the roots of the young Lombardy. This was one of two rats he had trapped the day before in the rat runs which infest the banks of the Cam and its ditches. The other rat had been buried under Gwen's tree. Both her tree and Jim's flourished, and this we attributed entirely to the nourishment they drew from the corpses of the rats, as the other two ratless trees did not long survive their planting. Gwen's prospered for some years until it too died, probably from being barked by the cart horses on the Lammas land. Jim's Lombardy, however, grew into a magnificent tree, a landmark from Silver Street Bridge, until, after some forty-five years, it succumbed to the erosion of the bank on which it stood. My son Stephen remembers that, in 1948 when he was up at King's, he and his brother Milo helped his uncle Charles cut down the dead giant.

CHAPTER FOURTEEN

Ducks and Swans

THE willows were planted on the Fen in March 1903 and in October of the same year we introduced the first Muscovy ducks to the Cam. They had been bred for us at Great Shelford, where our friends the Gadows lived on one of the small chalk hills. Dr Hans Gadow, F.R.S., was a zoologist of repute and a most interesting and delightful man. Though born and educated in Germany, he described himself as a Pomeranian. After a couple of years in London, writing part of the British Museum *Catalogue of Birds*, he was invited to Cambridge and in 1883 was appointed Strickland Curator of the birds in the Museum. The following year he became University Lecturer in Morphology and a Member of King's. In the obituary notice written for the Council of his College he is said to have had 'a great affection for living animals, especially birds, amphibians and reptiles, and an unusual knack of establishing confidential relations with them'. In 1889 he married Maud Paget, sister of Mrs (later Lady) J. J. Thomson and eldest daughter of Sir George Paget, F.R.S., Regius Professor of Physic, brother of the even better known Sir James Paget, Surgeon Extraordinary to Queen Victoria. Accompanied by his wife, Dr Gadow made several expeditions to Mexico, where the dictator Diaz employed him on occasions to visit its remoter regions and report on things of zoological interest there. He published two excellent travel books, one on Spain, the other on Southern Mexico. It must have been from one of their earlier expeditions to Mexico that the Gadows brought back the Muscovy ducks from which ours stemmed.

Mrs Gadow too was a remarkable and intrepid person. Mr R. Weeden Butler, as an undergraduate after the First World War, used sometimes to bicycle over to tea with the Gadows at Great Shelford. He has a vivid recollection of their first meeting:

she took me out into the garden and we sat on a seat in the sun waiting for her husband who had gone to shut up the cockatoo. All at once she said: 'Keep quite still—don't move', and produced a pistol from underneath the cushion at her end of the seat. I was a little alarmed at this till I saw that she was not pointing it at me but was looking to the right into the rockgarden overgrown with lavender. She raised the pistol slowly and fired—and I saw a large rat roll over dead into the lavender. 'Such a lot of rats', she said, 'one must try and keep them down.'

Her prowess with a pistol once stood them in good stead in Mexico. They had been attacked by brigands and the soldiers supposed to defend them had hastily decamped. Whilst Dr Gadow was still groping for his spectacles, she seized a pistol and fired at the bandits, hitting one in the leg; whereupon they promptly fled, leaving their wounded comrade to be taken prisoner by the soldiers, who returned as soon as all danger was over.

Like her husband, Mrs Gadow was passionately fond of birds. Her house was always full of parrots: she left instructions that when she died (in 1949) a favourite one was to be killed and buried with her.

It was in the sixteenth century that the Spaniards discovered Muscovy ducks, domesticated by the Indians in Peru, and they soon introduced them to Spain. In England they owe their name of Muscovy, it is believed, to the fact that from Spain they spread through Mediterranean countries to the Levant and even to Russia; from whence they were brought back by ship to England and so were regarded as having come from Muscovy. When Dr Gadow at the turn of the century imported his Muscovies from Mexico, they were still uncommon birds in England, though common in Spain and Southern France.

When word came from the Gadows that they had some Muscovy ducks ready for us, my sister Gwen, Billy and I were sent out in a cab to Great Shelford to fetch them, as I recorded in my diary on 6 October 1903:

Nine big beauties not full grown yet but getting on for the size of a goose. After catching them we put them in an enormous hamper and took them to their new home [in a corner-enclosure of the fowl run on the Big Island]. . . . We have to keep them shut up for a week or so.

Next day I regret to find that I wrote: 'the ducks are an awful bother'. One got loose and we only recaptured it after a long chase: the others all had to be lifted out of their house to feed and 'then they wouldn't touch a scrap of food. What can be up with them?' Their hunger-strike continuing next day, Gwen and I 'byked' over to ask advice of the Gadows. They assured us that Muscovy ducks often behave like this on being moved to a strange place and that they might not eat for a week or so. It proved to be a whole fortnight before they touched any food and we were much impressed by their self-martyrdom.

After this bad beginning, they settled down happily in their new home. They took to the water with enthusiasm but it was a long time before they took to the air. Their wings are rather small for their heavy bodies and they are said never to be strong fliers, though ours used sometimes to fly along the river or up into low trees. They soon, however, began to hold what I can best describe as silent conversaziones. One of the favourite places for these meetings was on the corner of the Lammas land opposite the copper beech. Here they would assemble, generally all nine of them, for they were a most united family, and one of them, frequently but not always a drake, would stand up very straight and tall, throw his head back and begin 'chittering' with his beak, but no sound except sometimes a faint hiss could be heard. Then others would be seized by the spirit, as in a Quaker meeting, and rise to address the assembly, flapping their wings and posing in strange attitudes; or sometimes they would carry on the debate seated, extending and retracting their long necks, as if to emphasize the points they were just making. The conversazione might last for ten minutes or more and then would cease as mysteriously as it had begun. We could never find any explanation of it, nor any set times for its performance.

Delacours, in his book *Waterfowl of the World*, gives a very similar description to mine of 'this curious habit, unique among the ducks, of standing together . . . holding their heads and bills vertically while they make snapping movements with their bills'. He adds that 'Muscovies are usually silent. The hissing of the drakes is barely audible, while the females' quack is short and weak.' Except perhaps for this discussion of their affairs in public, Muscovies show no other sign of particular intelligence; indeed, one of our ducks proved singularly obtuse in her choice of a pollarded willow for her nest, as there was a hole in it through which her eggs always fell into the river below. The gardener used to fish them out and take them home to eat.

We did not fancy Muscovy eggs ourselves, as they were said to taste fishy when boiled, nor for a long time would my mother countenance killing any of the ducks for food. She was fond of the amiable lumbering creatures and she admired their dark green and white plumage and even the red wattles at the base of the drake's bill—an adornment I never can appreciate. The Muscovies amused her, and she was proud to be their owner, believing them to be much less common in England than they really were. I believe it was food-rationing during the First World War that broke down her principles and she began not only to allow their eggs to be used in the kitchen, but even at times entertained a guest at dinner with home-produced roast duck.

Luckily, she never heard about the night-raid made years later on the Big Island when undergraduates captured a Muscovy. One of the marauders boasted of the feat in the hearing of a friend of my son Stephen and so in time it reached his ears, but he wisely refrained from telling his grandmother about it lest she write to the Vice-Chancellor in protest against such an outrage. I hope that the undergraduates concerned suffered pangs of conscience afterwards, unless they really believed, as I have my doubts, that the duck was wild and belonged to no one.

Muscovies are long lived and they look so much alike that I always assumed that I was looking at the original ducks when I returned home to Cambridge on visits. But they must have been either replacements made by my mother or remote descendants of the Gadow Muscovies that I saw and that my brother inherited when he took over Newnham Grange in 1947. The end of the ducks' long tenancy of the Big Island was by then in sight, for my brother and his wife were not interested in keeping poultry and rightly decided that the fowl-run was so ugly that both it and the chickens must be banished from the island. My sister, however, was interested in having new-laid eggs, so the hens were removed to new quarters in the kitchen-garden near the Old Granary where she could be responsible for them. At first the chickens must have missed their bridge and the freedom of the Lammas land, but at least they were now provided with a home above flood level and safe from the incursions of boys or dogs.

Immediately after the hens and their sheds had gone, the few remaining Muscovies decided to leave too and join the tame ducks downstream. Thereafter they only returned to the Big Island for rare calls on their old home. In time they probably mated with some of the other ducks but, as the resulting hybrids are never fertile, no lasting cross-breed could be established.

For years after we introduced the Muscovies to the Cam they were almost the only aquatic birds on the river. A couple of white Aylesbury ducks would appear occasionally in Newnham Millpool, or a pair of swans having escaped briefly, we supposed, from their captivity in the Wilderness might be seen swimming below St John's College with one or two semi-tame mallard. A few of the latter also sometimes came to Jesus Green, but that was all, until after the First World War. Then the number of ducks began slowly and steadily to increase; but in the last twenty or thirty years, there has been a veritable population-explosion and now at times there are scores of them to be seen, by or on the river, or overhead flying in. Some of the more politically advanced even come upsteam to hold sit-ins on the lawn of the Little Island. It is useless to try and turn them off: there they sit tight, in serried ranks, until they decide that they have demonstrated their right to the island and depart, honour satisfied.

I asked Mr R. W. Butler if he could explain the continuing increase of ducks in Cambridge, semi-wild and wild, and he kindly allows me to quote his letter in answer:

To see wild or half-wild mallard flying over the Cam and Coe Fen was uncommon in the early twenties. Now they are everywhere. There seem to be two general causes of this. Firstly, since the First War there has been a great increase of interest in, and appreciation of, birds among all kinds of people, even if they are not particularly expert in their knowledge of them.

In the early years of this century when there was still a good deal of poverty in Cambridge, a tame and confiding duck which did not appear to have any particular owner would have been in considerable danger of finding its way into the pot for somebody's dinner and if it were bold enough to nest near the river its eggs would likewise have been appropriated. Nowadays, with the great rise in the standard of living over the past fifty years, the children of Cambridge feed daily the descendants of the ducks that their grandfathers as boys would have tried to take home for their dinners. Wild mallard frequently nest in College and private gardens and the gardeners, who in the old days would have transferred the eggs to their luncheon haversacks, now put wire around the nests to keep cats away from them.

Secondly, many wild mallard have for the past forty years come increasingly to the pond in the Botanic Gardens where a certain number of tame duck were introduced in the twenties. The wild mallard fly in and pair with the tame ones and with the black Indian duck, themselves bred originally from mallard, producing with the latter, strange dusky mallard ducklings which grow up to fly away and confuse amateur bird watchers.

Wild and half-wild mallard and other duck also come to the old gravel pit off the Barton Road and to the pond in the Bird Sanctuary off Adams Road where they also breed. Outside Cambridge itself there are good haunts for wild duck on the low-lying fields beside the upper river and its tributaries above Grantchester, while the Quy pits and Fulbourn fen to the northeast and the new mere at Wicken fen are within easy flighting distance, as are indeed the big flood washes along the course of the Ouse, channelled into a straight line from Earith to Denver which, when flooded in winter, often form a home for thousands of duck.

From all these sources wild duck have been brought in increasingly to Cambridge by their association with the tame and half-wild duck on the river and in the Botanic Gardens.

Mr Butler's reference to the Bird Sanctuary off Adams Road reminds me of the famous long frost of 1895 when my father took me there to watch skaters, not birds, for this was long before birdwatching became a national sport. Adams Road was not yet in existence, and the path to the rink branched off a track leading from Grange Road to the Coton footpath. The pond stands in a field of about four acres belonging to St John's. In 1894 the field had been let by the College for twenty-one years at a rent of £8 to A. Austen Leigh, Provost of King's, J. B. Lock, Bursar of Caius, and J. N. Langley, Fellow of Trinity, 'to dig out and excavate . . . for the purpose of using the demised premises as a skating pond'. We children always called it, and believed it to be, the Trinity Skating Rink, perhaps because it adjoined the Trinity Playing Field on one side, or more probably because so many of the skaters were our Trinity friends, including J. N. Langley, later Professor of Physiology, who, as an athlete and first-rate skater, had no doubt taken the leading part in its acquisition and making.

He was there waiting for us that day. I can still see him doing fancy figures on the ice, whilst my sister and brother, aged nine and seven, wobbled about on their old-fashioned, wooden-soled skates attached to their boots by wide straps and a screw in the heel. Soon I was put in a chair on runners and in the proud position of being pushed round the pond by Mr Langley. After this the picture fades and the next memory I have of the rink is when I was old enough to skate there myself.

In 1935, the present bird sanctuary came into official existence on the site of the 'skating rink'. I say 'official' because the birds had long since taken over unofficially, and for some years it has been used as an ecological station by the Bird Club under the auspices of Mrs Brindley, a biologist like her husband, Mr H. H. Brindley, and a keen ecologist.

According to Mr Butler, there has also been a great increase in the number of swans all over England during the last thirty years. I should have liked to believe that some of the swans seen on the Cam now are remote descendants of Newnham Grange Swans, as they might have been, had my father accepted the kind offer made him in the following letter:

Dec. 13. 1888   St John's College,
                                                          Cambridge.

Dear Darwin,

Would you like a pair of swans to give picturesqueness to your ornamental waters? If so I am empowered to offer you a pair of

young well-grown birds on behalf of the College. Kindly send me
a note by return.

                                        Yours very sincerely,
                                             D. MacAlister.

The writer of this letter was the Tutor of St John's (later Sir Donald
and Chancellor of Glasgow University), mentioned earlier as having
built the Duffs' house in Lady Margaret Road. My father however
refused the gift, probably because he knew that swans could be
dangerous if they nested on the islands and from there might attack
his children or passers-by on land or water.

If, in 1888, St John's failed to find any home for these young
swans, they may have become the mature swans we were taken to
see on our walks along the Backs in the mid-nineties. They used to
swim slowly along the ditch, round and round the Wilderness (the
Fellows' garden of St John's), as we gazed down at them between
the uprights of the painted iron railings. These railings, surmounted
by 'families' of large and small balls, fascinated me even more than
the swans. The Victorian railings are still there, not looking a day
older, but the swans apparently disappeared from the scene a lifetime ago. When I sent a copy of Donald MacAlister's letter to the
Bursar of St John's, he found that not a soul in the College, no
matter how old, except the Master, knew that St John's had ever
possessed swans. The Master, Mr Boys Smith, however, does remember having heard long ago that once a pair had been kept in
the Wilderness: the ditch was covered over with wire-netting to
prevent them from escaping. I do not remember any netting over
them, so perhaps in the nineties they were pinioned instead.

Miss Porter of the Folk Museum tells me that St John's did once
have the right to own 'a game of swans'. In volume III of Willis
and Clark's *Architectural History of the University* (1886), it says that

at the present time swans are kept at St John's College and at
Emmanuel College; but we believe that at both these colleges the
introduction of them is of comparatively recent date. Willis and
Clark also refer to the keeping of swans by King's and Trinity
Colleges in the sixteenth and seventeenth centuries. In 1601, the
Jesus College accounts make mention of the payment of a

'Swanherde' for wintering eighty-three swans; it is evident that the birds were kept at a distance from Cambridge, probably at Willingham, for the purpose of supplying the Fellows' table with a delicacy on special occasions.

In 1942, swans even nested near Silver Street Bridge among the reeds on a little island of mud opposite the Millpool. Their nest was in full sight from the bridge but they throve on publicity and seemed to delight in having become one of the sights of Cambridge. This happened once again years later, when I saw them myself. Nests are found in several other places along the Backs; swans arrive by air or perhaps more often by river, but whence they come is seldom known. From their winter quarters they go out 'to the rivers around and to a very considerable distance', Mr Butler says. 'After all, they can now fly, as no one pinions them. . . . Cygnets can fly by the late autumn of the year they are hatched. They often keep with their parents for their first winter but several families may join in a larger flock. They move about but are not migratory.'

It is an enthralling sight to see these most beautiful of all birds, their feet held out in front of them to serve as brakes, alighting on the Cam with a great splash and then sailing majestically up and down the river past the ancient college buildings.

CHAPTER FIFTEEN

Life at Newnham Grange: 1895–1905

I CANNOT end my history of the nineties without giving some account of bicycling, because bicycles played such an important role in our lives at Newnham Grange.

Much to the alarm of his wife, our uncle Horace owned a penny-farthing bicycle in the eighteen-eighties, and may have used it occasionally to ride to and from the Cambridge Scientific Instrument Company, then in Tibbs Row off Downing Street; however, in 1886 after a bad fall in which he broke his arm, he gave up riding it, to the relief of Aunt Ida. It was his brother's penny-farthing no doubt that my father told us he had ridden once or twice long ago; but the invention of the 'safety' bicycle in 1885 meant that when he first bought a bicycle for himself it was one of the new type which was rapidly superseding in popularity the awkward and dangerous penny-farthing.* It was this 'safety' bicycle that turned him into an ardent cyclist. My mother had to content herself with owning a tricycle, as bicycling was still considered a strictly male sport. I believe it was during her tricycling days that the following dangerous incident occurred.

My parents were out for a cycle ride in hilly country when they came to the top of a hill down which the road zig-zagged steeply. My mother, who was leading the way, continued riding ahead, and, as she disappeared round a corner, my father saw with horror by the speed at which she was going, that she had completely lost control of her tricycle. He pursued her as fast as he could, but as he neared a hairpin bend, was not reassured by over-hearing two labourers

---

* The penny-farthing owed its name to the fact that the huge front wheel bore the same relation to the size of the little rear wheel as did an old-style penny to a farthing. Mr J. C. D. Howes, an authority on the history of bicycles, tells me its original names were the 'ordinary' bicycle, to distinguish it from its predecessor, the 'bone-shaker'. The 'safety' bicycle was so named because its stability was much increased by its having wheels of equal and moderate size.

148

A family outing

discussing what they should do when they found 'the lady's body'
on their way down. His relief can be imagined when, soon after, he
perceived her standing by her tricycle at the side of the road, calmly
waiting for him. She had somehow managed to negotiate the corners
without overturning and, as the road flattened out at the bottom,
regained control of the machine. In this happy end to her adventure,
she had been luckier than Charles Smith (Master of Sidney Sussex
College from 1890 to 1916). When his tricycle ran away with him
down Madingley Hill, he had been thrown off and had suffered
severe concussion.

There was an amazing boom in bicycling during the years 1895 and 1896 owing to the invention of pneumatic tyres, or Dunlop tyres as we always called them because they were made by the Dunlop Pneumatic Tyre Company. My father, of course, soon bought a bicycle equipped with these wonderful smooth-running tyres and then it was my mother's turn to be promoted from her tricycle to a bicycle with Dunlop tyres. She was apparently the first woman in Cambridge to ride a 'female' bicycle and was the object of such curiosity that she had to wear a thick veil to hide her blushes when she rode in the town.

Hard rubber tyres, however, were still considered good enough for children's bicycles and they did indeed make bicycling hard work for us, especially down hills, where the feeble front brakes had often to be supplemented by vigorous back-pedalling. On the other hand, children now know nothing of the glory of flying down a slope with one's feet up on the foot rests attached to the front forks of fixed-wheel bicycles, especially after Dunlop tyres came into use. It was only when the free-wheel was introduced that coasting down hills in this way ceased to be possible. But I also remember how hot and tired we became on those old hard-tyred bicycles as we toiled along the white dusty roads to a picnic on the Roman Road or at the Fleam Dyke. Sometimes our lot was ameliorated by sharing a bicycle with another child, so that we could take turns in driving with the non-cycling ladies, in the open landau or wagonette hired to take them to the picnic place. Yet I do not envy modern children their too easily won picnics made by means of a car. *We* had to earn our picnics by bicycling to them and this made them a rarer and much more valued treat. However, it was not very long before we were given bicycles with lovely squashy tyres like those of the grown-ups and then going for quite long rides became a pleasure instead of hard labour.

Chambers's Encyclopaedia, in its 1910 edition, gives a long and glowing account of 'the development of the pastime of bicycling in all classes of the community, including ladies', which was especially marked in 1895–96. In one passage the author becomes truly eloquent on the subject:

[The bicycle] has become the poor man's carriage, and the rich man's hobby in more senses than one. Royalty disports itself, at any rate in quasi-publicity, upon it, and the nobility and gentry make no secret of their love of the wheel. Clergymen visit their parishioners; medical men their patients; and tens of thousands of the middle classes transact their business or follow their pleasures by its means; while it is next to impossible to pass through any of the streets of our chief towns without seeing that the cycle . . . is ably ministering to the wants of the community.

This last sentence is certainly still true of Cambridge, even out of term time.

Later in his article, the writer quotes from the Local Government Act of 1888 in which bicycles, tricycles, and velocipedes were declared to be carriages within the meaning of the Highways Act. One of the provisions made was that cyclists 'upon overtaking any cart or carriage, or any horse, mule or other beast of burden or any foot passenger . . . shall . . . by sounding a bell, or whistle, or otherwise, give audible and sufficient warning of the approach of the carriage'. A bell fixed to the handlebar soon took the place of the bicycle whistle, if indeed such an instrument ever existed, but what kind of noise was 'otherwise' emitted I do not know.

After the boom of bicycling caused by the advent of pneumatic tyres had subsided, free-wheels with rim brakes were gradually introduced. I have a vague memory of my father's once having owned a dark green bicycle called an Elswick and was delighted to find that Mr J. C. D. Howes's father confirmed that Elswick bicycles of the time were green. According to some correspondence, my father late in 1898 sent his bicycle, presumably the Elswick one, up to the Elswick Cycle Company at Newcastle upon Tyne to have it fitted with a free hind wheel and two brakes, at the cost of two guineas. It was returned to him early in 1899 and was said to have been the first bicycle in Cambridge to be fitted with a free-wheel. Characteristically, later on he was also the first owner in Cambridge of a three-speed-gear bicycle: he was always in favour of innovations that seemed to him sensible.

His Elswick free-wheel must have pleased him, for some letters in May of the same year from the Singer Cycle Company at Coventry show that he had recently bought my mother what must have been a free-wheel bicycle and had had it fitted with a Singer Doolittle brake, but unfortunately the brake was living up to its name in not functioning properly. The Company, in answer to my father's letter of complaint, wrote indignantly that 'this must . . . be merely a matter of adjustment, as both our Managing Director, our Manager and others of our staff are using machines fitted with this brake, and find it in every way satisfactory and reliable'. However, they agreed to adjust it, but when the bicycle arrived they wrote they 'could find nothing much wrong with it'. In their letter after returning the bicycle they seemed to imply that the fault lay not in the brake but in my mother's injudicious use of it. 'The brakes', they wrote, 'are of necessity very powerful and should never be applied suddenly *but very judiciously* or accidents will assuredly happen.'

After this unfortunate experience with the Singer Doolittle brake, my father always bought our bicycles in Cambridge from J. Howes and Sons of 44 Regent Street, where the first John Howes had founded a coach-building and wheelwright's business in 1840. It was there in 1869 that he had produced his first 'bone-shaker' bicycle with its steel tyres and wooden wheels, having memorized one he saw in 1867 at the Paris Exhibition. This 'bone-shaker' marked the beginning of the bicycle-building firm which J. Howes and Sons eventually became. Here it was that their first Granta cycle was produced, still well known for its excellence, and here it is that Mr John C. D. Howes, great-grandson of the founder of the firm, still runs the cycle agency of his forefathers. He distinctly recalls dealing with my mother's and sister's bicycles; Newnham Grange bicycles were always brought there for servicing and repairs. I was touched to hear from him too that he remembered his grandfather talking sometimes of my father with whom he had had so many friendly dealings long ago. My father had a great respect and liking for this Mr John Howes and shared my engineer Uncle Horace's admiration for his remarkable knowledge of bicycles.

My father's interest in bicycling was so keen that, in 1898, he joined a Cambridge Cyclist's Protection Committee which had recently been formed. He was of course already a member of the Cyclists Touring Club, founded in London in 1878. The moving spirit of the new Cambridge Club was a Mr John H. Barker and the meetings took place in his office at 26 Park Parade. Professor Darwin kept a copy of the minutes of the meeting on 2 December 1898, over which he presided. The chief business was the passing of the Constitution. The Society had two principal objects in view: the first was 'to keep a watchful eye on the streets and roads in and near Cambridge . . . and to prevent illegal or unreasonable restrictions'. The second object was to 'render legal assistance to Cyclists who are the victims of assault, injury by drivers of vehicles . . . or who meet with accidents owing to the defective state of the streets or roads, or . . . where . . . legal assistance should be required, including to such persons who may be injured by cyclists riding furiously or neglecting the rules of the road'. I have found no further papers about this society, but until recently one had only to see the row of comfortable wooden bicycle stalls in the covered part of the Newnham Grange backyard to know that the Darwins were indeed a bicycling family.

In November 1904 my father had abundant cause for launching yet another of his protests. It was probably his last. This time it was against the preposterous plan for running electric trams down Silver Street and along the Backs. I found a copy of the printed manifesto among his papers.

MEMORIAL TO THE TOWN COUNCIL
OF CAMBRIDGE
We the undersigned residents in Cambridge have heard that a Bill is about to be presented to Parliament for the establishment of a system of electric trams in the borough, and we learn that it is proposed that a line should pass through Silver Street, and thence along the Backs of the Colleges.
We desire to protest against these portions of the suggested plan. Even at present Silver Street scarcely suffices for the traffic along it, and the additional obstruction caused by a tram-line would very much increase the existing difficulty. The passage of cars along so narrow a street would indeed be an absolute danger to the public. We base our objection to the other portion of the plan on the fact that the Backs of the Colleges furnish a unique charm to Cambridge, which would be in great measure destroyed by the proposed line.

We therefore beg leave to submit that the interests of the Town and University will be best served by the abandonment of these portions of the scheme.

The Town Clerk replied that the Memorial was presented to the Town Council, but I have no further correspondence on the matter, and as there never have been any electric trams in Cambridge, the affair had a happy ending. It is odd that such an undertaking was even suggested, as there were plenty of buses running in Cambridge long before 1904 and even the poor old one-horse trams continued clanking along the streets until 1914, though it is true that by then they were barely paying their way.

In October 1902, Professor Darwin had written to ask the University Press if they would consider giving up some ground to the Town Council at the corner of Silver Street 'with a view of improving the street', but he had been curtly refused by the Syndics. Perhaps two years later he was glad of this, as the narrowness of Silver Street was a useful point to raise against the introduction of electric trams. It has also preserved Queens' and Darwin Colleges so far from buses being routed past them, even though the new Lutyens bridge is wide and strong enough to take the weight of a bus, unlike the former narrow cast-iron bridge, removed in 1959.

Some time before the electric tram protest, my parents had decided to make a bay window in the dining-room. The strip of freehold ground in front of the house, on which the box hedge grows, made this project feasible. The two double windows were removed and rebuilt at an angle to form the sides of the bay, the middle part consisting of a blank wall along the edge of the path, parallel to the main line of the house. The lack of a central window no doubt was intended to prevent people having a direct view into the dining-room as they passed close by it. A ventilator high up in the wall kept the room aired whilst it excluded noise and dust. Now that one window faced further west, it admitted some late afternoon sunlight.

To Georgian purists the new bay was a crime. Had there been a third window in the middle of the bay, they might have regarded the crime as less heinous and even have forgiven it, as the bay does have the merit of enlarging the room and makes it look more spacious than it really is.

A few years later my parents, delighted with their new bay in the dining-room, decided to restore symmetry to the house by adding a similar bay to the other sitting-room facing the Backs. This room has often changed its name. When my parents bought the house in 1885 they named it the Smoking-room, a name it may well have had in the time of the Bealeses, for in Victorian days the gentlemen in most 'good' houses were confined to a special room for their smoking and would never have dreamt of so polluting the ladies' drawing-room. Later, it was called the school-room because we children used to have our lessons there. After we outgrew the Nursery, it became our sitting-room but retained its former name for the next forty years or so until rechristened the music-room by my brother's family. Then in 1964 it became the College Council room and now it is part of the Library.

As well as the bay, a tall new window was put in the west wall of the school-room near the fire-place. It looked across a small lawn at an old cherry tree and the side of the Hermitage behind its garden wall. This wall was demolished in 1967; and soon after, the erection of the Rayne Building of necessity blocked up this window as well as all the other windows on the west side of the house. However, the place of the window was soon filled to the ground by a large book-case matching those already there, for the Council room was in process of being turned into part of the College Library. The dining-room and the outer hall between the two rooms were ingeniously included to form the rest of the Library premises. The old front door was permanently closed, and the main entrance is now in the tower of the Rayne Building. The outer hall was partitioned off from the inner hall to form a lobby, and a door opening through this partition gives access to it and the new Library. The original doors of the dining-room and school-room opening on to the passage-way of the inner hall are now also closed; bookcases standing on the floor make the doors invisible from inside the Library. The entrance to these two rooms is through the small newly opened arches facing each other in the inner walls of the lobby.

These round-arched entrances had been filled in by my parents in 1885, as is shown by the architect's estimate on page 55, but it remains a mystery why they were ever made, for they were not needed as doors and the draughts they admitted from the front door must have been terrible. Nor is it known why two much larger arches were built above them, unless it be because the architect in 1793 was so enamoured of round arches that he put them in every possible place all over the main house, where they often serve no functional purpose at all.

My father's third building operation was undertaken, I believe, at the same time as the work on the school-room; it was done during the summer holidays whilst we were away, to save turning us out of our school-room and my father out of his study. For the next building planned was that of a book-room to adjoin his study. The main part of this was constructed from the storeroom behind the study; its floor was on the same level as that of the domestic part of the house, so that steps down to it were needed, and a window on its outer wall lighted it. I have found no architect's letters about these alterations, so perhaps my parents employed none. If so, my mother must have enjoyed the ingenuity required to plan the book-room with the help of the builder only. My father used to say that she was never so happy as when she was dealing with bricks and mortar. Perhaps Mr Saint had not yet retired, and was in charge of the work; if so, he would have had some check on her wilder architectural inspirations.

Recently, when I approached the secretary's room from what I still think of as the kitchen passage, I was so confused in my geography that I could not decide if I were standing in the store-cupboard my mother made into a telephone-cupboard, or if I were in the safe-room. (This had a heavy steel door which, if had it shut on me, would have instantaneously suffocated me, or so I believed.) But wherever it was I was standing, I could see that the Bursar had made an excellent office out of the old book-room in which to conceal his secretary, and that the accountant was even better housed alongside in the ex-pantry, though it gave me a pang to see that the old lead-lined sink had been taken away.

CHAPTER SIXTEEN

George Darwin's Later Years

In 1898, the British Government, having decided to join the International Geodetic Association, appointed my father as their delegate to the forthcoming meeting at Stuttgart. He preferred these congresses to all the others; the small number of delegates were all experienced geodesists and went straight to work without waste of time. We too as a family highly approved of the Geodetic Congresses, as they met, generally every three years, during our holidays in September, at interesting places, and we knew and liked so many of the members. Gwen and Charles accompanied my father to his first meeting at Stuttgart and then in 1900 my turn came, as the next Congress was to be held in Paris after an interval of two, instead of three years. By so doing it would enable the delegates and their families to see something of the Great Exhibition with which Paris was celebrating the new century. Accordingly, my mother and I spent an exciting week at the 'Exposition', joined by my father when he had time. We ended our stay in France by a visit to La Flêche (near Le Mans), where my father's old friend, Baron Constant d'Estournelles, had his country house. Here we all three had the thrilling experience of being taken for our first drive in a motor car. The automobile was open and we rushed through the air at what seemed to me to be a reckless speed, perhaps as much as 30 kilometres an hour. On our safe return my mother exclaimed at the wonderful driving of the chauffeur: how he had even managed to avoid a loose stone on the road!

The secretary of the Geodetic Congress was a small elderly Dutchman, Dr van de Sande Bakhuyzen. He and his large and amiable wife once came to luncheon with us at Newnham Grange and, when the parlourmaid offered them bread sauce to eat with their roast chicken, they burst into uncontrollable laughter, in which we soon joined, at being served with such 'baby food'.

The next meetings were held at Copenhagen (1903), Buda Pesth (1906), and Cambridge (1909), where my parents were the hosts.

This proved to be my father's last Geodetic Congress, as by September 1912 he was already too ill to attend the meeting at Hamburg, though he managed to get his reports ready to be presented by another British delegate.

The most memorable event in the lives of my parents occurred in 1905, when the British Association for the Advancement of Science — the B.A. or the British Ass., as it is still sometimes called — met in South Africa for the first time. The election of Professor Darwin as President of the Association for 1905 had already been made before the 1904 meeting in Cambridge under Arthur Balfour. G.H.D. knew well what an arduous task the presidency in Africa would be, especially for a man of sixty who had never since his youth enjoyed robust health: nevertheless he accepted the post with enthusiasm. Buoyed up by the excitement of the undertaking and sustained by his intense love of travel, he showed remarkable resilience in the way he stood the heat, the fatigue of the long journeys by train, and above all the ceaseless entertaining, at which he always had to make the chief speech. I have a copy of the diary he kept during the expedition, typed out when he got home, and incorporating relevant documents and press-cuttings.

On 29 July 1905, Professor George Darwin, as he still was, and Mrs Darwin with their son Charles sailed from Southampton on the Union Castle liner, *Saxon*, and arrived at Cape Town on the morning of 15 August. The same evening Professor Darwin gave his presidential address on 'Cosmical Evolution'. After four days of meetings, honorary degree-giving, and sight-seeing, they again took ship, to Durban, to begin their extensive tour of South Africa by special train, sometimes as many as four such trains being needed to convey the huge B.A. party. On their way they saw some splendid African dances and toured the battlefields of Colenso and Ladysmith. At Johannesburg, Professor Darwin gave the second half of his presidential address and the formal meeting was wound up, though further lectures were given at various stopping-places. On 12 September, they reached the furthest point of their outward journey at the Victoria Falls, where my father opened the single-line railway bridge just built over the Zambesi. They returned by Portuguese East Africa and the East Coast route, reaching Suez on 4 October. After a few days at Cairo, they arrived home, via Marseilles, and

Paris a fortnight later, having travelled nearly continuously for over two and a half months.

Soon after he got back my father was knighted. He appreciated the honour all the more from having learnt of it first in a private letter from his friend Arthur Balfour, the Prime Minister. He was also particularly gratified at being made a Knight Commander of the Bath, as he loved belonging to an Order with such a proud and ancient history. In those days full court dress had to be worn for the investiture and when the time came for him to be dubbed, on approaching the King (Edward VII), he tripped over his own sword — or so he told us to his own and our amusement.

Three years later, in the spring of 1908, he attended another conference abroad: this was the International Congress of Mathematicians at Rome. He had been charged by Oxford and Cambridge mathematicians to invite the Association to hold its next international meeting in 1912 at Cambridge and London.

Charles and I accompanied our parents to Rome. I remember an evening party the Mayor gave in the Capitoline Museum amongst the marble statues, the Dying Gladiator lit up, and how my father was told in a horrified, hushed voice by an Italian member that the Mayor was a Freemason. This puzzled me, because hitherto I had thought of Freemasons as harmless men who devoted their lives to the support of charities; but here in Italy they appeared to be regarded as politically subversive and evil people.

On the final day of the Congress, the meeting was held in a grand hall, into which we were ushered up a long staircase between the naked swords of two rows of Bersaglieri in their famous cock-plumed hats. We had seats near the front, facing the King, for Victor Emmanuel III was there, taking an active part in the Congress, as he had a passion for mathematics. He was a small man with legs so short that his feet as he sat in the enormous, gilt-armed chair, could not reach the floor; I longed to get him a hassock on which to rest his dangling legs. After the meeting, my father was kept behind to be introduced to the King. The invitation to England for the next meeting had been cordially accepted and Sir George Darwin had been nominated President of the fifth International Congress to be held at Cambridge and London in four years' time.

After the meeting was over, we stayed on a couple of days longer at our friendly 'Hotel de Londres et de l'Univers' at the foot of the Spanish Steps. We had all been reading G. M. Trevelyan's recently published *Garibaldi's Defence of the Roman Republic* and Charles and I were almost as excited by the bullet marks on the walls of the Monte Janiculo houses as we were at seeing the Forum. However, there was still time left to do more orthodox sightseeing with my father and take an enchanting walk round Lake Nemi among the spring flowers before leaving Rome.

Four years later, when the Congress of Mathematicians was meeting at Cambridge, I did not remain there to help my parents with the entertaining of the foreign members; this I regretted afterwards but I was not to know then that it would be my last chance of attending one of my father's international congresses. So I missed seeing many eminent foreign men, although the following year I met someone even more interesting to me than the mathematicians would have been. This was Professor Ernst Haeckel, the famous German naturalist. He had been a correspondent and friend of my grandfather's, and the most ardent exponent of the theory of evolution in Germany.

This is how the meeting with Haeckel came about. Having left Winchester in the spring of 1913, my brother Billy was boarding with a schoolmaster's family at Jena to improve his German before coming up to Trinity in October. I was having a holiday with a Somerville friend in Germany that July, combining it with a few days in Jena to see how Billy was getting on. His host, the schoolmaster, insisted on our meeting Professor Haeckel whilst we were there, and arranged for us to call on him next day in his home.

We found him sitting at a table in his large study, engaged in painting a landscape he had drawn for one of his many books – he was a competent artist as well as a prolific author. (I still have the copy of one of his coloured illustrations of Ceylon that he gave me as a souvenir when we left.)

He welcomed us most kindly, speaking in excellent, if rather formal, English. By way of entertaining us he produced two enormous albums of pictures he had made of every known species of jelly-fish, or so it seemed to us as we turned page after page. We were thankful when he stopped explaining the pictures and asked Billy what he was going to read at Cambridge. 'Mathematics', Billy replied, on which

Professor Haeckel paused a moment and then remarked reflectively: 'Ah, that is the one subject in which I did not excel.' It was a pity that I was not aware then of his having stayed more than once with my grandparents at Down, as it would have been so interesting to have got him to tell us about his visits there.

He said he would show us his museum the following morning. When we arrived at his house we found him sitting in a wheeled chair outside the front door with a stout lady in attendance to push him to the Museum not far from his home. A middle-aged woman, dressed aesthetically in green flowing robes and sandals, was hovering nearby, carrying a large laurel wreath. Haeckel was annoyed at seeing her, and with some difficulty she was shoo-ed away, his attendant explaining that the woman was a dreadful nuisance, always lurking about to try and crown the Professor with laurels whenever he appeared out of doors.

I remember nothing about the Museum itself except that it had four lofty rooms, each presided over by a full-length portrait of one of the protagonists of evolution: Lamarck, Goethe, Charles Darwin, and Haeckel himself. The portraits made them all look incredibly tall but after he had begun on the legs, the painter seemed to have lost interest and had ended them in a kind of forked mist, vaguely suggestive of a mermaid's tail. I regret that I never had the opportunity of going to Jena again to see how correct my memory is of the four protagonists' legs.

Sir James Jeans states in the *Dictionary of National Biography* that

although the main stream of George Darwin's work was always associated with the evolution of the solar system, yet no small part of his time was spent on quite other problems, many of which were brought to his notice through his membership of various scientific committees. He dealt as a recognized authority with a very wide range of subjects, including tidal theory, geodesy and dynamical meteorology.

Of all the scientific committees he attended in England, those at the Meteorological Office probably came first in his regard. The Royal Society had appointed him a member of the Governing Body

of the Meteorological Council, as it was then called, as long ago as
1885. No doubt the Council had a special attraction for him from
the first, as it had been founded by Captain Fitzroy of the Beagle
and reorganized by George's cousin, Francis Galton, after Fitzroy's
suicide in 1865. It was Galton who had developed the work of
studying the weather, and he remained on the board until 1900 as
one of its most distinguished Commissioners. Darwin had a great
liking as well as admiration for his cousin and was proud to associate
with him in the work. 'George's attendance at the Committee
meetings was very regular', wrote Sir Napier Shaw, Director of the
Office, to my uncle Frank in 1915, 'and all questions involving
measurements or mathematical reasoning were referred to him.'
Shaw's first recollections of G.H.D. had been the thrilling production
of a new version of the annual report of the Council which he had
written because the original was more 'scissors and paste' than he
could endure.

It was not only the Meteorological Office or meetings of the
Royal Society that drew George up to town—he was also a member
of the Cambridge University Association, an unofficial body founded
in 1899, largely on his initiative, to promote the further endowment
of the University in the great expansion which the scientific progress
of the age demanded. He used to enjoy having 'to run up to London'
to see the Duke of Devonshire who, as Chancellor of Cambridge
University, took a strong lead in the matter. Sometimes G.H.D.
would combine business with pleasure by lunching with Arthur
Balfour, visiting Francis Galton, or dropping in at the Athenaeum
for a meal and a game of billiards.

He sat on many boards and syndicates at Cambridge, but never
became what his brother Frank described as a 'professional syndic'—
one of those virtuous persons who spend their lives in University
affairs. Nor apparently did he display the patience he showed in
private life at some of the committees, where, according to Professor
Newall, 'his direct progress may at times have seemed unsympathetic
and hasty'. Dr Shipley described him at meetings as 'often rather
distrait but when anything of real importance came up he was of
extraordinary use. . . . He was especially interested in the Appointments Board. A good many of us constantly sought his advice and
nearly always took it', continued Shipley, 'but . . . I do not think he

cared much about the parish pump, and was usually worried at long meetings.'

The Research Defence Society was a movement that attracted his support in his last years. He invited Lord Cromer, President of the Society, to come and address an evening meeting of the Cambridge branch on the subject, dining with us first at Newnham Grange. I well remember the sight of his massive figure. Though his manners were so gentle and modest, he gave the feeling of being a Great Man. He amused us by the astonishment he showed at hearing that my mother and other Cambridge ladies had joined the society. He was apparently convinced that all ladies would belong to the Anti-Vivisection Society.

Sir James Jeans calls my father 'a recognised authority on tidal theory' and the whole of volume I of George Darwin's collected scientific papers is devoted to the subject of Oceanic Tides. He organised and greatly extended the systematic observation of the tides, and tide-tables were in constant use in his work. There is an amusing reference to this in a letter he wrote to Caroline Jebb in about 1883:

Oh dear, I've made a little tiny mistake in my great tidal work and I find that the people in India have been acting on it and have printed a numerical table based on the false formula. Well, last night I couldn't sleep a wink and at 1.30 I got paper and pencil and began working the theory out and satisfy myself of what it ought to be.

The only book he ever wrote was *The Tides* (John Murray, 1898). It was founded on the Lowell lectures he gave at Boston in 1897 and soon became the standard work on the subject. Jeans calls it 'a masterpiece of semi-popular scientific exposition'. Such was his life-long interest in the behaviour of tides and his passion for tidal bores, that he took us in 1904 for an Easter holiday to Cauxdebec-en-Caux to see the famous bore sweep up the Seine at the highest spring tide.

In his book he gives over ten pages to an account of the great Chinese bore at Tsien-Tang-Kiang, and he also tells briefly of his own attempt to see the humble English bore:

In general . . . it is only at spring tides and with certain winds that the phenomenon is at all striking. In September 1897 I was on the banks of the Severn at spring tide; but there was no proper bore, and only a succession of waves up-stream, and a rapid rise of water level.

This failure determined him to try his luck again but next time with the French variety.

I described the event in my diary written at Cauxdebec-en-Caux on Sunday, 3 April 1904:

This morning the bore came at 10.30. Lots and lots of people came in motors and on bikes to see it. We stood in a cart so as not to get wet — it came slowly at first, we saw it coming by the foam at the side of the Seine, and with a rush when it was near us. It was a jolly sight — a great wave dashing over the quay (more than 10 feet higher than the river). A great many people got wet — one man in a thick motoring fur coat was taken right off his legs and could not get out at first. It was so funny — especially because a man seized him round the waist after he was quite safe in water only up to his knees. His motor *was* cheered when it departed. The Seine was much rougher after the tidal wave had passed.

I recollect the incident vividly. The man, said to be a reporter, had rashly taken up his observation post on the jetty much too close to the river. The bore picked him up neatly and whirled him right round before depositing him again on the quay when, the danger over, his friend rushed in to rescue him.

Important as the tides were in Professor Darwin's work, his theories about the moon and the moon's genesis held the supreme place in his thought. It is fascinating to envisage what his excitement would have been had he known that man would be landing on the moon only fifty-seven years after his death, but I believe, romantic as he was, his excitement might have been tinged with a slight private regret at the violation of the moon.

I am told that present theories of the origin of the moon differ from each other in postulating either that the moon was formed from the protoearth (as my father believed), or that it represents captured ex-territorial matter. Some geophysicists today still consider much of G. H. Darwin's theory valid, although its dependence on tidal forces is disputed by others who look to gravitational irregularities to explain the breakaway of the moon. In his passage on the genesis of the moon, he wrote with his customary honesty that 'there is nothing to tell us whether the theory affords the true explication of the birth of the moon and I say that it is only a wild speculation, incapable of verification'. Perhaps, now that man has brought back rocks from the moon for investigation, his theory will some day be proved or disproved, but, even if disproved, I think that he would not have minded, so eager was he always to know the truth.

I have one curious memory of my father as a man of science. ('Scientist' was a new and mongrel word he abhorred and never used.) The incident occurred towards the end of his life. One morning he came down to breakfast in a strange state of elation because, during the night, he had either dreamt of or been inspired by—I cannot remember which expression he used—a new theory which, if true, would have solved some hitherto insoluble problem of vast magnitude. I imagine it was something to do with the solar system and the moon but he did not tell me what it was, as I should not have understood him. I accompanied him into the town that day and retain a mental picture of him crossing Silver Street Bridge, bowed in thought, entirely oblivious of the outer world. His state of abstraction continued for a day or two, until he found some fatal flaw in his calculations and had to abandon the theory. His disappointment was pitiful to see. At first there had evidently been no doubt in his mind but that he had lit upon the solution to some problem of enormous scientific importance.

I wish I had told my brother Charles about this episode; he would probably have known or guessed what the theory had been. That it came to my father in a blinding flash of inspiration I have no doubt, yet this was the very opposite of his usual method of work. One of his favourite quotations was from Anthony Trollope: 'It's dogged as does it.' For example, Sir J. J. Thomson commenting on the extremely laborious nature of his work, wrote that

[George] Darwin possessed to the full the Darwinian characteristic of sticking doggedly at a problem until he had found a satisfactory solution. . . . For example his celebrated paper on orbits, in which results of the highest scientific importance and suggestiveness are obtained, is a kind of apotheosis of arithmetic.

During his later years, many honours were bestowed upon him. He and Sir David Gill, the former Cape Town astronomer, used to have a friendly rivalry or 'race', as they called it, to see which of them had collected most memberships of foreign academies. One honour that gave him the greatest satisfaction was the decision of the Cambridge University Press Syndics, in 1907, to publish an edition of all his collected scientific papers, prepared under his own supervision. The fourth of the large volumes appeared in 1911; the fifth and last was posthumous and did not come out until 1916. It includes Frank Darwin's delightful memoir, from which I have quoted so much.

In 1911, G.H.D. was awarded the Copley Medal, the highest distinction the Royal Society can confer. When he was given it, he protested that its bestowal was due to the merely practical applicability of some of his earlier investigations. One of these was concerned with the pressure of loose earth; the Institute of Civil Engineers also gave him a medal for this work.

His experiments were made in his rooms at Trinity with a wooden box, a piece of tarpaulin, a heap of sand and a biscuit tin. One day when he was ladling sand from box to biscuit tin, he said to his observant bedmaker: 'This is a funny sort of job, Mrs Pleasants.' 'Oh, yes Sir, but it amuses you' she answered. 'That' remarked Sir George to his audience 'was the attitude of the British public towards Science.'*

Perhaps this simply made experiment comes into the category of what his father called 'fool's experiments'. Charles Darwin himself sometimes had recourse to these apparently childish experiments, as when he told his son Frank to play his bassoon in 'the loudest and deepest tones' to some earthworms to discover if they had any sense of hearing. The answer, confirmed by other experiments, was that they had none.

* Anecdote quoted from a biographical sketch of Sir George Darwin by Philip Jourdain in a monthly magazine, *The Open Court*, Chicago, April 1913.

G.H.D. took such a transparent pleasure in his honours that some people may have thought him conceited, but his open expression of satisfaction in his successes was largely due, I believe, to his innocent assumption that others would want to rejoice with him, just as he would have rejoiced with them in similar circumstances. He was free from envy or jealousy, ready to help younger men in their work and infinitely patient in reading and criticising their theses. His friend and pupil, Professor E. W. Brown, writing to Frank Darwin, said: 'He was always modest about the importance of his researches. He would often wonder whether the results were worth the labour they had cost him, and whether he would have been better employed in some other way.'

All the obituary notices mention not only his modesty about his work but also his great energy. Jeans wrote:

To the end of his life, Darwin's personality suggested a certain boyish eagerness, he seemed always on the lookout for adventures. He conveyed no suggestion of midnight oil; his own estimate of his average hours of work was only three a day. That he achieved so much must be ascribed first to a flair for starting each problem in the right way, and secondly to an obstinacy which insisted on probing every problem to the bottom.

His brother Frank observed:

Of George's energy we have evidence in the amount of work contained in the five volumes of his published papers. There was nothing dilatory about him and here again he resembled his father who had markedly the power of doing things at the right moment and thus avoiding waste of time and discomfort to others.

Their sister, Henrietta Litchfield (Aunt Etty in *Period Piece*), in her book *Emma Darwin* (John Murray, 1915) also spoke of his remarkable energy and persistence as a little boy, and added that he not only inherited his father's power of work but also much of his 'cordiality and warmth of nature, combined with a characteristic power of helping others'. Like his father too 'he worked under a constant strain from ill-health of a most wearing nature'.

In sorting G.H.D.'s files of correspondence, it was astonishing what evidence I found in them of the time he spent in helping other people. Many are generous with their money but there was literally no end to the *personal* trouble my father would take over someone he had decided needed his aid. The assistance, whether monetary or not, would always be given with the touch of human sympathy which removed the stigma of charity from it. To him, everyone he came across was a separate individual to be respected as such. I remember once witnessing the warmth with which he greeted an old servant from Down he had not seen for a couple of years and the perfectly genuine concern he showed in enquiring about her health and circumstances, every detail of which he seemed to remember. If he liked someone, his liking would soon grow into affection. Of course he had his dislikes but there were not many people whom he shunned with ill-concealed horror. 'Few people can have taken more pains to cultivate friendship', wrote Frank, and friendship included most of his near relations. After his mother was widowed and spent the winters in Cambridge, he hardly ever missed a day without walking or bicycling up the mile to her home at The Grove off Huntingdon Road, to spend a few minutes with her, however busy or tired he might be.

George had no obvious aesthetic interests; he did not care for music nor much for paintings, but he had a passion for the country, especially for its wilder regions, and his romantic nature showed that he had an unconscious love of beauty. He was by no means a materialist, in spite of his scientific approach to many things. Frank said that 'although he read much good literature with honest enjoyment, he had not a delicate or subtle literary judgment. . . . He was interested in travels, history and biography and as he could remember what he read or heard his knowledge was wide in many directions. His linguistic power was characteristic.' He read aloud supremely well and as we grew up there was always a 'reading-aloud book' on hand during the holidays, such as Kipling and W. W. Jacobs's short stories, and novels, especially Thackeray. I remember how he broke down in reading the death-scene of Colonel Newcome and could not continue. Best of all the reading-aloud books to my mind was when Frances happened to be staying with us, and she read us a Jane Austen for the first time, and we talked and thought of nothing but Emma for the rest of those holidays at Uncle Leonard's house in Sussex.

We were indeed fortunate to have him for a father. Though naughty enough with our governesses and sometimes with our mother, I never remember our being naughty or even *wanting* to be naughty with him. During the holidays, often spent in the wildest parts of Yorkshire, he used to take us long exploring walks cross-country, sometimes through bogs and mud, regardless of pouring rain and our squelching boots—there were no wellingtons in those days—climbing dry-stone walls, trespassing through woods or enclosed fields, but always careful to shut the gates and do no damage. We never objected to going these walks with him. He had a useful axiom in which I, at least, devoutly believed; it was that no Darwins were ever tired until they got home. This kept me from flagging many times.

We loved him dearly but we were not the least in awe of him, nor thought him infallible. We would argue with him freely; sometimes we would even laugh at his crotchets behind his back and did not take his fits of depression, when feeling ill, too seriously, as we knew he would soon emerge from them. I suppose he unconsciously treated us in the way his parents had treated him when young, and the system worked as happily with us as it had done with him and his brothers and sisters at Down many years before.

CHAPTER SEVENTEEN

Two Darwin Celebrations
and Sir George Darwin's Death

G. H. D. had a number of Charles Darwin's characteristics but he differed from him in physique, his father being much the taller of the two. However, they resembled each other closely in two respects, as they were both very thin and had the same kind of small slender hands with long thin fingers.

After Charles Darwin's death in 1882, the Royal Society raised a large sum of money for a memorial to him. Contributions flowed in from all over the world and Joseph Edgar Boehm (later Sir Edgar Boehm, Bart.), a well-known sculptor in London of Hungarian origin, was commissioned to make a seated statue of him in marble for the Natural History Museum in South Kensington.

The statue was unveiled at the Museum in June 1885. Professor T. H. Huxley, the then President of the Royal Society, gave the opening address and asked the Prince of Wales to accept the statue on behalf of the Trustees of the British Museum. The Prince 'made a suitable reply', according to the *Graphic* of 20 June. The statue was placed on the landing of the first flight of stairs at the north end of the great Central Hall and remained in that dominating position until 1927, when it was moved down to a bay in the Hall opposite Huxley. Darwin was dethroned in order to make place for Sir Richard Owen, who had himself been dethroned to make place for a particularly valuable fossil elephant. There was much public opposition to this 'dethronement' of Darwin, but the trustees were obdurate. The statues of Darwin and Huxley remained in their 1927 positions until 1971, when they were moved again, this time to the North Hall near the Education Centre. Owen, however, remains where he was on the landing.

Mrs Charles Darwin had preferred not to be present at the unveiling ceremony on 9 June 1885, but three weeks later she wrote

to her daughter-in-law Sara (Mrs W. E. Darwin) that she had been
to see the statue:

> The situation is unique, and I liked the attitude, but I do not
> think it is a strong likeness. George has been with Mr Boehm
> to have a cast of his hand taken as a sort of guide to altering the
> hands, but I believe if he attempted to make them as small as
> they really were, they would look out of proportion with the size
> of the figure. I also perceived the defect in the eyes that you
> attempted to get altered. However I never expected to be satisfied
> with the likeness and the general look of dignity and repose is of
> more consequence.

My grandmother's letter is of interest because of her statement
that Charles Darwin had such small hands. Had Boehm made them
the size they really were, they would have looked out of proportion.
The family were not the only people to criticize Boehm's representa-
tion of Darwin's hands. On 11 June 1885, *Nature* published an
account of the unveiling ceremony and praised the statue as a noble
work of art, but added that the hands 'do not bear the smallest
resemblance to those of Mr Darwin but are of a kind which, had
they been possessed by him, would have rendered impossible the
accomplishment of much of his work'.

Some years later, G.H.D. came into possession of what I believe
to be the half-life-sized clay model for the marble statue, dated 1883.
This small statue came to us from George's eldest brother, William.
He probably gave the statue to George when he moved to London
from Southampton in 1902, perhaps not so much because George
was the next heir, as because there was more room for it at Newnham
Grange than in his house in Egerton Place. I know nothing of its
earlier history, nor how William got it. The clay looked so discoloured
and fragile that my father soon had the whole statue bronzed
over and an iron guard fitted to the front of the pedestal to protect
the feet and legs from injury. The effect is slightly comic because it
makes Charles Darwin look as if he were warming his feet at an
imaginary fire. This was a thing he frequently did, but it never
occurred to my father that people might mistake the guard for a
fender. The statue was kept in the dining-room (now part of the
Library at Darwin College) until, some fifty years later, my brother

Charles gave it to Down House as the original model of the Boehm statue.

G.H.D. always said that the Museum statue was copied from this clay one. Some doubts that have been cast on this attribution were due to the existence of a miniature bronze statue, 16 inches high, also at Down House, but this was made by Horace Montford for Shrewsbury, where Charles Darwin was born and went to Shrewsbury School. It was unveiled in 1897. The clay and bronze statues do superficially resemble each other because, in both, Darwin is seated in an upright armchair with his legs crossed, but the posture in Montford's statue is different and so are many details, such as his hands not being clasped, and there is no cloak over his knees. My cousin Christopher Cornford and his wife Lucy, both of them artists, have compared the Museum statue with the photographs of the Boehm clay statue, and report that the statues 'seem to be alike in every particular except perhaps the hands in the photograph might be slightly smaller than those of the Museum statue. The hands of the (Museum) statue are quite large—a normal masculine size. The statue itself is about $1\frac{1}{4}$ times life size.'

Miss Jessie Dobson, Curator of the Hunterian Museum and of Down House, thinks that the only difference between the marble and the clay statues is that the hands are *not* identical—'those of the Down House statue seem to be much more carefully executed and more natural'. That is also my impression.

I remember my father saying on more than one occasion with a touch of pride, that Boehm had taken his (G.H.D.'s) hands as his model: they certainly do seem to resemble his 'proper Darwin hands', as we held them to be. Most of his generation of the family had similar thin brown hands with long slender fingers. We at Newnham Grange associated this type of hand particularly with my father and our aunt Etty (Mrs Litchfield). However, the Museum has no record that Boehm altered the hands in situ. Perhaps after criticism of the size of the hands by the family in 1885, he did, merely out of politeness, take a cast of my father's hand. He probably ruled out any alterations to the statue as inadvisable.

I think I know the photograph from which Boehm worked.*

* This photograph was engraved for the *Century Magazine* (January 1883) and forms the frontispiece of Vol. II of Francis Darwin's *Life and Letters of Charles Darwin*.

In about 1874, Charles's son Leonard had photographed his father sitting on the verandah at Down. The basket chair in the photograph has been transformed into a kind of throne in the statue and Darwin is not wearing his overcoat, but the posture is identical: his legs are crossed and his hands clasped. When I showed my cousin, Nora Barlow, the photograph of the clay statue now at Down House, she exclaimed that his hands were clasped in exactly the same way as her father, Horace Darwin, always clasped his—and so too did my father in repose. It was evidently a family habit.

When Boehm was finishing the marble statue he may not have taken great pains over the final carving of the hands. I am told, however, that it is most unlikely that a Victorian sculptor would have acted thus. So perhaps the real answer to the enigma of the hands is that Boehm left them large on the Museum statue because, like Mrs Darwin, he thought they would have looked wrong on a tall man like Charles Darwin, had he made them the small size they really were.

In June 1909, the University of Cambridge celebrated the centenary of Charles Darwin's birth and the fiftieth anniversary of the publication of *The Origin of Species*. There was a large international gathering to mark the event and among the many distinguished people invited were Mrs T. H. Huxley and the botanist Sir Joseph Hooker who, though much younger, was Charles Darwin's greatest friend. To my family's gratification, these invitations were both accepted, though being ninety-five, Sir Joseph did not attend many of the functions. Sir Julian Huxley, in his *Memories* (1970), describes having seen his grandmother 'then rising eighty-five and the bewhiskered and heavily-eye-browed Sir Joseph Hooker, sitting side by side on a dais, at the opening ceremony'. Later on, the Vice-Chancellor in his speech at the Banquet referred 'to the great delight we have experienced on seeing the remarkable Sir Joseph Hooker walking about Cambridge as if he were thirty years younger than he is'.

Sir Joseph and Lady Hooker were the guests of my aunt Bessy at Traverston in West Road for the celebration, and Mrs Huxley stayed with the Horace Darwins at the Orchard. One day the Hookers went up to the Orchard to call on their old friend Mrs Huxley, and a photograph was taken of Sir Joseph inspecting the first Darwin great-grandchild, Ursula, daughter of Bernard Darwin. (Mrs Huxley is holding the baby on her lap, Sir Joseph is seated by her with Lady Hooker leaning over them from the back.) This photograph is reproduced in Sir Julian's book.

When Gwen and I went round to aunt Bessy's to be introduced to Sir Joseph, we thought him such a friendly sweet old man that we tried to get him to tell us about our father and uncles when they were children at Down, but all we could elicit from him was a cryptic remark about Uncle William as a small boy: 'He used to stick pins into people', he said, chuckling over the remembrance. This seemed a most inappropriate memory to have of our much-loved and kindest of uncles and when we told uncle William about it later, he could throw no light on the incident.

It was this uncle of ours who was chosen to make the speech for the family at the great banquet held in the brand-new Examination Hall off Bene't Street on 23 June 1909. William Erasmus Darwin was the eldest child and the least well-known of Charles Darwin's five sons, but the most charming. As his brother Francis writes, William's early childhood had one point of distinction,

> for no sooner was William brought into the world than he was used by his father as scientific material; a minutely detailed diary was kept of the child's faculties, afterwards utilized in *The Expression of the Emotions*. But Charles Darwin was a devoted father and the most tender-hearted of men, and when (for instance) accurate notes on the act of crying were needed, the man of science disappeared and became the gentlest of nurses.

Uncle William was educated at Rugby School (where, as he told us, he and the other boys used to be intensely bored by the sermons of Thomas Hughes, author of *Tom Brown's Schooldays*, when he came to preach). William went to Cambridge in 1858 as a scholar at Christ's, where he read mathematics, and rowed. On leaving he became a partner of Grant and Maddison's Bank at Southampton, and eventually the manager of Lloyd's Bank which had swallowed the first-named bank. For forty-one years he was treasurer of the Hartley Institute (later University College) and the College became his chief interest in public life; it owes much to him. It is now the

University of Southampton. In 1877, he married Sara Sedgwick, daughter of a New York lawyer and an English mother, Miss Ashburner, and sister-in-law of Charles Eliot Norton of Cambridge, Massachusetts.

William was totally lacking in ambition, and was content to work as a bank manager for most of his life. He had, however, many interests: he was a keen amateur geologist and a great reader, as well as a lover of music and pictures, with a consuming passion for fine architecture. To make his speech at the banquet in 1909 must have been a fearful ordeal, but 'by common consent it was held to be the speech of the evening', as his brother Frank wrote.*

I was among the female Darwins who were admitted to the balcony of the Examination Hall to hear the speeches that evening. After the Chancellor, Lord Rayleigh, had proposed the King's health, Arthur Balfour spoke at length for the University, proudly recalling that he had met Charles Darwin personally. He was followed by Dr Arrhenius, representing the foreign delegates, who ended his speech by proposing the toast to the memory of Darwin, drunk in silence. Then it was the turn of Uncle William. He had a shiny bald head; blue eyes, a rosy complexion, clean-shaven except for the token white whiskers by his ears. He was only of middle height and looked very small and lonely standing up in that big hall to address the large and distinguished audience seated in front of him. His voice was pitched rather high; he did not have the deep warm voice of most of his brothers, but he spoke slowly and distinctly so that every word could be heard. The main themes were his father's hatred of cruelty, especially his abhorrence of slavery, his enthusiasm for the liberty of the individual and 'the natural' joyousness and gaiety which made him such good company not only to visitors but to his children as a playmate. Then William spoke of 'the very hackneyed subject of his loss of interest in poetry and art'. This lack he thought his father had exaggerated. As regards imagination, 'scenery, the beauty of flowers, music and novels were sufficient to satisfy it'. Nor could he have written the last paragraph

---

* In his obituary of William for the Christ's College magazine in 1914: 'In his modest and respectful manner of referring to the distinguished guests and still more in the pathetic charm of his words about his father, his audience had revealed to them the essence of his nature in a way which no description can emulate.'

or two of *The Origin of Species* or the passage in a letter to his wife about falling asleep in Moor Park when he 'awoke to a chorus of birds, with squirrels in the trees and the laugh of a woodpecker, and he added that he did not care a penny how the birds or the beasts were made. I think he could never have written either of those two passages without a deep sense of the beauty and the poetry of the world and of life.'

William ended by thanking the University for the celebration and the delegates for coming to it. He added that he thought his father would have said,

'though perhaps with a tone of apology in his voice, that if there was to be a celebration there could be no more fitting place than Cambridge . . . He valued more than any other honour the degree that was conferred on him here and he spoke to me with pride and pleasure of walking, dressed in his scarlet gown, arm in arm with Dr Cartmell, the Master of Christ's College.

The Vice-Chancellor, A. J. Mason, wound up the banquet by reading the telegram to be sent to Alfred Russel Wallace: 'The naturalists assembled at Cambridge for the Darwin Celebration cannot forget your share in the great work which they commemorate and regret your inability to be present.'

Sir George Darwin's last public appearance was as president of the meeting at Cambridge of Mathematicians from 22 to 28 August 1912. Sir Joseph Larmor wrote in his obituary of G.H.D. in *Nature* (12 December 1912) that 'though obviously unwell during part of the meeting, he managed to discharge the delicate duties of chairman with conspicuous success and guided with great *verve* the deliberations of the assembly of what turned out to be a most successful meeting of that important body'. As soon, however, as the Congress was over, he took to his bed and lay there for days hardly speaking. He was only too rightly convinced that he was suffering from some form of malignant disease. It came almost as a relief to him, I think, when at last our doctor and friend, the surgeon Arthur Cooke, decided to make an exploratory operation. This took place at Newnham Grange, for until after the First World War those who could afford to pay for trained nursing almost always had their

Charles Darwin, from a photograph (1874?) by Captain Leonard Darwin,
R.E.   Engraved for the *Century Magazine*, January 1883
(note the small hands)

Sir George Darwin, by his daughter Gwen, *c.* 1908

operations or illnesses in their own home. Nursing homes or hospitals were not generally for them.

The operation revealed that he had cancer of the pancreas and nothing could be done to save him. He was only sixty-seven and he wanted to live, feeling his power of work and enjoyment of life was as strong as ever; also, as he told me later on, he had so wished to see us more 'settled in life' before he died. Gwen indeed had already made a happy marriage the year before and Charles had begun his scientific career well at Manchester as Schuster Reader in Mathematical Physics, but I was still at Oxford, reading history, and Billy was a schoolboy at Winchester. My father had hoped to live long enough to see his sons established in professions and all of us married with children of our own. He would have loved being a grandfather.

In order to be with him and help my mother I did not return to Somerville for the autumn term. Sometimes I read to him, as he rapidly grew too weak to do that for himself. I remember his once asking me to read him the leaders in *The Times* on the Balkan War, though he told me to skip through one of them, as it was too dull, but he took an interest in outside events almost to the end. Most of the time he lay quietly in bed, suffering much from nausea and other discomforts, though never, mercifully, from any bad pain. The days and nights were very long for him — and for us, as we watched him dying by inches. It soon became too great an effort for him even to see his oldest friends, though he was not too far gone to be touched and pleased when Arthur Balfour came from London and did see him. I remember Mr Balfour's tall figure with his sloping shoulders silhouetted against the bay windows of the drawing-room as he bent towards my mother, talking to her in a low voice about my father before going up to his room. Once, too, G.H.D. asked if Mrs Sidgwick would come and see him, not that he had anything he wanted to say to her, but he just wanted to see her once more. So she came down from Newnham to spend a few minutes with him, and he was satisfied. She was that kind of person; one felt strength coming from her, even though she did not say anything. His brother Frank wrote of George that

his nature was simple and direct with a pleasant residue of the innocence and eagerness of childhood. In the manner of his death these qualities were ennobled by an admirable and most unselfish courage. As his vitality ebbed away his affection only showed the stronger. He wished to live . . . but his resignation to the sudden end was complete and beautiful.

He lapsed into unconsciousness and died on 7 December 1912. The funeral was at Trinity with the customary long procession of black-gowned Fellows following the coffin round from the far side of the Great Court to the packed Chapel for the service. The burial, attended only by the family and a few old friends, was in the grave-yard at Trumpington where parishioners of St Botolph's Church are now buried.

When my father died, my mother was only fifty-one. He had left her the life interest in Newnham Grange and she remained there for the rest of her life: thirty-five years. She missed him terribly, not only because she was entirely devoted to him but also because, in spite of her independent spirit, she had relied upon him in all matters. She really believed him to be the wisest as well as the best of men. She had no head for business and was lost when it came to money matters; she had, however, a kind of mystic belief that if she kept strict cash accounts of her expenditure and was exceedingly economical, she would survive all the difficulties that beset her.

Newnham Grange was an expensive property to run and her income none too large for the task, especially as she was so hospitable; but she never contemplated leaving the house, even after the Second World War when domestic difficulties became so great. Newnham Grange was her life.

Some weeks after my father's death, she was persuaded to make a long visit to her family in America. Her parents had died in the nineties but she had a brother and sisters and many other relations and friends to see. It was hoped that the change of scene would help her to get through the first painful months of her bereavement and give her strength to face the dreary prospect of living at home without her husband. She was not, however, to be long on her own, because in June I returned home from Somerville for good. Like my sister Gwen, I had no wish to lead the idle and boring life of a young lady, but luckily a part-time job in the Boys' Employment Registry soon came my way.

This voluntarily run employment exchange, founded in 1907, deserves a mention, not only because it anticipated Beveridge's Labour Exchanges by two years but even more because of its connection with Eglantyne Jebb, long before she achieved world-wide fame in 1919 as the founder with her sister, Mrs C. R. Buxton, of the *Save the Children Fund.*

In 1907 Eglantyne Jebb, a niece of Sir Richard Jebb, the Professor of Greek, was living with her widowed mother in Cambridge. She had recently published an excellent survey of Cambridge charities, and this, as well as her friendship with Margaret Keynes, had brought her into contact with Margaret's mother, Mrs J. N. Keynes, the mother of Maynard and Geoffrey, who was herself the pioneer of much valuable social work in the town and, in 1914, the first woman to be elected to the Borough Council, becoming the Mayor of Cambridge in 1932.

For some time, Mrs Keynes had been wanting to do something about the future of boys in blind-alley jobs and to help promising boys into skilled trades or find them good permanent work. In 1907, she asked Eglantyne Jebb to assist her in setting up a Boys' Employment Registry of which Miss Jebb would be the first secretary. (When girls were included, in 1911, it was renamed the Juvenile Employment Registry.) Having spent eight months in giving the Boys' Registry a good start, Eglantyne Jebb resigned her post to return to more congenial literary work. She had persuaded Margaret Keynes to succeed her as honorary secretary and under Margaret's spirited if unorthodox management, the Registry flourished exceedingly; so much so that, a couple of years later, the Borough Education Committee took it over. This is not surprising, for their former Chairman, the Rev. C. A. E. Pollock, was also serving on the Juvenile Employment Committee as Chairman and took a great interest in its work among boys. Such close co-operation as then ensued between a purely voluntary committee and the local education authority is surely unusual.

Their first act was to install the Registry in a suitable room in the old Guildhall. Hitherto it had operated from 82 Regent Street, where Mrs Keynes had her Charity Organization Society office. It was of course an immense advantage for the Registry to be under the same roof and sponsored by the Education Authority, and later on, when the latter financed the Registry entirely, it set our small subscribed fund free to be spent on such things as outfits for needy applicants, or help with apprenticeship premiums. When in February 1911 the Labour Exchange was opened at Cambridge, it too co-operated with the Registry, notifying vacancies and dealing with all boys over seventeen whom we referred to them. The number of juveniles we dealt with increased greatly but not nearly so fast as did the number of vacancies: in 1913 there were 838 of these, far more than we could fill.

When I returned to Cambridge in 1913, Margaret Keynes, a family friend and later my sister-in-law, had given up her post as honorary secretary of the Cambridge Juvenile Employment Exchange on her marriage to A. V. Hill, the physiologist, in June 1913. She wanted me to succeed her in the boys' department. Miss C. L. Digby, a much-liked and experienced social worker, was honorary secretary for the girls; there was also a good (paid) secretary, Miss E. Sturton, to assist me with the boys. I had had some experience of the work already, as before I went to Oxford I had occasionally helped Margaret at the office. In the autumn I was duly appointed by the Committee, though I was a very poor substitute for her. I took up my work as honorary secretary later that year. The office by then had been moved to another room in the Guildhall where it led direct on to the pavement of Peas Hill. I still remember the icy draught which blew through the door when it was opened, or under the door when it was closed, but it was an excellent central address from which to work. What a small place Cambridge was in those days! Every shop seemed to employ an errand boy to deliver its goods on foot or on bicycle and I nearly achieved my ambition of getting to know by sight, if not by name, all the boys who worked within half a mile of the Market Place.

CHAPTER EIGHTEEN

Cambridge and the First World War: 1914–16

I W A S in Cambridge, still working at the Registry part-time, when the 1914 War began. I shall never forget the evening of Bank Holiday Monday, 3 August, when I accompanied my brother to the Union to hear the latest news come through on the ticker-tape. Sir Edward Grey had been making his famous speech in Parliament from which the declaration of war resulted at 11 o'clock next morning. The Union was packed with men, dons and undergraduates standing in complete silence to watch the fateful words being spelt out. Here was no glorification of war but dismay and horror unspeakable on every face.

I had spent the day in an agony of indecision trying to make up my mind whether our entry into the war could be justified. It was the invasion of Belgium that brought me to believe, as it did so many others, that the Germans must be stopped whatever the cost.

Within a few days the Sixth Division of the Regular Army began to assemble in and around Cambridge. It seemed that on every open site men were living under canvas. Before the mobilization was complete, however, we left Cambridge to join our Uncle William at Sedbergh in Yorkshire, where he had rented one of the School houses for our joint summer holiday. We were loath to leave home at such a time but there was nothing as yet that we could do to help the war effort. Charles was already in France as a Territorial postal censor; Billy was up north in training as a Second Lieutenant in the Durham Light Infantry; only Gwen and Jacques Raverat remained free to join us as arranged, Jacques still hopeful that he might prevail upon the authorities to take him on as interpreter in the French Army.

I mention our stay at Sedbergh because it was there we came into direct contact with the rumour which was about to spread like wildfire all over the country: it was that Russian soldiers were landing in the north in large numbers to join our forces. (That they arrived with snow still on their boots was a later improvement.) The rumour had just reached Sedbergh and we were told that if we

hurried down to the junction at once we should see trains full of the
Russians on their way south. So off we rushed to a point from which
we had a close view of the main railway line and there we hung about
for a good two hours, but in vain, for all that we saw were a few
passenger trains and, in those going south, not a glimpse of Russian
soldiers to be had, though how we should have recognized them as
such I cannot imagine, especially at the speed most of the trains
passed us.

We were far too anxious about the war to enjoy our Yorkshire
holiday and in our last week there our beloved Uncle William fell
suddenly ill. He was only seventy-four but the doctor, hastily
summoned, pronounced him completely worn out and he died the
next morning. Later on, although we missed him sadly, we were glad
to think he had not had to endure any more of the war.

When we returned home early in September we found that the
Sixth Division had left Cambridge, I believe for France, but that the
place was still full of soldiers and war-time traffic. Gun carriages
drawn by horses trotted past the house and army vehicles, sometimes
pulled by mules, helped to churn up the mud on the unasphalted
roads in wet weather. I remember a particularly revolting stretch of
liquid mud which was inches deep and remained opposite the Old
Granary for weeks. It made bicycling very tricky. I suppose it was
in the autumn of 1914 that wounded soldiers began to be sent to
Cambridge. The hospital trains always seemed to arrive in the late
evening. Ambulances were by then motorized; they constantly passed
Newnham Grange on their way by the Backs to the First Eastern
General Hospital. I remember sitting in the school-room listening
in misery to the sound of the ambulances passing the house. When they
succeeded each other at frequent intervals for some time I knew that
there must have been heavy fighting in Flanders or France.

The first Eastern General Hospital, or the Open Air Hospital, as
it was called at first in Cambridge, has an interesting history. It
started here as a Territorial unit of the R.A.M.C., intended to
expand into a General R.A.M.C. hospital in the event of war. The
skeleton staff, a number of whom were local doctors, were called up
on 5 August and at once set up a temporary hospital at the Leys
School in North House, empty for the school holidays. Here the first
patients were admitted, coming mainly from the Sixth Division; the

Hospital did not remain there long, however, as in September it was removed to much larger premises in Nevile's Court at Trinity. Two hundred and fifty beds were provided in wards under the Library and along the north cloister; these were left open, though awnings were provided to give some protection from the weather. The Hospital offices were in New Court and a temporary operating theatre and other offices were set up in the south-east corner of Nevile's Court. The Hospital remained here until, in March 1915, it moved into the hutted hospital built for it on the King's and Clare cricket-ground where the University Library now is.

The Hospital had every right to continue being called the Open Air Hospital, as one side of the wards – I assume the south side – was left open. Presumably on the analogy of the beneficial effect of fresh air on tuberculous patients, it was thought, as Florence Nightingale had believed in the Crimea, that fresh air might also help the recovery of wounded men. The Commanding Officer of the Hospital was Colonel Joseph Griffiths; in 1914 he had been the obvious choice, as he was both a Territorial officer and a surgeon on the staff of Addenbrooke's. I am told that he had an almost fanatical belief in the curative value of direct sunlight and if he had a hand in the design of the wards, this might have been one of the reasons they were left open to the sun and air. The Hospital remained open-sided for nearly two years, the nursing and medical staff suffering even more from the draughts and terrible cold than did the patients tucked up in bed, but at last the authorities were persuaded to have the open sides glassed in, to the immense relief of everyone concerned, and the hospital gradually lost its name of the Open Air Hospital.

Our first encounter with Belgian refugees led to a most extra-ordinary coincidence. Soon after the fall of Antwerp the Belgian Refugee Committee in Cambridge were told to expect a large number of refugees. This must have been in October 1914. My mother offered to help the Committee by providing luncheon for a dozen refugees on their reaching Cambridge. This was before rationing had begun and our cook, Mrs Phillips, could be relied upon to give them an excellent and substantial meal. I remember seeing the party in the kitchen passage on their arrival. They were a group of heavily built elderly men and women all looking very respectable and Flemish in their warm overcoats, but also very much depressed and worried. However, they were also extremely hungry and ate up everything set before them in dead silence—at least I heard no sound issuing from the room next the kitchen in which they were dining. When the meal was over I went down to talk to them and finding that they all seemed to understand and speak some English I did not use my French. This was just as well, as I was told afterwards that the French language was anathema to Flemish-speaking Belgians.

I began by asking them from where they came; 'Antwerp' was their reply. I then told them that, though I had never been there myself, I had had an old Uncle who used to enjoy going to Antwerp to attend board meetings of the Antwerp Water Works Company, the company being British and he one of the directors. 'What was his name?' they asked. 'Mr William Darwin', I replied. 'He was rather a small old man with white hair and a rosy face and walked with a stick.' At this the men exclaimed that they were all employees of the Antwerp Water Works and had known him well. The ice was broken, and when they left to be assigned their new homes, they looked distinctly the better, not only for their dinner, but also for having met the niece of someone whom they had occasionally seen at Antwerp.

Our next encounter with Belgians occurred on 2 November 1914, when the Committee asked my mother to put up two young Belgians who had escaped to England to join some military force here. As far as I remember, the Belgian Embassy had sent them to Cambridge to stay until such time as this could be arranged for them. They were well-mannered nice young men but very home-sick and unhappy.

Cambridge was still trying to lead its normal life and the Gilbert and Sullivan company was giving its annual performance at the New Theatre (long since pulled down) in Regent Street. Thinking to entertain the poor boys and keep their minds off the war, my mother and I took them on their third evening to see *The Mikado*. They knew little English and were utterly bewildered by the performance. They evidently thought the audience quite mad to be amused by such a silly light opera at this time of public anxiety. They grew increasingly gloomy and I was ashamed at our having subjected them to so unsuitable an entertainment. However, the very next morning they were summoned to London and we never saw or heard from them again until the following September when one of them sent us a photograph of himself in a Belgian uniform, looking much older and even more serious than when we had last seen him. On the back of the photograph he had written his name: Antoine della Faille d'Huysse, and his home address: Château de Deurle les Cand, Belgique, adding: 'En souvenir de mon passage à Cambridge, le 2, 3 et 4 Novembre 1914.'

It was probably soon after these young men had stayed with us that my mother made a home at Newnham Grange for a Belgian widow and her small boy. Madame de Schietere de Lophem had escaped from Brussels in a farm wagon with her five-year-old son, Fernand-Ulric, concealed among bundles of hay like the little Duke escaping from France, in Charlotte Yonge's book. (All well-brought-up late-Victorian children were reared on *The Little Duke.*)

It was a pity that Madame de Lophem knew no English and made no effort to learn any, as this made her a dull companion for my mother, but Madame was a polite amiable lady and took good care of Fernand-Ulric, except, I thought, in the way she taught him religion. I remember once listening in amazement to her putting him through his Catechism (in French, mercifully not in Latin). He must merely have learnt most of the answers required of him by heart, repeating them parrot-like to his mother, for no child could possibly have understood the intricate theological and dogmatic questions propounded to him.

They only stayed with us for two or three months, as my mother became increasingly annoyed by Madame de Lophem's refusal to do any form of war-work, preferring to stay comfortably waited upon at home to making the slightest effort. At last my mother could bear her idleness no longer and asked the Committee to find her another home. She departed, however, on perfectly friendly terms with us, probably unaware of the exasperation she had been causing my mother.

My mother-in-law, Mrs Keynes, in her book *Gathering Up the Threads*, wrote about the refugee Belgians in Cambridge as follows:

They provided difficult problems throughout the war. They were of all grades and all classes, from University professors and their families to fisher folk from the coast, and were no more willing to overlook social distinctions in exile than in their own country. A separate committee fortunately undertook the arrangements for the University section and eventually a miniature Belgian University with its own professors and students was successfuly formed under the aegis of the University of Cambridge.

Its chief object was to enable Belgian students, either those under age or those not medically fit for military service, to complete a course of university training.

The Belgian University Committee was headed by Mrs Verrall, the widow of Professor Verrall, and Mrs Tilley, wife of A. A. Tilley, Lecturer in Modern Languages, a Fellow of King's since 1876. They were given a room in Gibbs Building at King's for their office; this was probably not so much because of Mrs Tilley's connection with the College as because the then Provost, M. R. James, took a keen interest in the University of Belgium, and as Vice-Chancellor in 1914 and 1915 carried on much correspondence with the Belgian Ambassador about the affairs of the new war-time University.

My cousin Ruth Darwin (later Mrs W. Rees-Thomas) spent most of her time in the early part of the war at the office in Gibbs Building, helping to establish the miniature University. She remembers sometimes looking out of the window and seeing the foreign lads walking across the sacred grass precincts. The old Porter was grieved to the heart. He shook his head over their impenetrable stupidity: 'These young foreign gentlemen,' he said, 'they don't know the difference between right and wrong.'

There were some delightful people among the University Belgians. I remember in particular the Dejace family from Liège where Monsieur Dejace was a Professor of Law. His elder daughter, Manette (long since Madame Paul van Gehuchten), has written me a short account of how she, with her parents and younger sister, came to live in Cambridge. Both her brothers remained at military camps in Northern France as volunteers training for the Belgian army.

Early in August 1914, the Dejace family had left their country house in the neighbourhood of the Liège forts to seek safety near the Belgian coast. In September, M. Dejace decided to accept the generous invitation from Oxford and Cambridge to all Belgian professors to come over and make their homes at one or other of the two universities for the duration of the war. In contrast to the great difficulties of communication during the last war, how easily the two countries seemed to communicate with each other in the First World War. In October 1914 when the Dejaces migrated to England, they came comparatively comfortably and safely by Ostend and Folkestone. On their arrival at Cambridge, the Belgian University Committee provided them temporarily first with lodgings near the Round Church and then with a furnished house until they moved into 57 Bateman Street where they remained for the rest of their time in Cambridge.

One of Manette's early memories of her sojourn is of a party for the Belgian colony given on 15 November by the Committee at the Red Lion Hotel in Petty Cury to celebrate the Belgian King's birthday. Manette, a good musician, was immediately installed at the piano to play the accompaniments to the Brabançonne and other patriotic Belgian or Flemish songs the loyal company were to sing.

I remember later on going to another Belgian social gathering at the Red Lion where the proprietor, Mrs Moyes, always seemed glad to let her room in a good cause, I believe at a special low rate. It is some years since the Red Lion Hotel was demolished but the name of Lion Yard still persists as the name of the Civic Centre and its multi-storeyed car-park.

From the very beginning of the Belgian University at Cambridge, Professor Dejace was regarded as its Rector, so when he heard that Professor Arthur van Gehuchten had arrived at Oxford it was he who at once telegraphed to the neurologist to beg him to transfer to Cambridge. They urgently needed more professors from different faculties to lecture to the students under military age, who were joining the university in numbers. Professor van Gehuchten agreed to come, especially as Professor Langley undertook to supply him with laboratory facilities for his research. It was a grievous blow to all who knew van Gehuchten and his work when, only a few weeks after his arrival, he fell suddenly ill and died a few days later at the Research Hospital.

His son Paul had been fighting in the Battle of the Yser as a volunteer with the Belgian Army when, on account of his father's grave illness, he was recalled and sent over to Cambridge. He

arrived however only in time for the funeral. He did not return to
the army afterwards, as special arrangements were made for him to
continue his pre-medical training at the First Eastern General
Hospital. This enabled him to qualify after a few months. He
rejoined the Army as a doctor early in 1916. After the war he became
a neurologist like his father and has ever since played a leading part
in the development of neurological science in Brussels.

In 1919, he and Manette Dejace were married in Belgium but
their marriage remains closely connected with Cambridge since it
was there they first met and there that they became engaged. 'In
spite of the sadness of the war', Manette writes, 'we shall always
think of Cambridge and of the friends we met there with affection
and gratitude.'

It was some time after the departure of Madame de Lophem and
Fernand-Ulric in the winter of 1915 that my mother undertook to
make a home for the two youngest daughters of my cousin Josiah
Wedgwood, during his absence abroad serving in the Gallipoli
campaign. My mother was always at her best with small children
and especially enjoyed the company of Betsinda, aged eight, and
Gloria, aged six, as they were entertaining little girls and the actual
care of them did not devolve on her, because their nurse came with
them. Their eldest sister Helen (later Mrs Michael Pease) was in
her second year at Newnham and could also keep an eye on them.
They remained with us for some months.

Josiah Wedgwood, in 1914 a Lieutenant-Commander with the
R.N.V.R., had been on friendly terms with Winston Churchill in
the House of Commons before the war, and now that Churchill was
First Lord of the Admiralty, they kept in close touch with each
other. Wedgwood highly approved of Churchill's plan to take
Gallipoli; it was just the kind of daring enterprise that appealed
to him. He was therefore delighted when Churchill sent him to the
future scene of battle with the Naval Brigade. He was to start by
helping to prepare the wreck-ship *River Clyde* for use in the landing
on V Beach at Gallipoli. On 24 April 1915 he began writing a letter
to Churchill from Sedd el Bahr with a full account of the disastrous

landing. In the later fighting on Gallipoli he was himself severely wounded on 6 May. Churchill had the news telegraphed at once to Helen Wedgwood at Newnham.

Some days after she had received this telegram, Helen burst into the drawing-room at Newnham Grange one afternoon to show us a note that had just arrived from Churchill enclosing a copy of the long letter her father had written him on 24–7 April. It is a wonderful letter, detailed and down to earth yet glowing with the account of the heroic deeds he had witnessed during and after the landing, and burning with sympathy for the terrible ordeal of the wounded whom they could not save but had to leave, many to drown in the shallow sea within sight and hearing of the *River Clyde*. He tells how after dark for three hours he stood on the end of a spit of rock in two foot of water, helping the heavily laden men jump ashore on the submerged dead bodies, monotonously repeating: 'Give me your rifle, and your shovel', 'Your left hand, jump wide', 'It's all right, only the kits', 'Keep clear of that man's legs, can't you?'. He ends his letter by saying 'I am going to lie down and sleep, the first sleep for three eternal days and nights.'

I have never forgotten the impression this letter made on me, coming hot from Gallipoli.* It was all the more poignant because barely two weeks before, on 23 April, Rupert Brooke had died on his way to Gallipoli with the Naval Division, and my cousin Erasmus, only son of Horace and Ida Darwin, had been killed near Ypres the day after. Reading the appalling list of casualties in *The Times* had become a daily terror lest it contained the names of friends or acquaintances, as it so often did.

My recollections of 1915 nearly all relate to Cambridge in wartime. However, I have found a correspondence between the Town Clerk and my mother written in this year, but which might have occurred in any other. Here is a draft of her letter (printed with the omission of a few redundancies):

---

* It is printed in full in Josiah Wedgwood's autobiography, *Memoirs of Fighting* (1942), as well as in Dame Veronica Wedgwood's biography of her uncle: *The Last of the Radicals* (1951).

10 July 1915   Newnham Grange.
                                                   Cambridge.

Dear Sir,

I am writing to ask you kindly to bring before the proper
Committee the following question. Is it possible for them to
regulate the weight of the steam and motor traffic that passes my
house?

During the last month or so a steam engine drawing three
trucks has passed, often every day twice, carrying paving stones in
two of three trucks. The name plate on the truck is Cherry
Hinton. The weight is so great that it not only must be very bad for
the bridge but it is very bad for my property. It shakes my house
and makes everything tremble. In the Old Granary, I am told the
pictures swing out from the wall. Would it be possible to have
only one truck hauled at a time? Otherwise could a regulation be
made to reduce the speed? When the bridge is reached and the
road becomes broader, speed is put on for the rest of the way. The
engines and trucks certainly do harm to the tarred road. There is
not much tar left. I wish also to ask if the motor buses that pass can
be made to go slower? They are very heavy; they go fast enough
to shake my house. On their return to the town they are compelled
to keep nearer to my side of the road because the boughs of the trees
growing beside the road would brush the faces of the passengers
on top of the bus. I ask that these boughs should be removed. I
could let my gardener do it. One of these trees in the autumn might
be cut down as it is preventing the younger trees behind it from
growing into a good shape.

My mother's remark about the 'trees brushing the faces of the
passengers' is a reminder that for years the two-decker motor buses
had no roofs over them. It was not until the end of the twenties, I
think, that covered buses were introduced in London and possibly a
little later in Cambridge. Passengers riding on the top deck found the
roof a boon in cold or wet weather, but in fine weather to sit on top
of an uncovered bus tearing through the streets of London (particularly along Piccadilly past Green Park) was a most exhilarating
experience.

My mother's mention of the trees growing beside the road refers
to a few old gnarled limes which grew opposite Newnham Grange

and the Hermitage on a bank between the road and the path along-side Queens' Green. Eventually all these trees were removed and a kerb replaced the untidy but grassy little bank with its scattered lime trees.

The Town Clerk replied politely three days later. He said that as the use of locomotives on highways was regulated by statute, he could not help her about the steam engine, since what it was doing was legal. He recommended her to write to the Manager of the Bus Company who would bring the matter of the trees before the Paving, Drainage, and Lighting Committee but some time ago when the Committee had 'contemplated the removal of some of the old trees next to the roadway. . . the proposition seemed to meet with so much disapproval on the part of those resident in the neighbourhood that . . . the Committee were led to modify their views'. So it appears that my mother's letter to the Town Clerk was written in vain.

It was the opening of Fen Causeway in 1926 which altered the flow of traffic past Newnham Grange. Through-traffic was no longer dependent on Silver Street Bridge, as it could now cross the river by the Fen Causeway instead of Silver Street. The City Surveyor believes there was some restriction in the use of Silver Street during the years before the Second World War, and in 1952 an order was made prohibiting the use of Silver Street Bridge by vehicles in excess of 2 tons. This was because Silver Street Bridge was wearing out, and a grand stone bridge, designed by Lutyens, was to be built to replace the old iron one. The new bridge, capable of taking any weight, was opened in 1959 and the ban on Silver Street was removed. However, by then Queen's Road and Fen Causeway had for so long been the sign-posted and recognized main road for through traffic, that little, if any, heavy traffic has returned to Silver Street. Hence the cessation of the minor earthquakes in Newnham Grange and the Old Granary. But even so, it will be a happy day for Darwin College when the Backs are no longer used as a by-pass to Cambridge.

By 1915, the Juvenile Employment Exchange and its predecessor had been running successfully for nearly eight years, and I had no scruple in leaving it in the competent hands of the paid secretary so that I could take up massage as my form of war-work.

The artist, Miss Mary Greene of Harston, whose drawing classes we had attended as children with such profit and enjoyment (see *Period Piece*), had a much younger sister, Helen, who was well-known in Cambridge both for her Swedish gymnastic classes and for her excellent massage.* In those days massage consisted mostly of rubbing, with the addition of remedial exercises, especially if, like Helen, the masseuse had also been trained as a gymnast. Massage was in much greater demand during the First World War than it is now, when so many other far more effective forms of physiotherapy are available.

Early in 1915, the Red Cross opened a small convalescent home for wounded soldiers at St Chad's, a house in Grange Road near the Open Air Hospital, as it was still familiarly called. Helen Greene was put in charge of the massage. She soon found herself in such urgent need of help that she began training some educated Cambridge women to act as her assistants. One or two of the younger members like myself had once attended her gymnastic classes. After I joined the other trainees in the spring of 1915 we numbered about seven.

She gave her corps some preliminary instruction in the technique and French nomenclature of massage; the only two names I now recall are *effleurage* and *petrissage*. After telling us the Latin names of the principal bones in the body and how they function, she bade us teach ourselves as much anatomy as we could, as she had no time to give us regular anatomical lessons herself. I managed to get hold of a second-hand copy of Gray's *Anatomy* and enjoyed learning something of the subject. I felt greatly privileged later on when I was allowed to examine pickled human muscles and their attachment to bones in

* Helen Greene (1870–1960) was in many ways a remarkable woman. She was the youngest sister of Sir Graham Greene, K.C.B., Permanent Secretary to the Admiralty 1911–1917. (Graham Greene the novelist is their nephew.) She was the favourite pupil of Madame Bergman-Österberg, the Swede who introduced Swedish gymnastics into England, at Hampstead in 1885. Ten years later, Madame Österberg founded her College of Physical Education at Dartford where it still flourishes, but since 1947 it no longer teaches massage. Helen Greene was Principal of the College from 1917–1920/21. After her resignation, she returned to Harston where the Greene family had made the red-brick William and Mary Harston House their home since 1891. She devoted the rest of her long life to social work. In 1922 she produced the first of three Harston Pageants, all of which proved most successful. She died aged ninety at Harston in Orchard Cottage where she had lived with her friend and companion, Miss Marie Hall, for the last twenty-one years of her life.

Looking along the Old Granary wall to Lutyens's Silver Street Bridge

Margaret Darwin, by Gwen Raverat, *c.* 1910

the almost empty School of Anatomy, though it put me off eating mutton for some time. I say 'almost empty' because nearly all the undergraduates who would normally have been there, had either joined the Forces or had gone to London to qualify as doctors as quickly as possible.

My remarkably brief introduction to massage over, I began work immediately at St Chad's. Miss Greene demonstrated on the patient himself what the treatment should be, after which I was left to carry out her instructions as best I could under her occasional supervision. No doubt she always kept the difficult cases to treat herself and only let us loose on the limbs of such wounded men as we could not further injure.

I liked making friends with my patients. I remember a splendid-looking young Scottish miner in particular because of the intensity of the pride he took in his calling and his great wish that his own small son should follow him in the family profession. The men at St Chad's were on the whole a cheerful lot, most of them with Blighty* wounds severe enough to ensure that they would never be sent on active service again. There was however one unhappy Sergeant, by name Purdey, whom I cannot forget. He was a man of great natural dignity who never complained but was so profoundly depressed by his war experiences and the fact that he was losing his sense of hearing that nothing I said or did could cheer him. I only hope he realized my sympathy, as I rubbed his shoulder week after week.

I had been doing massage for about a year when Miss Greene resigned her post at St Chad's; I believe she feared a breakdown in her health if she continued working so hard. But she must have recovered, for the following year she accepted the strenuous post of Principal of Madame Bergman-Österberg's College of Physical Education at Dartford. It was lucky that she had, as partner in her gymnasium and massage practice, an able young Swede called Signe Lavèn, willing and competent to carry on the training of the assistant masseuses at at St Chad's.

Before Miss Greene finally handed over to Miss Lavèn, the Incorporated Society of Trained Masseuses came to inspect our

* 'Blighty', an army slang name for England or home, was derived from a Hindi word. A 'blighty wound' indicated a wound severe enough for its victim to be sent to hospital at home.

unorthodox School of Massage. I had just forsaken massage myself to take up work at the Admiralty, but was still in Cambridge when the inspection took place on 6 May 1916. I was handing over my place to a young connection of mine, Kitty Farrer, who had been living at the Orchard with her aunt, Mrs Horace Darwin, helping her cousin Ruth with arrangements for the Belgian Refugee University; and I had to see Miss Greene about the arrangements for her to replace me. I happened to arrive at St Chad's just as the inspection was over. Miss Greene introduced me to the senior of the two examiners,* a stout and formidable lady, explaining that I had resigned to take up other work. She was in the act of shaking hands with me but promptly dropped my hand, exclaiming, 'but this is no hand for a masseuse! What *she* needs is a wide strong hand with broad fingers' — like her own, she implied, not like my narrow Darwin hands with their long bony fingers.† So it was just as well that I was giving up massage, since my own anatomy was so ill-fitted for the job. Apart from this defect, the Inspectors approved of the school.

I was delighted when Kitty Farrer proved to be one of Miss Lavèn's successes, especially as it was I who had been largely responsible for her having taken up massage. In 1917, though still under age, she sat the I.S.T.M. examination successfully from Cambridge and followed it up with a three-month course in the theory and practice of Medical Electricity at Guy's Hospital. She ended the war working at a Red Cross Hospital at Royston as a fully qualified masseuse.

In 1922, she married Edward Bridges (later Lord Bridges and Secretary to the Cabinet during the last war) and so it was not only

* The I.S.T.M. did not teach massage themselves but set examination papers in the subject and issued qualifying certificates. A few teaching hospitals in London besides Guy's may by this time have had courses in massage and held their own examinations, as did Dartford College until it gave up teaching massage in 1947.

† This was the second occasion on which my hands might have disrupted my career. At Levana, the boarding school near Wimbledon to which I was sent in 1905, the elocution teacher was Miss Elsie Fogarty. This must have been long before she founded her famous Dramatic School. Every three years she produced a Shakespeare play at Levana. In 1906, it was *Love's Labour's Lost*. I was cast as Costard the Clown, perhaps because of my healthy appearance. All went well until at the dress rehearsal she noticed my Darwin hands, so totally unsuitable for a rustic clown. All she could do at this, the eleventh hour, was to bid me keep them out of sight as far as possible. The play was otherwise a great success.

because of her relationship to the Horace Darwins that she is connected with Darwin College but still more on account of her marriage. It was Lord Bridges, as Chairman of the Syndicate on the Relationship between the University and the Colleges, who most strongly recommended the setting-up of Graduate Colleges. I know from Lady Bridges that he took a very special interest in Darwin College as the first to be founded at Cambridge. I was looking forward to giving him a copy of this book, but I have been too slow in its writing, as he died in 1969.

CHAPTER NINETEEN

The Admiralty and Room 40: 1916–17

ONE Sunday afternoon in the spring of 1916 when Sir Alfred Ewing, then Principal of Edinburgh University,* was spending a week-end at Cambridge, he called unexpectedly for tea at Newnham Grange. He had been a friend of both my parents ever since 1890, when he first came to the University as Professor of Mechanics and Applied Mechanics, but in 1903 had left Cambridge to take up an appointment as Director of Naval Education. The Admiralty had chosen him as the right man to reform the antiquated education of naval officers by introducing practical science and engineering into their training. This reform completed, and most of the boys over fifteen being on active service, Sir Alfred Ewing, though still D.N.E., was now occupied in the Admiralty on some top secret work — it had to do with wireless, we believed.

My irrepressible mother at once began to cross-question him about his present job, but with his quick wit and characteristic twinkle he soon routed her. Then some other callers arrived and the conversation became general.

After tea, Sir Alfred drew me aside and put me through a brief examination. First, he asked me how good was my knowledge of German? (He knew that in 1907 I had spent three months in Berlin staying with Freifrau von Richthofen in order to learn German.) I said I could still speak and read German fairly well. He appeared satisfied with my answer but his next question was more surprising: How good was I at our favourite family game of Word-making and Word-taking? I replied that of course I had often played it but never

---

* Sir Alfred Ewing, K.C.B., F.R.S., born at Dundee 1855. Won engineering scholarship at Edinburgh. Held professorships in engineering at Tokyo and Dundee before he came to Cambridge in 1890 as Professor of Mechanics. Later Fellow of King's. Director of Naval Education 1903. Started deciphering enemy wireless 'intercepts' on 4 August, 1914, and soon after organised Room 40 for the work. Principal of Edinburgh University 1916. Retired to Cambridge 1929 and died there in 1935. Phenomenally successful in every post he ever held.

with the diabolical proficiency of Gwen or Charles. His final question went something like this: Could I keep a secret that was so secret that to keep it, one had to pretend there was no real secret at all? I said I thought I could as long as I understood what it was that I had to keep so secret. He thereupon asked me if I would like to take a job at the Admiralty which he was sure I should find interesting, but he could not tell me what it was until I had accepted it. He gave me a couple of weeks to think it over but I never had any hesitation in accepting his offer. I was sorry to drop massage but I was not advanced enough in my training to be a loss to the team, nor, with my unsuitable hands, should I ever have made a good masseuse. So, in the second week of May 1916, I began work as a very minor civil servant in London.

My office was not in the Admiralty but nearly opposite it in a narrow building above a shop, where the existence of a small office run by a woman was not likely to arouse the suspicion of enemy spies. This was vital, as at all costs the Germans must not know that we could read—or were attempting to read—their codes. The secret was kept so well that it was not until some time after the war that the German Foreign Office was surprised to learn that this was exactly what we had been doing throughout the war. They thought that the French might have been reading some of their codes, but not the British—we were too stupid—so, as Sir Alfred put it, the British reputation for stupidity was an invaluable asset to us.

We had strict injunctions from Sir Alfred not to tell anyone where our office was. I remember one absurd occasion when Jim Butler took me out to lunch and, not being in a hurry to return to his work at the War Office, said he would accompany me back. I could not think how to shake him off until, in desperation, as we were walking down Whitehall, I told him that I must try and get a cake for the office tea and, wishing him a hasty goodbye, plunged into a con-fectioner's shop nearby, where I remained in hiding until he was safely out of sight.

On becoming a temporary civil servant attached to Naval Intelligence, I had to go over to the Admiralty to sign a formidable document, or book, in which in my excitement I thought I read that I should be hung, drawn and quartered did I betray any Govern-ment secrets—but I must have imagined this, for old-fashioned as the wording of the document was, I cannot believe it was quite so archaic as that.

The office was run by Miss Greta Robertson, a delightful middle-aged woman who had been up at Oxford and had first-class brains. She was in some way related to the Bismarck family and was bilingual in German and English. When I joined the office, the staff under her numbered only three or four women, two of them wives of young men employed in the Foreign Office. Early in August 1914, Sir Alfred had given instructions to our wireless stations that all enemy messages should be intercepted and sent to the Admiralty for deciphering. If the telegrams were in one or other of the two *Hat* ciphers with which our office dealt, they were to be sent on to us.

Hat ciphers were so-called because the 4-figure groups of which they consisted were apparently chosen at random, like lots picked haphazard out of a hat. Each name, word, syllable or letter had to be guessed separately since there was no kind of system in their selection. I remember my secret pride when I discovered a hitherto unread group for *Konsul* in Code 0053 and proved my guess correct by referring to other messages on our index cards where the group occurred and the word *Konsul* obviously fitted.

Early in 1917 we were moved out of our humble office in Whitehall to better premises on top of the Admiralty, where an additional wooden storey had been built on the roof to provide more offices. The view of London over the Horse Guards was splendid and I enjoyed feeling that I now really belonged to the Admiralty. It was interesting, too, to have a chance of seeing important naval people. I remember the Director of Naval Intelligence, Sir Reginald Hall, coming up to join our office tea on two or three occasions: once he was accompanied by Captain William James, R.N. The office was agog to see him because we all knew Millais' painting of him as Bubbles from the Pears Soap advertisement, in which he appears as a beautiful fair-haired child in green velvet, blowing bubbles.

Soon, however, the process now known as Parkinson's Law began to operate: a couple of girls were added to our staff though we were not aware of needing more help, and presently two dons from Cambridge appeared: Ernest Harrison, Fellow of Trinity and future Registrary of the University, and (Sir) Frank Adcock, Lay-Dean of King's and later Professor of Ancient History. They had been

THE ADMIRALTY AND ROOM 40: 1916–17   199

working in the Admiralty, presumably as cryptographers, since 1915, and came up occasionally from an office below to see Miss Robertson in an advisory capacity. Our work was reorganised on rather more scientific lines, so that our index cards multiplied till we felt more and more like human machines. Gone were the exciting days when the breaking of the *Hat* codes depended so much on inspired guessing.

I do remember, however, the satisfaction I felt when Miss Robertson gave me a few of the old *Lusitania* letters to work on in our new office. They were in the *Hat* cipher 0064 which our fore-runners had been breaking in 1914–15 and we in our Whitehall office had continued working on, until it was almost completely solved. My job was, I think, to redecipher the letters with the use of our constantly revised index cards in the hope of filling in some of the few remaining blanks.

These letters had been discovered on the *Lusitania* concealed among goods being exported to the U.S.A., and were sent to the Admiralty for deciphering. They were addressed to Count Bern-storff, the German Ambassador at Washington, and were political in character, coming from Zimmermann, the German Foreign Secretary. (Our wireless intercepts were also often signed Zimmer-mann in clear.) I remember hearing that the revelation of the content of these would-be smuggled-in letters had done as much to bring America into the war as the sinking of the *Lusitania* on 7 May 1915.

The reason that I so enjoyed revising these letters was because the groups of figures were so clearly and accurately typed in black on sheets of thin white paper, unlike those hasty scrawls of wireless operators on telegraph forms, with which we usually had to deal. When the wireless intercepts were headed 'Fierce Jammings' or marked with a row of crosses — XXXXX — we knew that we could not rely on the accuracy of the figures and that some of the groups might have been missed altogether. Such warnings were generally unnecessary, for by then we had become so familiar with the chief groups in the two *Hat* ciphers that we could tell at a glance if there were faults in the transmission. Indeed, we could often correct a wrong figure in a group without having to refer to the index cards. It was only on rare occasions that we had the luck to work on telegrams from Mulay Hafid, the Sultan of Morocco: one I remember particularly enjoying was when he demanded a First Class Iron Cross instead of the Second Class one that he had been awarded.

Our familiarity with the groups was of great service to us in our first Whitehall office when on one occasion Miss Robertson was away ill, and the task of decoding the day's intercepts fell on our senior member, Frances Orde. We looked in dismay at the apparent gibberish sent us to decipher, unable to recognise a single group. We knew that sometimes the Germans *keyed* their messages by shuffling the numbers, retaining only one figure the same as in the unkeyed code. We assumed rightly that this is what they had done to our 0064 code that day. So Mrs Orde and I set out to discover what the key was. By then we knew the kind of things that the wireless telegrams would say. Out-going ones would be from Zimmermann probably giving instructions to his consuls in neutral countries; in-going ones would be demands from the consuls for more money, presumably to pay the spies.

At long intervals we consulted each other to see if either of us had made any lucky guesses to be put to the test — it was all a matter of trial and error. By tea-time, however, we were triumphant, able to un-key the groups and decipher the messages which now made sense. They were delivered to the Admiralty as usual that evening. Mrs Orde and I were exhausted but happy: I thought we might even be thanked by the Admiralty for our achievement. Next day Miss Robertson returned to work and Mrs Orde reported what we had done — only to be told that the Admiralty knew the German method of keying their codes and if we had enquired they would have supplied us with the key. So we got no kudos at all for it; but I still think it was rather a praiseworthy effort on our part.

Although an account of my time at the Admiralty and in Room 40 may seem quite irrelevant to the history of Newnham Grange, I have included it because it was entirely due to Sir Alfred Ewing that I went to work at the Admiralty. He was the creator of the mysterious Room 40, staffed by so many Cambridge men that its connection with the University must have been very close. I have no means of checking my recollections of my time in the Admiralty: with one exception I depend on my memory throughout; but I am always surprised to find how accurately I remember events in my early life when I find evidence with which to compare them.

I still have a feeling of guilt when referring to Room 40, but A. W. Ewing has revealed so much about his father's work at the Admiralty in his book *The Man of Room 40: The Life of Sir Alfred Ewing* (1939) that there can be no need left for secrecy. Many others have written about Ewing, not least Winston Churchill in *The World Crisis, 1911–1918*, where he says that Ewing's 'services to the Admiralty were of the first order'. Churchill had watched the development of Room 40 with constant interest and did much to foster it.

The *Dictionary of National Biography* summarizes the beginning and early years of Room 40, as follows:

On the day of the outbreak of war in 1914 Ewing was asked by Rear-Admiral (Sir) H. F. Oliver, then director of the intelligence division of the naval staff, to decipher some wireless 'intercepts' from German stations, there being no department to which to refer them. This was the beginning of 'Room 40' in the Old Buildings of the Admiralty where the task of deciphering the German messages under Ewing's supervision was facilitated by the opportune discovery in 1914 of the 'highly confidential' Signal book of the German navy in the arms of a drowned signalman of the *Magdeburg*. . . . The breaking of other codes besides that of the Signal book was proceeding simultaneously and when successful led to the arrest of Roger Casement, the loss of his armament off Tralee and the revelation of the Zimmermann telegrams with their effect on the policy of the United States of America.

Casement was landed from a German submarine on the Kerry coast in April 1916; he was arrested by the police and taken to London on 24 April. It was a fortnight later that I began work at the Whitehall office and some time afterwards learnt from colleagues that it was Code 0064 (on which we were working) that had been used by Zimmermann in his interchange of telegrams with Casement. The interception of these messages led to Casement's arrest; this was effected by the police because if the Navy had acted, the German Foreign Office might have suspected that we were reading their code-telegrams. The necessity of keeping our code-breaknig secret constantly hampered us in taking desirable actions against the enemy. After Germany was blockaded it became increasingly hard for the Germans to use fresh codes owing to the difficulty of distributing new code books to their foreign stations.

The *Lusitania* letters from Zimmermann to Count Bernstorff were also in this code which seemed to be constantly employed for political messages. Later another *Hat* code, 0053, came into use and we worked on it as well, but I never became as familiar with 0053 as I did with 0064 — there were still too many blanks in its index cards. Little can be more frustrating than trying to decode a message when there is almost nothing but unguessed figure-groups to be seen on the paper.

One morning in June 1917, Miss Robertson told me to go down to Room 40 where they were in urgent need of extra help. An appalling thing had happened: the Germans had suddenly changed their Naval code from one which we could read, to one of which we could not read one single word. If the German High Seas Fleet were to emerge from its safe retreat in the Heligoland Bight before we could read the new code, it would be disastrous.

I was lucky even to have set foot in Room 40, the Holy of Holies, but luckier still, as I afterwards realised, to have been there in such a time of crisis. I entered the lofty square room apprehensively, but no one took any notice of me at first. Five or six young men were sitting at two tables working with entire concentration on intercepted wireless messages. No one spoke; the feeling of tension in the room was extraordinary. This department, dealing with the Naval code, seemed to be run almost entirely by Cambridge dons: two at least were Fellows of King's — Frank Birch and A. D. (Dilly) Knox, a friend of my recently acquired brother-in-law, Maynard Keynes. I remember my surprise when I found that the code they were trying to break was not a *Hat* code like ours but only became 'readable' once the rules governing the cipher could be discovered. My job, as far as I can remember, was to copy out guesses and keep them tabulated in some kind of order. The appalling thing for me was that these young academics were using the Greek alphabet to distinguish their categories and I did not know it! So I spent the next days trying to learn the Greek alphabet during the lunch hour.

Luckily for me they did not seem to get much further than delta, so I got through without disgracing myself nor my gross ignorance having been found out.

I had only been working in Room 40 for a very few days when a Zeppelin was shot down on 17 June at Theberton near the Suffolk coast. Next morning, soon after work had begun at the office, a very weary, unshaven Admiralty messenger walked in. He had been despatched the night before to Theberton to see if he could recover any fragment of the new code book from the still smouldering carcase of the Zeppelin. Out of his black satchel he drew a small charred piece of white cardboard and handed it in dead silence to the senior man in the room. The few printed words still legible on it, with their accompanying groups of figures, were enough to show that the guess-work in Room 40 had been on the right lines; and the new code book could now be quickly made up with the help of this evidence — the only fragment of the German code book that the messenger could find. I have never known a more dramatic moment. The relief felt by all present was indescribable. This is the one incident I have been able to verify. I remembered that it happened in June 1917. After searching through a long list of *German Naval Airships 1912–1918*, Mr Loukes, the assistant librarian of King's, found the only entry of a Zeppelin destroyed in England in 1917 was of the L.48 'Destroyed by British aircraft at Theberton, Suffolk, 17.6.1917'.

Shortly after this, I was returned to my own department as I was no longer needed, and I never went near Room 40 again.

CHAPTER TWENTY

The War: 1916–17

AFTER I went up to work in London, my mother continued living quietly at Newnham Grange; she was no longer required to put up Belgian refugees but instead she made homes for relatives whose husbands or fathers were abroad fighting, or invited old friends in need of a change of scene to come and visit her. Cambridge was a sad place in those days with the University deprived of most of its younger men, and the ever-lengthening casualty lists of its former members. Nothing seemed to happen to bring the end of hostilities any nearer until suddenly, on 1 July 1916, the terrible monotony of trench warfare was broken by the opening of the Battle of the Somme.

My brother Billy had recently been ordered to France with his battalion of the Durham Light Infantry and, as we knew that they were attached to the Fifth Army now engaged in heavy fighting, we were in great anxiety about him.

He was the youngest member of my family, a fair-haired boy of twenty-two, much loved by us all. He used to keep us happy with his nonsense and jokes, for at a remarkably early age he showed an original and delightful sense of humour. I remember a typical instance of his quick wit when he was only seven or eight. We had walked up to the end of the Backs where a large red-brick building (Westminster College) was in the course of construction. Billy asked what it was for? Father replied it was to be a college for a kind of clergyman. 'Oh', said Billy, 'we've got King's College and Queens' College, so this must be Knave's College', and Knave's College it has always remained to me.

On learning of the battle, my mother hastily came up to London to get our passports ready in case of need, for, odd as it now seems, in the First World War near-relatives of wounded men too dangerously ill to be moved to England, were sometimes allowed to cross to France to see them at a Base Hospital. However, when the dreaded telegram did come, on 5 July, it was only to tell us that W.R.D. had arrived at King's College Hospital (on Denmark Hill) with a wound in his arm.

I got leave from the office to accompany my mother to see him next morning. My memory of the visit is of entering an immense top-lit hall—perhaps the hall of the hospital—turned into overflow wards for the flood of wounded soldiers arriving from the Somme. But what struck me even more than the numbers of wounded men lying in the beds was the pall of silence that hung over the hall where not a man seemed to be talking. Their silence was probably due to their intense fatigue, many of them having only just arrived from the battle-front. All they wanted was to be allowed to sleep and forget for a while the carnage from which they had escaped. However, their silence seemed to me oppressive and unnatural.

When at last we caught sight of Billy and made our way to his bedside we hardly dared break the silence and left it to him to tell us in a low voice that he had been shot through the arm and thought he would soon be coming home on convalescent leave. He looked tired and as if he too were living in a world far remote from us and did not want to talk; so we soon left him. I was relieved to get away from the hospital and the sight of the haunted survivors of the Battle of the Somme.

When Billy was passed fit again, instead of rejoining the Durham Light Infantry he was transferred to the Sound-ranging Corps. He remained in France for the rest of the war, and on demobilisation returned to Cambridge to finish his course.

The next family event occurred towards the end of the same year when I became engaged to Geoffrey Keynes, younger son of Dr J. N. Keynes, the Registrary of the University. Our engagement and marriage took place under the terrible shadow of the war and this made our correspondence and meetings, when Geoffrey was home on his rare leaves, infinitely more precious than they would have been in the course of a peacetime engagement.

Geoffrey had resigned his post of House Surgeon at St Bartholomew's Hospital on the outbreak of war in order to join the R.A.M.C. He was in France by 24 August serving first in a Base Hospital at Versailles for some months, then on an ambulance train for three months, followed by a year as Medical Officer to a Brigade of Field Artillery. During the Battle of the Somme he was transferred to a Casualty Clearing Station as a surgeon and remained working in C.C.S.'s in France until the end of the war, eventually becoming a Surgical Specialist with the rank of Major.

It was during Geoffrey's ten days' leave late in November 1916 that we became engaged and decided to be married at the first opportunity. He would apply for marriage leave as soon as he could after rejoining his C.C.S. and meanwhile I should obtain the special war-licence which would enable us to be married without delay when next he got back to England.

I soon discovered that this would involve me in much 'pernoctating'. The licence had to be obtained from the surrogate of the bishop in whose diocese one wished to be married and the surrogate had to decide whether one did *bona fide* live in the diocese or not. At Cambridge the surrogate with whom I had to deal was the Vicar of St Paul's, the red-brick church on Hills Road near Harvey Road where Geoffrey's parents lived. He was a pernickety old man who would not allow that Newnham Grange, where I had been born and bred, was my home because I was temporarily living in London engaged in war-work. He ordered me to spend the next three weekends at Newnham Grange, but even that was not enough to satisfy him and he insisted that I must also come for a night during the middle of one of the weeks. Of course I had to comply, though with inward bad grace, as travelling in war-time was not easy. Then at last he gave me the licence. However, all my pernoctating did do some good, for soon after, when Mrs Keynes's cook needed a similar licence, my mother-in-law got hold of the Bishop of Ely and told him what an old pedant his surrogate was. So the bishop gave the Vicar of St Paul's a piece of his mind, as they say, with the result that the cook got her licence without having to do any pernoctating at all, though I believe she, unlike me, had never had a home in Cambridge but came from somewhere in the Fens.

In February 1917 Geoffrey applied for special marriage leave but it was refused on the grounds that just then there was too much activity at the Front. It was a bitter disappointment. Moreover, the licence only held good for three months and by May it would have only a fortnight left to run. I had begun to despair of Geoffrey's

ever getting back to marry me, when on the afternoon of Thursday
10 May as I was sitting at my table in the office, drearily trying to
concentrate on my deciphering, an Admiralty messenger brought
me a telegram, copied out on a long white form, headed *From
Folkestone Pier To Admiralty*; it was addressed to 'Miss Darwin c/o
Sir Alfred Ewing'. The message ran: 'Meet me 3.35 Victoria today.
Geoffrey.' I showed the telegram to Miss Robertson and she sent me
off at once with her blessing, arrangement having been made for
my release from work whenever Geoffrey appeared on marriage
leave.

I reached Victoria just in time to meet him and, after calling at
my flat to pack my luggage, we caught the next train to Cambridge
and were married at St Botolph's on the morning of Saturday
12 May 1917.

A friend, Dr Hugh Stewart of the Malting House, Newnham,
Dean of Trinity, married us, assisted by the Vicar, A. W. Goodman,
who later wrote his *Little History of St Botolph's* that I found so useful
when I began writing this book. There was only time to invite
relations and a few old friends to the ceremony. My mother described
it afterwards as a 'jolly wedding', it was so full of children 'conversing'.
I hope their talk was drowned occasionally by Dr Alan Gray's
playing of the organ. The youngest child there was my sister Gwen's
Elizabeth, born only four months before at Newnham Grange.
Maynard Keynes was best man and Uncle Horace, in the absence
of my brothers in France, gave me away.

A slight crisis occurred at Newnham Grange before the wedding.
I wanted to walk down to the church as it is so near, but when
Mrs Phillips, our well-known and indispensable cook, heard of this
plan, she said firmly, 'If Miss Margaret walks down to her wedding,
I won't come to it.' So of course I had to give in and drive down to
St Botolph's with my mother and Aunt Etty: but when we arrived,
the clock on the face of the tower showed that for once in my life I
had arrived too early for an appointment. So we filled in five minutes
by driving slowly round the market place — surely one of the oddest
drives I have ever had.

It was an exquisitely beautiful day. The appalling winter of
1916-17 with its incessant snow, ice, rain and fog was over at last —
spring had come on the very day of Geoffrey's arrival. The service

was at eleven o'clock, so that we could drive straight to the station from the church and reach by the late afternoon the house in Ashdown Forest which Uncle Leonard and my cousin-aunt Mildred had lent us for our eight days' honeymoon.

After we left St Botolph's, some of the relations in the congregation went to Newnham Grange to have a little celebration in our absence. Mrs Phillips had made a wedding cake, and a bottle of what my mother called *the Darwin Vintage* was opened to drink our health. It was made in 1909 of the small green grapes that grew (and perhaps still grow?) on the old grape-vine opposite the study, now the Bursary of the College. I hope it did not taste too nasty.

Our honeymoon being over on Sunday 20 May, Geoffrey took the afternoon Leave-boat from Folkestone, and I returned to London to be ready for work at the Admiralty next morning.

CHAPTER TWENTY-ONE

The End of the War and the Armistice: 1918

SOME three months after our marriage, Geoffrey was given ordinary leave again, and mine coinciding with his, we arranged to spend the first days at Cambridge. I was out when he arrived at Newnham Grange, and he was surprised to find my mother in bed recovering from an operation, with a nurse installed in the house. My mother's operation is worth mention as it demonstrates both her courage and her behaviour in an emergency; it is also of interest because it shows that voluntary war-work was being undertaken by older women in one of the University laboratories.

It may have been Sir Alfred Ewing's brother-in-law, Bertram Hopkinson, the Professor of Engineering, who invited my mother to engage in occasional work filling shells in his laboratory—for that is what she proudly described her job to be. It seems curious work at which to set an elderly lady, but as it turned out, her engineering job did not last long, for one morning she was suddenly seized by such violent abdominal pains that she had to stop work. Her companions wanted to take her home in a cab, but she insisted on bicycling back, no doubt refusing, even in such a crisis, to waste money on hiring a taxi for a short journey. She did in fact reach home before collapsing altogether.

Mr Arthur Cooke, the surgeon, was summoned at once. The nursery table was carried upstairs—the kitchen table traditionally used on such occasions being too vast to move—and a bedroom near her own was transformed into an operating theatre. Soon the house reeked with the smell of ether as Mr Cooke confirmed his diagnosis of a perforated duodenal ulcer, and proceeded with the usual operation. She made a perfect recovery and was soon able to eat what she liked with impunity, but her shell-filling days were over.

In December I fell ill myself and had to resign my post at the Admiralty to return home and be nursed. I was still at Newnham Grange on 20 March 1918, when the Germans made their final attempt to win the war by attacking the Allies on a very wide front.

We retreated strategically and our lines, though dented, held; however, the situation remained critical for some time to come. No news of Geoffrey came for over a fortnight and, aware that his C.C.S. was on an exposed site near Albert, we were exceedingly anxious about him by the time his first letter after the great attack reached me.

His silence was explained by his C.C.S. having had to evacuate all its patients to the base before the medical and nursing staff could set out for Doullens. Soon after they had left their C.C.S., its site became part of our front line. Many of the hospital orderlies were C3 men (unfit for active service) and barely capable of making such a journey on foot, so Geoffrey spent the night of 25 March—his thirty-first birthday—encouraging the exhausted men to struggle on to their destination at Doullens, which they did not reach until the next morning. He was relieved to find that no one was missing, and then flung himself down on a stretcher and slept for the next eighteen hours.

As soon as his C.C.S. hospital was re-established in the Citadel of Doullens, the surgeons began operating night and day on the wounded men that poured in from the Front. Geoffrey had no time or energy left for letter-writing until the flood began to subside, and then he wrote home at once. Several months, however, had still to be endured before the war came to an end.

In June 1918 I spent some weeks at Skipness Castle, Argyllshire, with the owner, Mrs Graham, and her daughter Frances, late of Newnham, now the wife of Cosmo Gordon, Geoffrey's closest friend. After Cosmo joined the Coldstream Guards in France, she and her small son Hugh lived at Skipness for the rest of the war.

I found Frances directing an unusual form of family war-work. This was the gathering of sphagnum moss as a dressing for septic wounds, said to be far more effective than cotton wool in absorbing discharge. I spent back-breaking hours in the bogs round Skipness pulling up the moss to put in a sack and carry back to dry in the Grahams' furnace-room. The billiard-room was given over to the moss; the table was protected by dust sheets, and when the moss was dry it was spread out on the sheets so that bits of heather and other scratchy objects could be extracted from it. When at last the sphagnum moss was ready to be sent to the Red Cross, it was disconcerting to find what a small amount one had contributed after hours of heroic work. I say *heroic* advisedly, as I often worked in a cloud of ferocious midges, especially on damp still days. They penetrated the finest bee-veil, in spite of our having rubbed lavender water all over our faces and necks; this was said, quite erroneously, to repel them, but there was no escape from a determined midge. It was years before the invention of efficacious insect repellents.

I returned home in August still unable to believe that the end of the war was approaching. I occupied myself in helping at my mother-in-law's Central Aid Society and took up massage again in a small way, under strict supervision of course. I forget the details, but the massage took place in the Newnham College Gymnasium where a small treatment centre for disabled soldiers must have been run on certain days.

One fine October Sunday I bicycled out to the Roman Road for a walk. I had a copy of *The Observer* with me and stopped to read it at a spot high up on the Gogs from where one could sometimes hear the guns being fired in Northern France (—or were they in Flanders?), but *heard* is not the right word for the strange vibrations one felt in one's ears, though occasionally one did detect a faint sound as well as feel the vibration. On this Sunday I opened the paper on one of Garvin's most flamboyant leaders, in which he positively asserted that it was only a matter of weeks, if not days, before the enemy would be asking for an armistice—and at last I believed in the coming of Peace. It was an extraordinary sensation to feel hope in the future again after the long years of despair—not that I ever thought the Germans would end by winning the war, but it seemed that the deadlock of trench warfare would continue for years to come.

The shutters close on my memory after this one blinding flash of hope and when they open again it is on Monday 11 November 1918 and I am sitting in the Newnham Gymnasium rubbing an old soldier's back, the other patients having left. Suddenly Great St Mary's clock began to chime followed by the striking of eleven o'clock (or was it the bells of the Roman Catholic Church we heard? I forget), and the striking of the hour was immediately followed by the clang of every church bell in Cambridge, or so it seemed, as discordant peal after peal rang out. The soldier and I knew what that meant—the Armistice had been signed. By mutual consent we stopped the massage and went our different ways. I felt I must see if anything was happening in the town and bicycled to the Central Aid Office in Regent Street, the bells still clanging in my head. The office was empty except for the paid secretary, Mrs Langdon, a war-widow left with two small boys to bring up. She was standing by the window looking aimlessly down at the street below. I could see what she was feeling: 'The Peace has come too late for me.' Mumbling something, I fled. What could one possibly say to comfort her?

On the way home through the Market Place I saw no signs of rejoicing—it was no doubt too soon to expect any. I felt a great need of activity, and remembering that I had made a vague appointment with my dentist for the late afternoon, I made this an excuse for catching the next train to London.

It was a gloomy drizzling November afternoon when I emerged from Liverpool Street station. None of the few buses I saw were going in the direction of Hanover Square where the dentist had his consulting-room, so I decided to walk there. Singularly little wheeled traffic was about and the ever-increasing crowds of people were walking in the middle of the streets as well as on the pavements. Then at last I saw and heard the first signs of public rejoicing. An empty open-topped bus careered along the street eastwards with two bugler-boys perched precariously on top, blowing the 'All Clear' as loud as they could over and over again; long after the bus had disappeared from view, the sound of the bugles lingered in the air.

I did not remember having seen bugler-boys in action before, except on one occasion at the Admiralty when they were used to summon us office-workers to take shelter in the vast basements below. My memory is not very clear on this point but I think the messenger-boys turned into bugler-boys for the occasion and blew their bugles down the corridors to inform us that the Germans were conducting one of their rare daylight raids and we must come down at once. In the basement allotted to us, the boys had climbed up on to the high sills of the windows to see the aeroplanes pass, standing so close together that no one else could get a glimpse of the Luftwaffe. I remember being annoyed at this, for though I had heard Zeppelins padding along on their way to London and had seen their immense cigar-shaped bodies outlined against the dark night sky, I had never as yet seen a German aeroplane.

As I trudged along towards Hanover Square, I saw another bugler-escorted bus and heard distant cheering, but on the whole it seemed rather a sombre and quiet lot of people that were making their way steadily south-westward. Until I read of it next day in the paper, I did not realise that a great crowd was assembling at Buckingham Palace to call for the King and Queen and to celebrate far into the night. I had no wish as yet to join in the cheering; indeed, I had been on the verge of tears most of that memorable day. I should surely feel more like celebrating the Peace, I thought, when Geoffrey and others were safely back from the wars, but the four last terrible years were too fresh in my memory for me to be able to take an active part in any light-hearted rejoicing.

I slept that night on the floor of a little house on Campden Hill belonging to some Irish friends. Next morning, I toyed with the idea of trying to get into St Paul's on my way to Liverpool Street station, to join in the Thanksgiving Service the King and Queen were to attend; but I realised I should have set out much earlier to have had any hope of being admitted to the Cathedral, so I wisely decided to go straight home where there might perhaps be a letter from Geoffrey awaiting me.

I remember nothing more about the Armistice until some days later when Geoffrey arrived home on unexpected leave. It was eight or nine months since I had seen him, but my joy in his return that evening was marred by his saying that he was feeling so ill he must go straight to bed. However, next day he had revived and showed no signs of having caught the dreaded influenza which had already cost the lives of thousands of soldiers in France. He has never forgotten the sight of the rows and rows of bodies covered by sheets lying in the tented mortuary of his C.C.S. at the height of the epidemic. Some of the stricken men had succumbed within a few hours of developing the disease.

On his way back home through Boulogne he had gone to the hospital to which Cosmo Gordon had been sent from Cambrai where Geoffrey had last seen him recovering from a large flesh wound in his thigh. But in Boulogne he realised that Cosmo was now extremely ill with pneumonic influenza. Years later he told Geoffrey that he believed his survival had been entirely due to his determination to live.

This type of influenza also had many victims in Great Britain. I remember one day that autumn bicycling in the Mill Road district of Cambridge on Central Aid business, and in every house I visited there seemed to be either a person very ill with influenza, or in great anxiety over the illness of some relation or friend. The most distressing case was that of a young woman who opened the door to me and told me in a numbed way that she had recently lost her new-born baby and now had just heard that her husband had died in France of influenza. I was reminded of Pepys and the plague in London he described so vividly after seeing a row of houses in Drury Lane marked with a red cross to show that they were infected with the Plague, and he added, 'writ under them was Lord have mercy on us'. This lethal epidemic of pneumonic influenza was our twentieth-century Plague and, when it was over, it was reckoned that more people had died from it all over the world than had been killed in the Great War.

After a short leave, Geoffrey returned to his unit, but not for long because, having attained the rank of Major and become a surgical specialist, he was wanted back in England to treat the wounded soldiers who were still filling the military hospitals. His recall meant that he spent his first Christmas at home since 1913, before reporting for work at the Woolwich Military Hospital at the beginning of the New Year.

We found comfortable lodging at Blackheath, within easy reach of Woolwich by bus, and settled there for the next three or four months. The winter was exceptionally cold and gloomy: the newspapers, no longer having war news to relate, were full of the great Coal Strike taking place, but in my ignorance I assumed that once the mines were nationalised there would never be any more trouble with coal strikes again. Fuel and some food were in short supply, but Geoffrey drew his rations from the military hospital, and the slab of meat he brought home weekly was larger than that issued to civilians. Green vegetables were hard to get and I remember having an unsatisfied craving for brussels sprouts. However, none of these very minor hardships mattered now that Geoffrey was back and would be demobilised at the end of April 1919. We celebrated his freedom by a long second honeymoon in Cornwall during most of May. In June, he returned to Bart's Hospital as Chief Assistant to George Gask, head of the first professorial surgical unit to be established at a teaching hospital in London. The war was over, there would never be another, and all was bliss in front of us.

CHAPTER TWENTY-TWO

Maud Darwin at Newnham Grange: 1919–29

THE end of the war finally severed me from Newnham Grange; henceforward we lived in London. When I did return to my former home it was as an accustomed visitor rather than as a regular inhabitant, and I still find it difficult to look at Cambridge with a fresh-seeing eye. My intense familiarity with everything about me made the place so full of memories that, when our four sons were in turn old enough to descend from their prams and begin to play in the house or garden, or accompany their intrepid grandmother on the river in the *Griffin*, my memories took shape and I saw them as the reincarnation of my brothers and sister and myself, beginning to do the same things as we had done as children long ago.

Having been in Cambridge during both World Wars, I can safely assert that the first was not nearly as disrupting to the pattern of our lives at Newnham Grange as was the second. In 1918, my mother emerged with two of the four maids she had had before the war. It should be remembered that in those times we depended completely on the resident staff for our home comfort. If one of the maids left, it was still usually possible to find a successor for her: this, however, after the Second War was no longer true. An end had come in most middle-class families to the luxury of being looked after by resident maids.

Our cook in 1918 was the Mrs Phillips who had entered my mother's service some ten years before the war. Unmarried cooks, if not too young, were often called Mrs to mark their position as head of the staff. Mrs Phillips richly deserved this honorary title, as her reign in our kitchen lasted for nearly thirty years. She died at Newnham Grange in 1935 and was buried in Trumpington Cemetery not far from my parents' grave. The tomb is inscribed: 'Louisa Phillips, 1872 – 1935. A valued Friend in the Family of Lady Darwin for nearly Thirty Years.'

I remember Mrs Phillips as a rather stout but very nice-looking woman; she was also an excellent housekeeper and a supreme cook of the English School; so outstanding a cook was she that the gourmet Professor A. E. Housman of the *Shropshire Lad* always accepted my mother's invitations to dinner. She said he hardly spoke a word on these occasions, but she liked him and was proud of the dinners she and Mrs Phillips concocted for him. My husband and I were great admirers of his poetry, so I begged my mother to invite him to dinner one evening when we were to be there. He accepted and to our gratification talked a good deal at dinner, and afterwards I remember sitting by him on the sofa in the drawing-room having an agreeable psychological discussion with him, he agreeing with me that we did *not* forget the horrid things that had happened to us, as psychologists said we do. I took great care not to mention the *Shropshire Lad*, having been warned that he disliked allusions to his poetry.

Mrs Phillips was not only a cook who could lure Professor Housman to Newnham Grange but she was also a highly respectable and well-spoken woman, so that I was startled one day—I think I was about eighteen at the time—at some unsolicited advice she gave me: 'It's the blue eye that does it, Miss Margaret', she said. 'Do your hair fussy when you're young and they'll all be after you.' I am afraid I never took her advice, but I am sure it would not have worked for me.

I have another more typical memory of her, in 1908, when Uncle William and my father jointly rented for the summer holidays a charming, though rather crumbling, Jacobean house called Vaynor Park in Montgomeryshire near the English border. Mrs Phillips came with us to do the cooking. There had recently been much talk about Summer Time, but it had not as yet become a law. My father liked the idea of not wasting early morning sunshine, so we decided to experiment with having our own Summer Time whilst we were isolated at Vaynor Park on top of a hill about a mile away from the village and other houses. But we had not reckoned with Mrs Phillips. She thought it both foolish and *Wrong* to tamper thus with Time and if we insisted upon doing it, Sir George must alter the clock himself. So he was summoned to the kitchen on our first evening at Vaynor Park to put the hands forward, whilst Mrs Phillips, sitting by the huge old kitchen table, silently watched him. However, next day she seemed to have forgotten our shocking behaviour and herself used the new Time as if it really were correct, and not telling a lie.

A few days later we arranged to make an expedition to Ludlow to see the castle where *Comus* had first been performed in 1634 by the Egerton children. We were too large a party for Uncle William's car to hold, so another car had been hired to take the rest of us. We had an early luncheon in order to leave by two o'clock and, when we came out of the house, there was Mr Hoskins standing by the spotless White Steam Car ready to go as soon as the hired car arrived; but where was it? We waited and we waited and we waited. There was no telephone yet at Vaynor by which we could make enquiries. We had almost decided to give up the expedition as it was getting so late, when at last the car arrived. We crowded round the chauffeur to discover why he was so late. Looking puzzled, he pulled out his watch to show us it was exactly two, but on our watches and the Vaynor clocks it was three o'clock. Not until that moment did we remember that we were on Summer Time. So Mrs Phillips had the last laugh that evening.

A second absurdity happened the same afternoon. Whilst we were looking at the Castle inside, the two chauffeurs were making friends outside and enquired each other's name. 'Charles Hoskins', said one: 'Charles Hoskins', said the other. A remarkable coincidence that really did happen on that day of misunderstandings.

This Summer Time holiday at Vaynor Park with Mrs Phillips there as cook happened in the care-free years *before the war*, and now I return to the subject of my mother at Newnham Grange *after the war*. She had suffered a serious personal loss when her aunt Caroline went to live permanently in America. Lady Jebb had been finding Springfield too large and empty a house after her husband's death, and life in war-time Cambridge was becoming increasingly dull for her, as more and more of her friends among the Fellows of Trinity were away on important war-work. So when her favourite niece Nellie Du Puy, in 1916, urged her to come and live near her in Washington, she gladly agreed, sold the lease of her house back to Caius College, the free-holders, stored most of her furniture and, early in 1917, set sail for the United States with one of her maids. In spite of the war she seems to have found no difficulty in carrying out her journey.

Though she had lived in Cambridge for over forty years, she showed no compunction in leaving the place, or Maud and her many friends; however, she wrote to Maud later on that she hadn't had a game of chess since she had played with her, and 'missed those late afternoon hours more than anything else'. But my mother missed her, not only on account of chess, but because when her aunt Cara was there, hardly a day passed without their meeting. Now she was left alone at Cambridge without any of her own relations near her, surrounded indeed by George Darwin's family of whom she was fond, but who could never take the place of her American relatives.

Lady Jebb greatly enjoyed the social life she led in Washington, meeting many interesting and distinguished people. After six or seven years, however, and the death of her favourite niece Nellie, she migrated to Erie where Maud's eldest sister Mary Spencer lived, and she (Mrs Will Spencer) took care of her for the remainder of her life. After the war, she returned several times to Europe to winter in the Riviera, and generally stopped at Cambridge on the way. I remember seeing her on one of her visits standing in the bay window of the drawing-room at Newnham Grange, welcoming the friends my mother had invited to come and see her that afternoon. She had put on a dazzling though most unsuitable dress of white satin and looked as young and Titianesque as ever, with her beautiful dark blue eyes, high colour and auburn hair only slightly grizzled at the sides. I can still hear her deep rich voice as she talked with her accustomed animation to her friends. In her last years she lost her memory entirely, but was said to have retained her gracious manner and her smile to the very end. She died at Erie in July 1930, aged ninety.

After the war, my mother was still on the right side of sixty and liked to take an active part in the life of Cambridge, so she was delighted when she was made one of the Governors of the Management Committee of the Cambridge School of Arts and Crafts. She had no kind of qualification for the job, but some of her friends on the Borough or County committees must have encouraged her to stand for election, thinking that she would be of use as a reliably independent member—sometimes, indeed, making the wildest and most impossible suggestions, but at other times producing a remarkably simple solution for a problem unsolved by any other member of the Committee.

In 1923, the new Principal was a young man of twenty-three, Mr (later Sir) Arthur Bryant. He told me he was appointed by Henry Morris,

the dynamic Secretary of Education in Cambridgeshire, who was always looking for a young man of like character to carry out his projects, and then, inevitably, quarrelled with him. I remember your mother with great affection; she was a remarkable character . . . and one of the Governors. I can still picture her in Committee or during her frequent visits to the School with some new advice or offers of help to the very raw young man who was its slightly bemused Principal! My function as Principal, and also as Principal for Further Education in the County, was to turn it into what was then called by the grandiloquent title of the School of Arts, Crafts and Technology and, in the course of the next rather hectic two years, we increased its members from about two hundred to over two thousand, studying almost every conceivable subject from motor engineering and plumbing to mother-craft. . . . Since those early days it has expanded into an enormous Technical College.

I remember how proud and pleased my mother was with the great success of the School; she seemed to attribute it entirely to young Mr Bryant; she had backed him from the first and, though he resigned his post as Principal after three years, the glory always remained his in her eyes.

One of the problems which soon arose was that of a Life Class. Mr Bryant, holding it to be a necessity for an Arts School, instituted one. Some of the Councillors were deeply shocked and determined they must get rid of it. Action was required at once to save it, and Mr Bryant had what he called 'a wicked idea'. He consulted my mother and they decided to invite the two chief opponents of the Life Class to attend the classes and see for themselves what went on in them. The Councillors accepted the invitation but after duly attending the class on two or three occasions, they found it so boring that they never went again. I believe that the Life Class has continued in existence ever since.

The next events of importance in the family were my brothers' marriages: Charles in 1925 and Billy in 1926. Charles met his future wife, Katharine Pember, in July 1925 at a Royal Society party for the International Astronomical Union. She and her father, Dr Francis Pember, Warden of All Souls College, Oxford, were the guests of Professor H. H. Turner of the Oxford University Observatory, under whom she had started astronomical work in 1921.

Only five days later they announced their engagement to their astonished but delighted families and friends. This was not the first association of Pembers with Darwins, for Katharine's barrister grandfather, Edward Henry Pember, had many years earlier been a friend of our Uncle William. This accounted for a number of slim green volumes given to W. E. Darwin by the author, E. H. Pember, kept on a bookshelf at Newnham Grange. They consisted of poems mostly on classical subjects, or translations from Greek and Roman authors.

The Pembers had one much earlier association with Cambridge: their direct descent from one Robert Pember, appointed Fellow of Trinity and the first Reader in Greek when Henry VIII founded Trinity College. Dr Pember liked to think that the pioneer of Greek teaching at 'the other place' was his ancestor, who had Roger Ascham as his favourite pupil.

Charles and Katharine were married from All Souls on 24 September 1925; the actual ceremony took place at St Mary's, the University Church in the High, and the reception was in the Codrington Library of All Souls, a suitable and lovely setting for such an academic gathering.

Two years before this, Charles had been appointed Tait Professor of Natural Philosophy at Edinburgh, and they looked forward eagerly to making their home in Scotland. All of their five children were born at Edinburgh and brought up there until, in 1936, Charles returned to Cambridge as Master of Christ's College. Charles and Katharine spent eleven happy years at Edinburgh, where they made many lasting friends.

Billy's wedding bore small resemblance to Charles's academic marriage, but its Yorkshire setting made it most enjoyable. On leaving Trinity, to which he had returned after the war for a year to complete his course, the Cambridge Appointments Board strongly recommended him for a post as trainee at Pilkington's Glass Works in Lancashire. After a year or two there, however, he found the work becoming more and more uncongenial, so when he fell ill with sciatica—as slipped-disc trouble was then called—he resigned his post and decided to become a stockbroker—a profession he pursued happily to the end of his working life.

In London his 'sciatica' worsened and he was kept in bed for months, until at last he was well enough to complete his convalescence by taking a voyage to Australia. On the ship he met his future wife, Monica Slingsby. They returned to England an engaged couple and some weeks later, on 8 April 1926, they were married from Monica's home, Carla Beck at Carleton-in-Craven. Her father was John Arthur Slingsby, a landowner and cotton manufacturer. Monica was the youngest of his twelve children; the death of three of her five brothers in the 1914–18 War was still overshadowing the family.

CHAPTER TWENTY-THREE

The American Interlude: 1930–38

AFTER the two Darwin weddings, the next event to chronicle is the visit of my mother's niece Louise Reed to Newnham Grange in the autumn of 1929. This was the first of many visits. A student at Wells College in New York State, she was now attending a year's course on French literature at the Sorbonne. Some knowledge of economics was also prescribed by Wells College, but as Louise could find no elementary teaching in the subject in Paris, somebody suggested (perhaps as a practical joke?) that she had better study *Le Charbon* instead. All that she remembers of this peculiar alternative to economics is the many journeys she had to take to coalfields in Northern France where, dressed in immaculate white overalls, she descended by lift down black coal shafts into the mines. What good this did her or the mines she failed to discover. No instruction on the subject was ever provided. However, the Sorbonne lectures on literature were excellent, and two vacations enabled her to escape from the coal mines to Newnham Grange where she spent a blissful fortnight with her aunt Maud Darwin in the autumn and again in the following spring.

Louise adored Cambridge from the moment she arrived, and when she left in 1930 at the end of her spring vacation, it was with the understanding that some time after graduating at Wells she would return to spend a whole year at Newnham Grange. As it turned out, however, she spent not one but four years there, only returning home to New York occasionally to see her family. During the thirties, other charming American girls joined her at Newnham Grange, and helped her to make this American Interlude probably the happiest period in Maud Darwin's long widowhood. She loved Louise, and Louise warmly reciprocated her affection.

My mother thought it her duty—but it also gave her much pleasure—to get to know most of the American students working at Cambridge. She had sometimes corresponded with them or their parents before the boys came over, and often she was able to give them useful introductions to University dons, preferably at the colleges they were joining.

Tall, strikingly good-looking, gay, and friendly, Louise enlivened life at Newnham Grange and acted as an invaluable second hostess for her aunt. They had the same liking for games and entertainments of all kinds and enjoyed planning ingenious parties to amuse the English as well as the American boys invited to the house. A fallen tree on one of the islands made a good excuse for a party to saw it up. Lady Darwin's reward for her hospitality would be a large pile of logs ready to feed the drawing-room fire and theirs the enjoyment of sawing and splitting logs in cheerful company, with a large and festive tea to follow.

My mother had a positive genius for 'fagging' — or slave labour as we called it when we were grown up. As small children she constantly fagged us 'to trot up on my washstand' and fetch her something she wanted, but later I emended her order to myself as 'trot up on my towel-horse', and still retain my mental picture of a trotting towel-horse jumping up the front stairs. When old enough to ride our bicycles through the streets, we were frequently fagged to deliver her notes by hand to save her having to put a red penny stamp on her letters or a green ha'penny stamp on her cards, for of all her economies I think postage was nearest to her heart.

It was after our youngest son Stephen was grown-up and an undergraduate at King's that she carried her fagging too far. He would have enjoyed dropping into Newnham Grange sometimes to see his grandmother but for her invariable habit of giving him some job to do on his way back to college. She began her fagging mildly by only asking him to deliver a couple of notes for her, but next time he was required to pay some of her bills or leave some orders at the shops, and the last straw was when she began asking him to do the actual shopping for her. Then he did rebel and seldom went to Newnham Grange again in her lifetime, unless it were on some special occasion when his grandmother would be too busy entertaining other visitors to give him any jobs to do. Luckily, she never realised how much time he spent next door with his aunt Gwen at the Old Granary when he might have been so much more usefully employed doing her shopping. My mother had a very strong will and it was almost impossible for anyone to refuse to do what she demanded.

A Rook Shoot, followed next day by a dinner of Rook Pie cooked by Mrs Phillips—though even she could not make a Gourmet dish of it—was the most popular entertainment my mother had to offer those of her fags who could get hold of suitable rifles. In early spring, the noise of rooks quarrelling over their nests in the small rookery on the Big Island became so intolerable at the Grange that Lady Darwin decreed that the rook population must be culled forthwith by a Rook Shoot. I avoided being there on the day in case some of the parent rooks might be shot before their young could fly and fend for themselves, for I was very rook-minded in my youth. This was because I associated the cawing of rooks with the intoxicating thrill of the beginning of spring, and even more because if the cawing was accompanied by the delicious gabble-gobble sound of the baby birds gulping down the food brought them, that meant spring had really come. But I was rook-minded most of all because I remembered Ralph the Rook whom (or which?) I had adopted when I was a girl of eleven. He had fallen out of a nest high up on one of the tall elms on the Big Island and must have lain where he fell for hours before he was found, for he was too exhausted to try and escape when I picked him up to show to my father. In his fall he had injured one leg badly so that he could not stand on it.

When I appeared in the dining-room with my rook, I found my father beginning his luncheon, so I seized a helping of mashed potatoes, laced it with some of my father's special Italian wine (sent him annually in a cask from Bologna), and began feeding the ravenous bird. He gobbled it down, flapping his wings, and making the right sound after each beakful. Then, when there was no mashed potato left, I put him in a packing case in the nursery to sleep off the effect of the wine, whilst I had my own luncheon in the dining-room (without any mashed potatoes). When I returned upstairs I found he had succeeded in getting out of the box and was hobbling round the nursery, dragging his injured leg and cawing vigorously for more food. This time I begged for some meat for him from the larder.

My father said it would be cruel to keep a badly injured bird as a pet and, if his leg showed no sign of mending after the end of a week or so, he must be destroyed; but when the week was over he said I might invite the University Librarian, Mr Francis Jenkinson, to tea to act as judge of whether the rook was really on the road to recovery.

Mr Jenkinson was not only a dear friend of all the Cambridge Darwins and their children but an authority on birds. In his youth, he had been an impassioned entomologist but now that his collection of moths and butterflies was nearly complete, he had taken to collecting flies as well, with equal passion. His tall and lanky figure with his drooping black moustache and side whiskers was one of the sights of the University, as he caught flies whilst walking the streets of Cambridge. He once accompanied the Horace Darwins on a holiday to Switzerland, where my cousins to their joy saw him catch flies on the backs of astonished strangers by clever manipulation of the pill-box in his left hand. . . . So now Mr Jenkinson came to tea and examined Ralph the Rook (as I had named him) and, since I was able to assure him that the rook was daily becoming less lame, I was allowed to keep him.

This was not the first time I had asked Mr Jenkinson for advice about a bird injured at Newnham Grange. I believe that one morning I caused a minor sensation in the University Library (then in the Old Schools adjoining the Senate House) by running in carrying a dying kingfisher in a cardboard box and imploring an assistant to take me up *at once* to see Mr Jenkinson. The kingfisher, only minutes before, had flown into our school-room through the west window (now blocked by the Rayne Building) and had dashed itself against the window pane in trying to escape. 'Could Mr Jenkinson please tell me how to save its life?' But when I showed him the bird, the lovely little creature lay motionless in my hand and it did not need Mr Jenkinson to tell me it was dead. With instant tact he advised me to take the body to Mr William Farren, the taxidermist, and have it stuffed. This I did later on that day and the case containing it stood on top of the bookshelves in our schoolroom for years. I hope members of Darwin College still occasionally see a flash of dazzling blue streak along the ditch between the Lammas land and the Big Island, and realise that they have just seen a kingfisher. Sometimes one could be more clearly seen from the drawing-room window flitting to and fro over the river near the copper beech.

My last memory of Mr Jenkinson is also connected with birds, for when I was rather older, he once asked me if I could keep a secret, and when I said I could, he told me that he had been born with webbed toes like a duck. Later on, I discovered by discreet questioning that this was indeed a known human deformity, so I decided that Mr Jenkinson had been telling me the truth, though why he had chosen me as his confidant I could not imagine. I wondered if I could get confirmation of his having webbed toes from one of his relations or friends, but the idea of asking his widow was out of the question. She was a fragile little old lady who looked as if she came straight out of a French eighteenth-century fairy tale with her white hair fluffed out below a large lace mob-cap tied on her head by a black velvet ribbon. She generally wore a long figured silk dress when she played Mozart to a favoured few, with such delicacy and beauty that it was considered an honour to be allowed to hear her. Boris Ord got up some little Mozart concerts for a tiny orchestra, with her as soloist, for performance in the small room at the Guildhall. She owned both a spinet and a harpsichord but generally used the spinet as the harpsichord needed such constant tuning. My cousin Nora remembers being taken to one of these Guildhall concerts and sitting by Mr Jenkinson, who listened with his eyes shut and ears cupped in his hands so that he could hear the music better, as he believed. He too was exceedingly musical. After her husband's death, she moved into a house near the Huntingdon Road end of Storey's Way and I remember seeing her once there in her mob cap. I have kept Mr Jenkinson's webbed toes a secret for the last seventy years or so and only now make the story public as I have recently come to the conclusion that Mr Jenkinson was pulling my leg, and deserves no further secrecy on my part. Another illusion gone.

Returning to the story of Ralph the Rook—he did make a complete recovery and our backyard became his home, with the bicycle handles as convenient perches—a messy proceeding of which the bicycle owners did not approve, but it was impossible to make the rook obey any rules, as the poor dog found out when Ralph evicted him from his kennel to turn it into his own bedroom at night. For Ralph feared no one and no thing; he was also most intelligent: he used to slip through the back door into the kitchen when he was hungry and peck on the larder door with such ferocity that the cook could not ignore him, and to get rid of him and save the larder door would feed him with scraps of meat. This was a lengthy operation as he insisted on her feeding him as if she were his mother, dropping each mouthful down his throat. He kept this habit for the remainder of his life, though when no one was about he must have sometimes had to feed himself.

Another clever thing he could do if he felt in the mood was to weed for the garden boy; the boy used to throw a pebble at a weed and Ralph would hop over and pull it up, but as he never would retrieve anything he was little help as a gardener. When it came to apricots, however, he knew how to collect and hide them in a pile behind a bush for future use, as we discovered when ripe apricots began disappearing from the old tree which grew against the high wall by the lawn tennis court. We had not suspected the carnivorous rook of being interested in fruit, but the hoard full of half-pecked unripe apricots was undoubtedly his doing.

The oddest phobia the rook had was his intense dislike of brown shoes — black shoes he ignored, perhaps because he was himself always dressed in ecclesiastical black. That summer we gave a garden party and, as the guests began to assemble on the tennis court for tea, Ralph decided to join the party. He waited quietly at the edge of the grass until a man wearing brown shoes arrived, when Ralph raced in front of him to peck his offending brown toe-caps. The hurried peck luckily did not injure the shoes and the wearer easily dodged his next assault. I was watching the scene from the gallery above enjoying the erratic movements made by the brown-shoe man side-stepping the rook, until I was ordered to remove him and keep him shut up till the party was over. But he could not have found many victims because in those days black shoes were still almost *de rigueur* at parties, though brown shoes were beginning to come into fashion for women as well as for men.

He never showed the slightest affection for anyone, unless he perhaps had a friendly feeling for me, as he allowed me to carry him about on my wrist like a hawk, without attempting to peck me. When his wing-feathers grew, he used sometimes to flop around the garden but he always preferred walking to flying, so we did not bother to confine him until one day he escaped from the garden, either by walking through the back gate when it happened to be ajar, but nobody saw him do this, or by flying over the gate by the

Old Granary. Luckily, he was seen about to cross Silver Street Bridge by a passer-by who knew we had a tame rook and reported this to the gardener who immediately went out and caught him. We decided after this escapade that it was wiser to cut his wing feathers but this proved his undoing, for one autumn day when no one was about in the garden, he fell into the river and was unable with his clipped wings to save himself from drowning. His body was found floating down the river near the boathouse. So we buried him in the flower bed near the Hermitage and gave him a handsome white-painted wooden tombstone with an epitaph, written by my sister, of which I can only remember the date — 1901 — and the final two lines:

> Ye passer-by in sorrow shed a tear,
> for Ralph the rook is buried here.

But I shed no tear for the little black fury. His permanent ill-temper may have been due to his having been too old on adoption to assimilate human behaviour. Perhaps he pined to be back among fellow-rooks on the high trees, leading the life he would have lived had he not fallen out of the nest, but he never seemed in the least interested in other rooks.

In the summer, out-of-door games took the place of useful employ-ment for the young gentlemen invited to Newnham Grange: lawn tennis was played on the court by the gallery, bowls on the small lawn behind the copper beech, and boat picnics were arranged on the Granta or the Ouse. In the evenings impromptu dances occasion-ally took place on the parquet floor of the school-room to music played on the wireless. The most ambitious of the dances was the one on 14 February when the girl-hostesses invited their partners in anonymous Valentines and the men answered in verse. It was all very gay and American and the participants appear to have much enjoyed the novelty of a St Valentine's ball.

Meanwhile Louise had many men-friends or *beaux*, as she called them in the evocative eighteenth-century way still being used in the United States. My mother took a great interest in Louise's affairs but on one occasion she blundered badly when Laurenz Rhinelander, a young Harvard lawyer, was courting Louise. He had previously spent two years at Trinity reading law and now, having got his final degree at Harvard Law School, he returned to Cambridge for the Long Vacation and had fallen in love with her. Sitting together on the Little Island under the leafy canopy of the old medlar tree one afternoon, he had proposed and been accepted. They decided to keep their engagement secret for the first few days. It was at this juncture that my mother drew Laurie aside to ask him, as if he were a Jane Austen character, what his Intentions were with regard to Louise. Laurie was furious. That he, a rising young lawyer and the son of the Episcopalian Bishop of Pennsylvania, should be accused of harbouring Dishonourable Intentions . . . he left the room speechless with rage. It took Louise considerable time to persuade him that her Aunt Maud had only been over-playing the role of Niece-Protector and all she really wanted was reassurance from Laurie that he had no intention of leaving Louise behind with a Broken Heart. When at last he was convinced that 'Auntie Maud' had not meant to insult him, they burst into uncontrollable laughter at the absurdity of her question and even now, after the passage of so many years, they still laugh affectionately over the incident when it is recalled.

They soon announced their engagement and her aunt gave it her unqualified blessing. I believe that its having taken place on the Little Island made her feel that Newnham Grange had set its seal upon their marriage.

My mother valued Louise greatly as a companion on all occasions, but most especially when she was acting as her chauffeur; for now at last Lady Darwin had a car of her own. She had intended to drive it herself but after making many gallant attempts she found, among other difficulties, that she never could master the art of reversing. In her first solo drive in the country—I believe it was along the Barton Road—she solved the problem of how to return home without reversing by deciding to take every left turn she met. Who but my mother would have discovered such a simple solution of her difficulty, and who but my mother would have had the luck to find that left turns in this case actually did bring her home? But except for this one miraculous success she had so many near-escapes from accidents that, after being summonsed for a collision with another car, she wisely, but sadly, decided that driving was not for her.

This summons was of special interest to me, as the magistrate before whom she had to appear happened to be my mother-in-law, but Mrs J. N. Keynes tactfully decided to absent herself from the Bench that day, so that those present missed the amusement of seeing one grandmother passing judgement on the other. I do not know what penalty she had to pay for her misdemeanour — this was long before the day of driving tests. Lady Darwin's decision to give up driving must have been noted with satisfaction not only by her relations and friends but also by such other local drivers as had met her frequently ignoring the rules of the road.

My mother had to find someone to drive her car and characteristically decided that her between-maid Lilian was the very person to train for the part. A sensible intelligent girl, she soon became proficient and acted as part-time chauffeur for some years until she left Cambridge to be married. She was succeeded by the new between-maid, Kathleen, but when, soon after, Louise came and settled down at Newnham Grange, it was she who became the head chauffeur and Kathleen was demoted to driving the car only locally or when Louise was absent. Long routes and motor-tours were henceforward left for Louise to drive.

There was nothing my mother enjoyed more than going these tours with her, and in the course of the next four years they must have covered a large part of England and Wales; even Scotland was not too distant. Their only serious accident occurred somewhere near Bath. They were driving up a steep hill when suddenly a car appeared round a bend. There was no time or space for Louise to take avoiding action before the car crashed into them and was sent flying over the edge of the embanked road to land in a field below. For a minute there was complete silence and Louise said to herself: 'I've killed Auntie Maud! I've killed Auntie Maud!' Then she saw that the seat beside her was empty and her aunt was standing at the edge of the road looking down at the driver of the offending car to scold him. He was evidently shocked, though uninjured, and was looking up at her pitifully through his broken window whilst she harangued him: 'Oh, you wicked man! Don't you realise you nearly killed us? You deserve to be punished. We shall report you to the police. I have never seen such selfish behaviour in my life'. Their car was also damaged but not seriously, and after a day or two they were able to continue their journey.

The ostensible object of most of my mother's motor-tours was to visit such friends as lived a long way from Cambridge and, if possible, in lovely country. One of her oldest friends was a cheerful elderly widow called Mrs (Nan) Gandy who satisfied both of these conditions by living in Westmorland in a beautiful old house near Kendal. She was an active Christian Scientist, but that did not militate against their friendship which rested firmly on a common addiction to the game of chess. Many were the games they played at Newnham Grange when Mrs Gandy was there on one of her annual visits and many were their attempts to continue their games by post. But the ladies lacked method and were apt to scribble down their new moves on old envelopes or scraps of paper easily mislaid or illegible when they did arrive. Sometimes the moves would get hopelessly mixed and a furious postcard would come from Mrs Gandy to ask why Maud had not yet sent the next move and Maud would assert, on another postcard, that she *had* sent it and it was Mrs Gandy who was to blame. The correspondence would grow more and more acrimonious until at last the game in question was given up in despair. However, they remained great friends and fervent chess players with each other for the remainder of their lives.

Another favourite stopping-place on the way north was Marnie Darwin's home at Elston Hall near Newark. This was the Elizabethan or Jacobean house where Dr Erasmus Darwin was born in 1731 and grew up. The place was now owned by a distant cousin of my father, a Colonel Charles Darwin. His wife Marnie was a handsome black-haired Yorkshire lady, who had twice been heiress to a considerable fortune. She amused us with her County way of pronouncing such words as huntin', shootin', and fishin', and we were fond of her and her family of three small boys.

I remember the house as always full of flowers beautifully arranged; even the lavatory had its vase of flowers. The garden itself was not spectacular, although an old ha-ha separated it from the rather flat surrounding country. Marnie was a skilled pianist and played Beethoven magnificently on her grand piano. Some years before my first visit to Elston she had bought another of these instruments from a dealer, second-hand, but as soon as she tried to play it, it developed a queer rattling sound. On lifting the lid she found a beautiful real pearl necklace concealed under the strings. She tried by every means to trace the original owner, but in vain, so she kept it to wear on special occasions (as she already had a fine pearl necklace of her own). She must have looked splendidly lavish and Oriental when she wore both. She died long ago, and Elston Hall no longer belongs to a Darwin; and I never heard what became of the necklace.

When Louise left Cambridge in 1936 to settle in the United States, the American Interlude at Newnham Grange, of which Louise had been the hub, was coming to an end. Louise had arranged for her younger sister Mary Reed to succeed her at the Grange, but though fond of her and aware of her intelligence and good qualities, my mother did not find her a substitute for Louise, nor had Mary any wish to take her place. It proved lucky for Mary, however, that she did come over in 1937 for her sojourn of nine or ten months in Cambridge, since it enabled her to visualise Springfield and the background of Lady Jebb's life in Cambridge, when she came to write her book, *With Dearest Love to All* (by Mary Reed Bobbitt, London, 1960), about her great-aunt Cara.

I believe some other American girls came over to stay with Lady Darwin after Mary Reed left in July 1938, but Munich soon after put an end to these visits. War was in the air; the happy life that Louise experienced when she first came to Cambridge over; the American Interlude a thing of the past.

CHAPTER TWENTY-FOUR

The Second World War and Two Years After: 1939–47

THE First World War had fallen on us out of a blue sky with appalling suddenness; the coming of the second was as terrible, but did not cause us quite such a shock, for Munich had warned us of the probability. Nor this time did we have any such hesitation about joining in the war; Hitler must be fought regardless of the cost.

The first duty of householders was to black out all their windows — and there are a great many large windows at Newnham Grange, including the huge round-headed one on the front stairs. Luckily, long before the war my mother had curtains made up for it from two long Persian rugs and these served the purpose of black-out well. The demand for black cotton material at the beginning of the war was immense; I remember seeing a large bale of it at Newnham Grange after the war, still lying unused — kept for emergencies which had never occurred. In spite of my mother's efforts, police or air-raid wardens still called from time to time to complain of a chink of light coming from such and such a window or escaping through a door carelessly left open.

Then there were hundreds of evacuee children, sometimes with their mothers but more often unaccompanied, to be billeted in or near Cambridge. Householders over eighty, if they pleaded their age and the impossibility of providing for these children adequately, were exempted I believe, but my mother was only seventy-eight and Newnham Grange was a large half-empty house affording plenty of room for billeting by the authorities if they so wished.

Bedford College was, however, in process of being evacuated from Regent's Park to Cambridge for the duration of the war, and my mother was asked to take seven or eight of the students. She agreed at once. The Principal, Miss G. E. M. Jebb (Gem to her friends), had been given Springfield as her headquarters, and the panelled library of her late uncle, Sir Richard Jebb, became her sitting-room and office. It must have seemed odd to Gem to find herself billeted in a house she had known so well in her youth.

Some of the students at Newnham Grange had to share bedrooms and sitting-rooms. Breakfast they ate in the Grange dining-room, but their two main meals they had next door at the Hermitage where Miss Cragoe was still running her admirable Paying-Guest House. Being a kind and co-operative woman, she was willing to provide lunches and dinners for the students, thus saving the Grange cook, Mrs Shirley, much work. Mrs Shirley was an elderly widow from Peterborough who, in addition to having a bad leg, was really too old for such a strenuous job, and would have collapsed had she been obliged to cook for the hungry girls as well as for Lady Darwin and her (at times) innumerable guests.

At first all went well. Most of the girls were well-mannered and helpful, though a few were noisy, untidy, and treated the house as if it were their own. But there were the drains; they had already been blocked twice since the Bedford College students arrived at Newnham Grange; now the trouble recurred a third time and the plumber came to show Lady Darwin the worn-out silk stockings that were the main cause of the trouble. She could not stand such stupid behaviour any longer and promptly marched over to Springfield to tell Gem Jebb she must immediately find fresh quarters for the Bedford College girls at the Grange.

As soon as the young women had left, my mother began filling the Grange again, this time with friends and acquaintances in urgent need of temporary homes. There was no lack of such people, the bombed-out among them, but some room had to be left for the summer visitors needing rest and change of scene. They would count on still getting it at Newnham Grange even in those grim days.

Since the death of Mrs Phillips, my mother had no one to assist her in the house-keeping—which rationing had made more difficult —and she badly needed more help. Like so many others in those hard days she turned to the mothers of illegitimate babies to get the cleaning done and to help Mrs Shirley in the kitchen. The room that had been our night-nursery in the past returned to its former use. If no illegitimate babies were to be found, Lady Darwin some-times advertised successfully in the Cambridge papers for a girl to do part-time domestic work in return for board and lodging.

The people who had chosen Cambridge for their war-time homes had done well for themselves as it turned out, for there were remarkably few air-raids on Cambridge and in only two of them had people been killed and much damage done.

My mother's reaction at the age of over eighty to her new responsibility of making homes for so many people was a loss of some of her former self-confidence. (I doubt if she would at this time have succeeded in bluffing her way through the Italian passport office without her passport, as she had done at the age of about thirty on her way to join friends in Italy. The train had stopped at the Italian frontier for passport examination, when she discovered that she had left her passport behind with the all-important Italian visa in it. With instant presence of mind she produced her English visiting card, presented it to the passport official and, proclaiming that she was Lady Darwin, swept through the barrier gate into Italy, leaving the officials bowing and wondering who the grand lady could be.)

But now she worried about things that had never bothered her before. This may have been due to her advanced age and the state of her health. She had developed serious heart trouble and often felt ill, though she ignored her symptoms as far as she could. Her doctor prescribed a weekly day in bed to give her a thorough rest. She disliked the idea, but reluctantly obeyed and I believe did benefit from the enforced rest.

Eddi Hambro, the Norwegian husband of Elisabeth (Raverat), my mother's granddaughter, told me recently that when they were in Cambridge in 1943, he accompanied my mother up the front stairs at Newnham Grange trying to make her move more slowly and rest with both feet on the same step before proceeding upwards. She stopped suddenly on the stairs and, slapping his hand playfully, said: 'Though I am old and ill and know I ought to be careful, I won't. I want to live in my own way to the end, whatever happens to me.' He remembers the incident very vividly because it struck him at the time as a splendid example of the spirit and courage of the old lady. She maintained this attitude towards illness for the rest of her life. She was a splendid antidote to the older Darwins with their exaggerated tenderness towards the slightest illness.

I was seldom in Cambridge during the war. Because my husband was Consulting Surgeon to the RAF, we were living in Buckinghamshire to be near the RAF Medical Centre. But I did happen to be at Newnham Grange on the day that the Government agents took away our front railings. My mother was having her day in bed when I went up to see her. As I sat talking to her, the front-door bell rang and one of the cleaners came up to announce that 'a lady had come with two men and a hand cart to take the front railings away'. My mother, much agitated, told me to go down at once to prevent them from taking the side railings by the front door steps, as she relied on them to pull herself up to the front door. So I hurried down and found 'the lady and the men', waiting by the steps. I explained politely why my mother wanted these particular railings left. The woman did not reply but turned to the men and ordered them to get on with the work of sawing off the iron railings. The woman had a sort of cold insolence in her manner that I did not like. She seemed to enjoy spoiling other people's homes. Of course if she had explained that orders were orders and she was sorry but she was obliged to take *all* the railings whether they were ornamental or for use, I should have been mollified.

When I returned to tell my mother the news, she thought I had been very weak to let the railings go, but I felt sure that even she herself could not have prevailed on that disobliging woman to leave behind the two short lengths needed. Nor were we comforted by hearing that the Government had taken our railings under the mistaken idea that we should think we were helping to win the war by giving them up to make munitions. In fact it soon became apparent that the iron was never used for this or any other purpose but lay rusting on scrap heaps in builders' yards. Then indeed we were angry, especially those landowners who had beautiful old wrought-iron gates and railings impossible to replace.

It was towards the end of the war that our (long-since grown up) first-cousin, Bernard Darwin, with his Irish wife Eily, took refuge at Newnham Grange from the bombing at Downe, the village in Kent where they had been living since 1925 in a small country house called Gorringe's. Bernard, like most of us, his Darwin first-cousins, had a great affection for Down House and garden, but his was a much deeper love than ours, for he had been born in the village, and owing to his mother's death soon after his birth, he had been brought up at Down House (which keeps its old spelling) by his grandparents, Emma and Charles Darwin. His father, Francis Darwin, had married again in 1882 and lived in Cambridge at Wychfield near the Huntingdon Road. I am sure dear old Conservative Bernard always believed at the back of his mind that one day he would return to live at Downe.

When the Second World War began, the RAF Fighter Station at Biggin Hill proved a favourite target for the Luftwaffe and therefore a most uncomfortable neighbour for Downe village. Matters became even worse when the new buzz-bomb (the V1) came into use. Barrage balloons were put up in Kent and Sussex to bring them down in the countryside before they reached London. One balloon was in Gorringe's field and several bombs fell very near the house, so that it was made almost uninhabitable. The Bernards then decided that they must leave Downe till the war was over and the house again made habitable. Down House too suffered even more severely, so that it took a very large sum of money to repair it.

My mother welcomed Bernard and Eily Darwin warmly on their arrival from poor stricken Downe. It would be a nice change to have a man in the house again, instead of a fourth old lady. They soon settled down in their new quarters. Bernard was assigned the dining-room as his study between meals. He was still golf correspondent of *The Times* and it was there that he now wrote his golf articles for it and other journals, such as *Country Life*. His prose was so easy, full of humour and delicate observation, that even I could read them with enjoyment, though I knew nothing and cared less about the game.

I remember staying at Newnham Grange when the Bernards were living there. I was warned by one of the old ladies not to go into the dining-room after breakfast because Bernard would be writing one of his Fourth Leaders for *The Times*. These brief light essays were much read on account of their wit and humanity, and his authorship of them was always recognisable. Darwins too were amused to find references to themselves or their affairs thinly veiled in *The Times* Leader, but the fun was poked at them so deliciously that the victims were seldom offended.

I am proud to say that Bernard once quoted a remark of mine in his Fourth Leader. I must have been about seven years old when I made the remarkable discovery that if Mademoiselle Kastler gave me my French lesson the day after *I* had been to a party, '*she* was just like an angry tiger'. I cannot imagine how Bernard wove the curious statement into his Leader, but apparently he did.

Another pleasant memory of Bernard's stay at Newnham Grange is of the way he used to read aloud in the evenings to the old ladies and to such other inmates as wished to come too. After dinner the party adjourned to the drawing-room, where they listened entranced to the passages he read them, usually from his favourite authors – Dickens (above all), Jane Austen, or Anthony Trollope. He read beautifully in his deep but soft voice. He generally knew the passages he chose almost by heart – he was a great re-reader of his favourite books – so he could bring out the sense and the non-sense in them to perfection.

The old ladies of course adored him but he did not always reciprocate. The truth is that he was easily bored, and although tolerant of them, the old ladies rather wearied him if he saw too much of them, as he often did at the Grange. Bernard and Eily were by now longing to live once more in a home of their own. So when their son Robin offered to lend them his house, Winson Manor, near Cirencester, they gladly accepted and spent the rest of the war there. They fell in love with the Cotswolds, as everyone seems to do who lives in or near them. But when the war was over and Gorringe's was ready for them, they kept their promise of returning to live at Downe.

Eily herself told me the following story of the comical scene in which she took part at Newnham Grange in September 1944.

My son Richard was working on naval radar at Admiralty Signals when he came over from Witley to spend a weekend with his grandmother at Newnham Grange. He had invited Anne Adrian to come for a river picnic with him on the Saturday morning, but when she duly arrived with a picnic lunch it was pouring with rain and no kind of day for canoeing. My mother advised them to wait in the drawing-room – in the bay window, I was about to add – for it is well known that when people first come into the Grange drawing-room they always go straight to the bay window, attracted by the shining view up the river. This is where Richard and Anne sat to wait for the rain to stop. But it never did and continued all that day.

My mother of course had scented a possible Romance, and determined that they must have the room to themselves. Then followed

an absurd comedy of which Richard and Anne were totally unaware. My mother shut the drawing-room door carefully on leaving
the room, and sat in the hall guarding the door. Presently Eily
entered on the scene. She was making for the drawing-room to get
a bag she had left there overnight. My mother at once took action:
putting her fingers on her mouth to show that silence must be kept,
she began making extraordinary gestures to show that she would
repel any attempt to open the drawing-room door. For a minute
Eily really thought that Maud Darwin had gone mad, so she decided
to humour her, and stopped trying to retrieve her bag. As soon as
my mother saw that Eily was no longer attempting to storm the
drawing-room, she began to shoo her into the school-room opposite,
then, after shutting the door carefully, she spoke at last. 'They are
in there', she said. 'Who are?' asked Eily, more mystified than ever.
'Richard and Anne', replied my mother, and then propounded her
theory that 'who knows?' they might become engaged if only they
were left long enough uninterrupted in the drawing-room. Meanwhile, as the rain still pelted down Richard and Anne slipped out of
the drawing-room, through the hall, and made their way to the
gallery to eat their war-time sandwiches in its shelter. When my
mother found the drawing-room door open, she realised that the
birds had flown. For once in her life her match-making had come
off, and Anne and Richard were already on their wet way up to the
flat in Grange Road to announce their engagement to Anne's
somewhat startled parents. I do not know how soon Richard's
grandmother was told of it, but we ourselves did not get the news
until Monday. I have never known a happier piece of news come to
me by post.

Richard and Anne were married a few months later, on 20
January 1945, in Trinity College Chapel. As the Chapel is not
licensed for weddings, they were first married legally in the Shire
Hall, so that took up half-an-hour of that endless morning. No
morning can ever seem as long as the morning before an afternoon
church wedding. Anne went home to change into her wedding
dress, but we continued to walk round Cambridge disconsolately
until Richard remembered he had some clothing coupons in his
wallet, and said he would buy a new shirt with them. So off we
wandered to Bodger's to find him a shirt, and that took another

twenty minutes. After this we gave up trying to kill time and went back to Newnham Grange for an early lunch.

It was a quiet wintry day with snow still lying on the cobblestones in the Great Court. There had been no reports of bombing in London during the night, and no alerts during the day itself in Cambridge. Both the silence outside in the Great Court and the small party given by the Adrians in the Great Hall gave us a foretaste of the coming of peace. It was so long since any of us had been at any party. Then Richard and Anne left for Sussex, where Maynard Keynes had lent them his house at Tilton for their honeymoon. When they got back, Richard returned to his naval radar and Anne to her work at the Ministry of Production.

Eily died at Downe some years later after a long illness, and life without Eily at Gorringe's was impossible for Bernard; he returned to London to share a flat with his younger daughter Nicola. Eily was irreplaceable, a 'very special person' as someone called her after her death, and Bernard had liked that description. She was an artist to her finger-tips. When a painter friend of her mother's family saw the drawings of animals she had made before she was fifteen, he had persuaded her mother to send her from her country home near Limerick to be trained at the Slade, and there she had made friends with some of the leading painters of the time. She was indeed a most unusually lovable and sensitive woman.

I found that the declaration of the German surrender in May 1945 bore little resemblance to the Armistice of 1918 — in my feelings at any rate; it was not nearly as moving and tremendous an event. This was partly due no doubt to the fact that it brought only a partial peace to the world. We were still at war with Japan and perhaps we had been anticipating the coming of peace for too long.

I was in Buckinghamshire at the time and remember nothing about the day on which the news came. What I do remember is the end of the black-out that evening and the excitement of looking at the night sky through uncurtained windows; 'letting the light escape into the outer world again', I felt.

Many people felt that the black-out was what they minded most during the war years. My own worst experience of this was at a pitch-black station on the Aylesbury line, when I scrambled into a train and sat down firmly on a stranger's lap. Fortunately I never saw his face.

In the early days of peace it was wonderful to look up at the sky and see a passing plane and know that one need not fear it any longer. I remember for months after the end of the war I used to mutter to myself as I walked along, 'The only thing that matters is that we never have a war again.' It is sometimes almost as difficult to get used to living in peace as it is to living in war.

Life at Newnham Grange soon recovered. Most of its temporary population drifted away, but a very nice helpful lady, Mrs Meyer, offered to take over my mother's housekeeping. This made life far easier, and enabled her to enjoy a fair amount of the last two years of her life, in spite of the bad condition of her heart, which made her doctor wonder how she was able to live at all. She liked meeting her friends, and still enjoyed a game of chess; and she used to enjoy seeing her many grandchildren, and two great-granddaughters, Elizabeth's and Sophie's children. She had by now twenty descendants, which in those days was considered a virtuous and not an excessive number on eugenic grounds. Gwen was living in the Old Granary and kept an eye on her, but Charles was still at Bushy as Director of the National Physical Laboratory for another two years.

In February 1947, my mother fell ill with bronchitis. She seemed to be recovering when I came up from London to see her, but for almost the first time she complained to me of feeling ill, asking me if I had ever had bronchitis; when I said no, the little frown of pain between her eyebrows deepened and grieved me. She said bronchitis was horrid, gasping a little as she spoke. I left her, however, thinking that she was going to recover, but she died a couple of days later. I returned for her funeral at St Botolph's, and saw her buried in my father's grave in the Trumpington cemetery. She had lived at Newnham Grange from 1885 to 1947 — for sixty-two out of her eighty-six years.

The Last of the Darwins at Newnham Grange

CHARLES and Katharine had long since decided that when he retired they would live at Newnham Grange if it were available. Now, owing to the death of his mother (the life tenant), the house had become his, but he still had to serve two more years as Director of the National Physical Laboratory before he could move to Cambridge. Fortunately, Mrs Meyer had agreed to remain in charge of the house, so that the family could begin to use it as their residence.

Charles was by nature rather reticent, and I had not foreseen how profoundly happy he would be to live at the Grange again. In the depth of his feelings for 'home' he resembled his cousin Bernard, who had insisted on returning to Downe where he had been born. In every other way the cousins were totally unlike. No one could ever accuse Bernard of having a scientific brain, nor could anyone deny that Charles had been born a man of science, as became the godson of Francis Galton and Lord Kelvin. Even during his childhood he was constantly trying to understand how things worked. One day at the age of six he cut his finger and ran up to the nursery to have it bandaged, explaining to his nurse that 'the juice of his body was running out'. I was nearly three years younger than he and remember him as a rather serious elder brother — good-tempered, tolerant and kind; sometimes we played with his beautiful hand-made polished oak bricks, or he used me as an adversary in games of chance when there was no one older or better to be had.

Later on my father would often read to the assembled family novels such as Thackeray's *The Newcomes*, or Kipling's *Kim* and other stories; most of us enjoyed this reading greatly but, not long before her death, Gwen told me that Charles had recently confided to her, as if it were some disgraceful secret, that he had often been so bored by the books that he had 'switched off' his attention, though if it were a history book or historical novel, he would listen intently.

As a boy, Charles often had a preoccupied expression on his face, probably because he was deep in thought over some scientific or mathematical problem. However, one of his contemporaries remembers him as 'a big cheerful energetic boy, humorous and scornful of nonsense'. He and his father had much in common and were great friends; they often had long talks together on subjects from which we others switched off at once, just as Charles had done from romantic novels. I recall an occasion when he was an undergraduate, and came abroad with us for a holiday. He was reading his leather-bound copy of Gibbon's *Decline and Fall* and somehow lost the central volume of the set; his dismay was extreme, not only because of the loss of a volume which it might be impossible to replace, but still more at being interrupted in the middle of the book, and having to wait some days before he could hope to get hold of another copy. He mourned the lost chapters almost as if he had lost a dear friend, so exaggerated was his grief.

He lacked my father's romantic sense of the poetry of life, but none the less had a strong appreciation of drama and went to the theatre as often as he could. He did not care greatly for pictures, but had a real love of classical music. Again, his deep interest in the world around him was already shown by his passion for travel and sight-seeing. Katharine fully shared in this love, and the number of countries they had seen was encompassed by their two journeys round the world.

Charles's school education began at Cambridge with two years at Ralph Goodchild's preparatory school, St Faith's, off the Trumpington Road. When he was nearing fourteen he entered Marlborough College with an entrance scholarship. His father had decided that this was the right school for him, just as George's youngest brother, Horace, had decided the same for his son Erasmus. The fathers both attached great importance to the situation of the school and thought that the country round Marlborough was of such outstanding beauty that their sons would benefit from being there. In addition, my father was greatly attracted to the neighbourhood by the number of prehistoric sites near by. Supreme among them, Stonehenge was of special interest to him as an astronomer, because of its probable association with sun worship and astronomy. As a family, we were made aware of the existence of Stonehenge from our earliest years, and when, in the summer of 1894, George took a house in Marlborough for the holidays, one of the first things he did on our arrival was to hire a two-horse wagonette from Mr Duck, proprietor of the Marlborough Livery Stables, to drive us over the twenty miles to Stonehenge. This journey was to be made so that eight-year-old Charles could be introduced to its wonders. Though only four-and-a-half myself, I was included in the party, with Nana our nurse, and the cook. There were as yet no cars, huts, or barbed wire round Stonehenge, and we came upon the huge stones standing in their earthwork ring with nothing else in sight on the great plain surrounding them. By the time we arrived it was raining heavily, but Charles jumped out to explore while the rest of us stayed for a time near the wagonette, sheltered by it and the horses' capes, and such macintoshes as we had with us. I have a mental picture of Charles being brought back to us in soaking clothes; and the female consternation at the idea of a child already wet to the skin being driven back through the rain all the way to Marlborough may be imagined; but to our surprise and delight Nana produced a pair of pyjamas which she had put in a bag at the last moment 'just in case Master Charles gets wet'. A tent of horse-tarpaulins was raised over them while the boy was dried with a tea-cloth and clothed in the pyjamas. Someone lent him a dry coat and he became the hero of the day, for surely he was the first boy ever to return from Stonehenge dressed only in pyjamas.

Another strong reason for sending Charles to Marlborough had been that there was a first-class mathematician, Herbert Savery, on the staff, whom his cousin Erasmus had praised as a most excellent teacher. However, when Charles first went to the College in the autumn of 1901 he had to go through two classical forms before he was allowed to specialise in mathematics and other sciences.

In the Lent term of 1902 an epidemic of measles had swept through the entire school, and Charles was one of the victims. He had a sharp attack but no complications, and soon recovered. Many others developed pneumonia and four boys died. A contemporary of Charles's at Cotton House was Siegfried Sassoon and, when Siegfried fell ill, he was given a bed next to Charles's in an improvised ward. Here he developed double pneumonia and nearly died. His mother was summoned and it is believed she had helped to save her son's life by making him the strongest beef tea ever brewed in the kitchens of the local Ailesbury Arms where she was staying. On arriving she had telegraphed immediately to Sir Thomas Barlow to come for a consultation. Sir Thomas was Queen Victoria's physician (and incidentally, some years later became my cousin Nora's father-in-law). Siegfried mentioned the consultation in his autobiography, *The Old Century*, and was told that he had been so ill that he was prayed for in Chapel, which was very gratifying. 'The Master might not remember me, but he had prayed for me by name and I felt none the worse for it.'

My mother also went to Marlborough to see how her son was getting on. Sitting facing the two boys in their beds, she and Mrs Sassoon made friends. They soon jointly discovered that the feeding of the boys was outrageous, so they united forces with other mothers and one Sunday afternoon, according to Siegfried's description of the incident, they swooped down on the Master and made him listen to their demands for reform in the diet (especially in the matter of meat). I am told that, since then, the feeding of the boys has been greatly improved. Charles and Siegfried had nothing in common, and seldom mentioned each other to us, but when they did they showed a curious kind of distant respect for one another.

In June 1903, Charles was awarded a senior scholarship, and a few letters sent to Cambridge from Marlborough College show that both Savery and the Master of the College, Frank Fletcher, were in close touch with Professor Darwin over the teaching of his son. Savery's letter includes a weekly timetable for his approval. Eleven hours were allotted for mathematics and eight for allied subjects in science, leaving two hours for divinity, four for classics, two for literature and essays, and two for history. The Master remarked in his letter that Savery would take care that the boy would not be overpressed, recognising that he was 'a willing horse, to be bridled rather than spurred'.

History, though a side-line, was a favourite subject for Charles and it was an achievement when, with so little tuition, he as a scientist won a history prize. Yet his pleasure in this was largely spoilt by the Master, who made some sarcastic remarks about scientists when handing him the books. He was deeply hurt, for although he always had an outward appearance of calm, he had a hidden sensitivity. He hated 'scenes', but endured them stoically in the knowledge that the annoyance would soon pass. After Charles got into the Sixth

Form, we began to notice a difference in him: he seemed to be much happier. He was no longer a solitary figure hanging about, making the best of it, for he had positively begun to enjoy Marlborough.

Then at last came the happy day when he won a major scholarship in mathematics at Trinity. How deservedly pleased Savery must have been and how happy it made all of us in Cambridge when at last he emerged fully from his chrysalis stage. He was soon very popular and made many friends among his fellow-undergraduates. As Sir George Thomson records, he became President of the light-hearted under-graduate Debating Society at Trinity, known as the Magpie and Stump. He was also an enthusiastic member of the Lake Hunt and did some climbing in Skye. Sir George also writes: 'a contemporary records the confidence he inspired as an immovable anchor', and adds that 'he had little or no benefit from his study of the classics and ended with contempt for them', this seeming to be an echo of his grandfather's even more critical words about the classical education he had endured at Shrewsbury School. The younger Charles, however, retained enough knowledge of Greek to be able to carry off successfully a variation of custom in Trinity College Chapel. In those days morning Chapel was compulsory and scholars took turns to read the lesson of the day. When his turn came he found a Greek testament on the desk open at the correct page instead of the usual Bible, and proceeded to read it, as if it were a matter of course, in well-pronounced Greek to the surprise and admiration of the congregation.

He read for the mathematical tripos in the last year in which candidates were placed in order of merit. His friends hoped that he would have been the last Senior Wrangler, but he was bracketed fourth. The next year, 1910, he was classed I.2 in Part II and was afterwards appointed Schuster Reader in Mathematical Physics under Rutherford at Manchester University, this being the beginning of his interest in nuclear physics. I can only summarise the high-lights of the scientific work that followed, being unqualified to attempt anything else.

When the 1914 War began, Charles happened to be in camp with the Manchester University O.T.C. and was shipped off to France at once. He was first employed at Boulogne as censor and in other administrative duties, but after about a year he was put to work more suited to his capacities, being attached to the Royal Engineers for research on artillery sound ranging. He was engaged on this type of work for the duration of the war and was awarded the Military Cross in recognition of his part in this often dangerous work.

In 1919, he became Fellow and Lecturer at Christ's College, Cambridge, and researched on statistics in collaboration with R. H. Fowler, this work impinging on the properties of the atom. He was elected F.R.S. in 1922. Two years later he moved to Edinburgh as Tait Professor of Natural Philosophy and in 1925 married Katharine Pember, as already described. This period coincided with the development of atomic theory and Charles visited Copenhagen in 1927 and 1928 to work with Niels Bohr on the quantum theory. He was greatly excited by the opportunities this gave him, producing scientific papers which are regarded as the most important contributions he ever made. The work led to further advances in particular relation to the work done by Dirac.

In 1936, Charles returned to Cambridge as Master of Christ's College, but two years later, foreseeing the outbreak of the Second World War, he accepted the post of Director of the National Physical Laboratory at Bushy Park in succession to Sir Lawrence Bragg, who had become Cavendish Professor of Physics in Cambridge. At the N.P.L. he supervised work connected with the construction of the Mulberry Harbour used for the invasion of France. In 1941, he was seconded to Washington for a year at the British Central Scientific Office and in this capacity became involved in the development of the atomic bomb. He never took part in the actual construction of the bomb, but foresaw the full consequences of the invention. Early in 1940 a body of scientists, known as the 'Maud Committee', was set up to examine the work in progress on the uranium bomb. As related in Margaret Gowing's official history of the bomb, *Britain and Atomic Energy* (London, 1964), a copy of the Report was sent to Charles Darwin, and among thousands of relevant documents which the author examined she found 'only two expressing doubt whether an atomic bomb should be used' (p. 170). The first of these was a letter written by Darwin in the autumn of 1940. As Mrs Gowing explains:

The Committee which had focused the scientific issues of a uranium bomb so brilliantly did not focus the larger issue: it did

Newnham Grange from the river, c. 1886

The Old Granary from the river

The Old Granary from Newnham Grange showing the gallery

not suggest that a single bomb capable of razing a large city was so different in scale as to be different in kind from all that had gone before. This point was seized by Dr Darwin as he read the Maud papers and talked to Dr Bush and Dr Conant in America. He wrote to Lord Hankey that the scientific work posed the question whether 'provided the thing can be made it would be used: for example are our own prime minister and the American president and the respective general staffs willing to sanction the total destruction of Berlin and the country round, when, if ever, they are told it could be accomplished at a single blow?'

I had never dared to ask Charles whether he had been compelled to share in the complicity for this appalling scientific 'advance' and years later was greatly relieved to find that he had only served to warn the highest authorities of what was being done.

On Charles's return to Cambridge in 1949, Newnham Grange became once more the home of a scientific family. His four sons all chose to do their two years' National Service before taking their degrees, and during this time all were at Trinity College, Cambridge. Three of the brothers, George, Francis, and Edward were scientists, and the fourth, Henry, read Classics and Law, and has become legal adviser to the Foreign Office with regard to scientific subjects. Cecily, Charles's only daughter, read chemistry at Somerville College, Oxford, under Professor Dorothy Hodgkin, O.M., and then took a research post in Philadelphia, U.S.A., where she married an American lawyer. Small wonder that all five children proved to be scientists, since their mother, too, was a qualified scientist. Katharine had studied astronomy with mathematics and physics at University College, London, and worked in computing, first for the British Astronomical Society, and during the war for Admiralty Radar Research; later, she worked at the Cavendish Laboratory in Cambridge. In 1951 her father, Dr Francis Pember, aged eighty-eight and a widower, came to Newnham Grange to live; the arrangement proved very happy. Charles and his father-in-law liked each other, and had a mutual interest in Court Tennis, the only game Charles really enjoyed and played well to the end of his life.

The years of his retirement were largely occupied in travelling. His journeys included a long visit to India, in 1946–7, and, in 1952, a period of several months in Thailand, where he acted as scientific adviser to the Government, concerned particularly with the organisation of universities. The people of Thailand he found specially congenial, their easy friendliness being due, he thought, to their never having been a conquered nation. In 1956, he lectured in New Zealand and Australia, and visited Ceylon.

Meanwhile, in 1952, he published a book which had occupied his thoughts for a long time, entitled *The Next Million Years*. In this closely argued work he set out to predict the future of the human race in relation to the enormous increase in population visibly taking place, and the limited resources available on the earth for their use and enjoyment. He chose to regard man as a biological specimen like any wild animal, and how he is influenced by the society around him. Here he was anticipating a theme now in the minds of many people and regarded as of paramount importance, but he made the mistake of estimating the critical period as a million years, whereas it is now seen to be only a few hundreds or less. Because of this, the book made little impression on contemporary consciousness. His conclusions can now be seen to be inescapable, but no one worries about what is going to happen in so distant a future.

During these years Charles's interests had continually widened. Sir George Thomson wrote that

He had an exceptionally wide range of understanding and a most unusual capacity for seeing the essential idea in a maze of complicated mathematics or conflicting experiments. . . . Tizard's remark that 'Charles was notably wise in dealing with things he knew nothing about' shows merely the limit to which this quality tended.

He was still in the fullness of his powers when he suddenly died, painlessly and without premonition, at Newnham Grange on 31 December 1962.

Postscript

'The announcement by the Masters and Fellows of the three
Founding Colleges, Gonville and Caius, St John's and Trinity, of
their intention to found Darwin College was published in a report
by the Council of the Senate of the University of Cambridge in
June 1963. Nearly six months before this, on 31 December 1962,
the death had occurred in Cambridge of Sir Charles Darwin,
K.B.E., M.C., F.R.S., grandson of the Charles Darwin of evolution
fame. His home, Newnham Grange and the Old Granary, which
had been made widely known by the publication in 1952 of *Period
Piece* by his sister Gwen Raverat, became available as the result of
the decision of the remaining members of his family to move from
Cambridge. During the early months of 1963 those who were
discussing the proposal for the foundation of a then un-named
graduate college learned of the coming availability of Sir Charles's
Cambridge property. Enquiries about the possibility of acquiring
Newnham Grange and the Old Granary for the housing of the
proposed new college revealed that Lady Darwin and her family
were warmly receptive of the idea. Furthermore they agreed with
the suggestion that in these circumstances it should be named
"Darwin College". So when, in June 1963, the intention to found the
new graduate college was announced, its name and its site had
already been agreed.'

From F. G. Young, *Darwin College, 1963–66, and the University of
Cambridge* (Cambridge, 1967).

Index

252